outcasts

outcasts

a love story

Susan M. Papp

To Dagman, with love

Hedy

DUNDURN PRESS

TORONTO

Project Editor: Michael Carroll
Editor: Barry Jowett
Design: Jennifer Scott
Printer: Webcom

Library and Archives Canada Cataloguing in Publication

Papp, Susan M
    Outcasts : a love story / by Susan M. Papp.

ISBN 978-1-55488-422-3

    1. Schroeder, Tibor. 2. Weisz, Hedy. 3. World War, 1939-1945--Personal narratives, Hungarian. 4. Holocaust, Jewish (1939-1945)--Hungary--Biography. 5. Soldiers--Hungary--Biography. I. Title.

DB999.N329 P36 2009   940.5482439   C2009-900284-1

1   2   3   4   5   13   12   11   10   09

 Conseil des Arts du Canada   Canada Council for the Arts

Canadä

 ONTARIO ARTS COUNCIL
CONSEIL DES ARTS DE L'ONTARIO

We acknowledge the support of the **Canada Council for the Arts** and the **Ontario Arts Council** for our publishing program. We also acknowledge the financial support of the **Government of Canada** through the **Book Publishing Industry Development Program** and **The Association for the Export of Canadian Books**, and the **Government of Ontario** through the **Ontario Book Publishers Tax Credit program**, and the **Ontario Media Development Corporation**.

Care has been taken to trace the ownership of copyright material used in this book. The author and the publisher welcome any information enabling them to rectify any references or credits in subsequent editions.

J. Kirk Howard, President

Printed and bound in Canada.

www.dundurn.com

Dundurn Press
3 Church Street, Suite 500
Toronto, Ontario, Canada
M5E 1M2

Gazelle Book Services Limited
White Cross Mills
High Town, Lancaster, England
LA1 4XS

Dundurn Press
2250 Military Road
Tonawanda, NY
U.S.A. 14150

This book is dedicated to the youngest member of the Weisz family who was killed simply because of who she was — a twelve-year-old girl named Icuka who was sent to the gas chambers on the day she arrived in Auschwitz-Birkenau at the end of May 1944.

contents

acknowledgements

THIS BOOK HAS ABSORBED my life for the past six years. I owe a debt of gratitude to so many people who provided support and encouragement, both those who are mentioned here and those whom I have inadvertently omitted. First of all, I want to thank my grandmother, Margit Hokky, who instilled the love of storytelling in me at an early age. I would also like to thank my husband, Bela, who has encouraged me to pursue this project for years and who has coped with the frustrations of living with a writer.

Dr. Sandor Szakaly was of invaluable assistance in researching the military history of Hungary. The collected academic publications of Csilla Fedinec were enormously valuable in providing a comprehensive history of Karpatalja. I relied on the research of many scholars and authors to authenticate the history of the era. These books are listed under Suggested Further Reading.

Eva Demjen, Tibor's wife of many years, was a source of inspiration, never failing to tell me that this is a great story and needs to be told. Special thanks go to the many people who read chapters and gave their feedback: Mark Lovewell, Ilona Mikoczy, Bobbi Speck, Eva Tomory, Helen Walsh, and especially to writing coach and editor, Myrna Riback.

Without the brilliant advice and assistance of Anna Porter, this project would have never come to fruition. I will always be very grateful to her for that.

Finally, many thanks go to all the people at Dundurn Press who have been so supportive and helpful: Kirk Howard, president and publisher; Michael Carroll, editorial director; and Barry Jowett, my editor, who so skillfully brought the manuscript together.

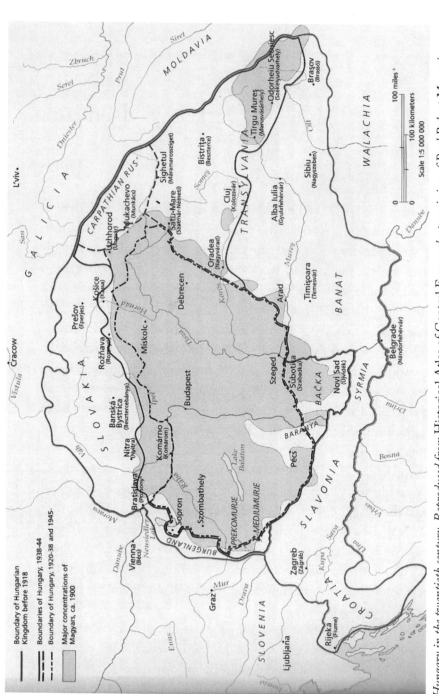

Hungary in the twentieth century. Reproduced from Historical Atlas of Central Europe by permission of Paul Robert Magocsi, revised and expanded edition (Seattle: University of Washington Press, 2002). Nagyszollos (Vinogradiv today) is now in Ukraine, just across the northeastern border of Hungary between Satu–Mare and Mukachevo.

introduction

THIS STORY MIGHT NEVER have been told had it not been for an incredible accident — one that can only be called serendipity ...

This incident occurred in 1988 in Toronto at a banquet to celebrate the successful completion of a new non-profit apartment building for Hungarian-Canadian senior citizens. The federal government and the Ontario Ministry of Housing were partners in funding the building, but my husband, Bela Aykler, the developer of the project, was sponsoring the banquet. For Bela it was especially important that the evening unfold without a hitch. The staff of the minister of housing for the Province of Ontario had announced that the minister, who had gained a reputation for her tough, intelligent, no-nonsense style, would attend the banquet. Bela saw this as a real opportunity to provide a positive impression of his company of developers and property managers.

The minister, Chaviva Hosek, arrived exactly on time at six-thirty with a very masculine-looking female assistant. My husband greeted them and introduced them to me and several other guests. We escorted them into the reception area and offered them each a glass of champagne and *pogacsa* (cheese biscuits) and, after a few minutes, Bela left to attend to other arriving dignitaries.

Events at the Hungarian Cultural Centre are notorious for starting late, and this evening would prove to be no exception. Left standing with the minister, I was relieved when several individuals approached her and introduced themselves. She was soon surrounded by people. Once I realized that, as a public person, protocol must require her to attend hundreds of such official functions each year, I stopped worrying about entertaining her. A trusted friend offered to give the minister and her assistant a tour of the artwork in the rooms, and I was pulled away by another group.

When Bela returned to check on the minister, he found her standing in front of a map of pre–First World War Hungary, examining it with great curiosity and pointing out something to her assistant on the map. When he joined them, the minister turned to him and asked, "Could you show me where you were born?"

Bela was a bit taken aback by the request and tried to shrug it off. "Trust me, you have never heard of it. It's a very small place that isn't even part of Hungary anymore."

"Try me," replied the minister with a little smile playing on her face. "What is the place called?"

"It was called Nagyszollos when I was born there, in a region Hungarians still call Karpatalja, though it's now known as Transcarpathia and is part of Ukraine."

The minister paused for an instant, visibly taken aback. Bela saw clearly from the expression on her face that she was stunned by his answer. "My mother was born in Nagyszollos," she answered calmly. "Did you know the Weisz family?"

Bela looked at her in disbelief. Not knowing what to say, he finally blurted out, "I was very young when I left to go to boarding school, but my older sister spent many more years there. Let me bring her over and introduce you to her." The minister nodded without saying a word and continued to study the map.

Bela hoped to find his sister quickly in the increasingly crowded room. She wouldn't be easy to pick out. Caroline — or "Picke," as everyone called her — was diminutive and, as she grew older, she seemed to shrink in height and weight. Soon he recognized her signature ash-blond, coiffed hair. She was chatting with a group of elderly friends when he politely interrupted and asked her to come with him. Elegantly dressed in a black velvet suit with rhinestone buttons offset by a string of pearls, Picke's face didn't show the years of hard work that had enfolded her life. Like the other members of their family, Picke and Bela had come to terms with the indisputable hardship of losing everything and starting anew. Each member of the family had developed a fatalistic attitude about life. Pulling her to the side, he looked intently into her eyes.

"Listen, you know the minister of housing? Her mother is from Nagyszollos. She asked me a lot of questions that I simply don't know the answer to. I need you to chat with her. She seems to know a lot about the place."

After introducing them, Bela left again to organize the seating. The banquet hall had almost completely filled up by then and it was time to introduce the minister. It couldn't have been more than ten minutes since Bela left them, but when he returned to the reception area he found Minister Hosek and Picke with their arms around each other. Bela was shocked to see that the minister's lovely, composed white face had turned beet red. Tears were rolling down her face.

What the hell has she said to the minister in such a short time to make her cry? Bela thought. They had to begin the formalities of the evening, the greetings and speeches, and now the minister was upset.

As soon as he had a chance, Bela pulled his sister aside. "What happened?"

"The minister is Hedy's daughter," she began.

Bela stared at his sister. There was only one Hedy he could think of. Their older brother, Tibor, had been passionately in love with a Hedy Weisz and had talked about her incessantly after the war.

"Isn't it unbelievable?" Picke continued. "She didn't know he was our brother but started telling me all kinds of stories about him. As soon as she said the name 'Tibor Schroeder,' we both started crying." Bela and Picke's mother had been married twice so they had a different last name than Tibor. "Hedy lives in New York and still remembers him fondly. Chaviva said she will bring us together." She stopped for a moment, lost in thought. "It's such a shame Tibor never lived to see this day."

THIS LOVE STORY THAT happened so long ago in such a faraway place called Nagyszollos has always fascinated me. It has taken me years to discover all the pieces of the story.

Nagyszollos is part of a region known as Karpatalja, a key geographic area bordering Hungary to the southwest, Slovakia to the west, Ukraine to the northeast, Poland to the northwest, and Romania to the southeast. Since the First World War, it has been claimed by six different countries.

Until the First World War, Karpatalja was part of the Austro-Hungarian Empire. The region was a place of acceptance, absorbing tens of thousands of immigrants from east and west. Jews came from the east escaping pogroms, and Germans, Hungarians, even Britons, came from the west to work as engineers in mines or teachers in the schools, or to buy relatively inexpensive lands. Whether they came from elsewhere or were among the ethnic groups who had already been working there for centuries, like the Rusyns, Hungarians, and Slavs, the people who lived there gained the respect of their neighbours and were welcomed to build their life there if they worked diligently.

Maybe because it is located geographically at the meeting place of the Hungarian Plains and the foothills of the Carpathian Mountains, or, possibly, because it was a point of conjunction for so many ethnic groups and religions, the area became very fertile ground for writers, poets, legends, and unbelievable happenings.

My mother, too, was born in Nagyszollos; my grandfather, a senator in the Czech Parliament, represented the region during the interwar period. As a child, I heard interesting, quirky, unbelievable stories of the place and, in my mind, Nagyszollos became a magical land of undulating, bountiful hills full of apple and peach trees and fields of vineyards — a place of majesty and mystery. There was a real baron who lived in a castle in the town. The children I grew up with only read about barons and lords in their fairy-tale books, but I knew of a real baron. He was named Perenyi and he lived in Nagyszollos. My grandparents often visited him and his family. I envisioned his castle, and heard about how our relatives went there each Sunday after church for visits and went horseback riding on the expansive grounds. In my imagination, I created a magnificent film about the place.

The region was famous for its viticulture. My grandmother's family owned forty-five acres of vineyards and dozens of acres of fruit orchards. By the time I heard about the privileged life of my mother's family, however, the vineyards, lands, and the elegant family home were just a memory. My family lived in a wood-framed, two-storey house in a low income neighbourhood of Cleveland, Ohio, where my parents rented out rooms on the second floor. My grandmother, the senator's wife, struggled to help support the family by working as a seamstress in a bridal shop. In addition to my sisters and me, my mother babysat other children as well to earn extra income while my father toiled at two shift jobs in different factories. He had a Ph.D. in law, but the degree was of little use in America. As he travelled from one job to the other, he studied the dog-eared English dictionary he carried with him, picking up English phrases while riding on the bus. During those early years, we hardly ever saw him.

We grew up realizing there was no easy road to success in the New World, but stories of the Old World still haunted my dreams.

At the end of the Second World War, Karpatalja was annexed by the Soviet empire and became a closed region where the Soviet troops and tanks were stationed during the height of the Cold War. Even if one was able to obtain a visa to fly to Moscow or Kiev, one still could not travel to the region without special government permission. Then, even if you acquired the right credentials, you would still be assigned a guide from the Ministry of Information to travel with you. Possibly, the fact that this region had been hermetically sealed off from the rest of the world for so many years added to its mystique. Only after 1989, when *glasnost* descended on the region, did it finally became possible to cross into Ukraine from Hungary and visit — if you were willing to wait seemingly endless hours at the border.

I visited Karpatalja and Nagyszollos for the first time in 1993. Married for the second time to a man whose family also came from this part of the world, I desperately wanted to see the place that had absorbed so much of my imagination as a child. The visit, when it finally took place, was incredibly disappointing.

By the time we crossed the border into Ukraine, darkness had fallen like a thick wool blanket. Streetlights, even on the main roads, were not working. The neglected roads were full of potholes and difficult to navigate and there were no hotels or restaurants to be seen. We found our way to a nearby village where the president of a local community organization offered us a humble dinner and a place to stay. We were grateful for the respite, although the Russian cognac our host offered us smelled a bit like rusty water. It was an inauspicious beginning to the trip.

The next day the sun was shining as we drove into Nagyszollos, but the disappointment I had felt the day before simply hung over me like an enormous fog as I stared at the Perenyi Castle of my dreams. The white-washed paint was peeling, the roof had been crudely patched, and the manor house stood silent and naked against the elements.

We approached the once-elegant home my husband was born in, but the two-storey house stood like a brick skeleton, stripped even of its window frames. We discovered that, during the communist era, it had been used as a private club for communist henchmen, a brothel, and later a restaurant. The family had never sold it or signed the ownership over to anyone, so the local government hadn't known what to do with it, considering that the former owners could come back at any time to claim what was theirs. They allowed local hooligans to smash it apart, brick by brick, and carry away what they could. In front of the expansive property, goats munched on grass where flowering plants and vineyards had once grown.

The gate enclosure was locked in front of my grandmother's ancestral home, and the main entrance to the house was on the side, away from the dusty streets. I gazed through the wrought-iron fence and tried to imagine what it might have looked like once. The courtyard was still the same, but the fertile garden, about which my grandmother had talked so much, was completely destroyed. Before our trip, my grandmother had reminded me to look for the enormous evergreen, lilac, and magnolia trees in the garden behind the house. I knew I wouldn't have the heart to tell her that the property had been subdivided in the back, a row of little ramshackle houses standing where the garden had once been.

A simply dressed, elderly man came by to ask us what we were looking at. When he spoke, I noticed he hardly had any teeth. I told him my family had once lived here. He stared at me sadly and walked away.

The entire town felt gritty with dirt, but there were some hopeful signs of reconstruction. The massive, Gothic, Roman Catholic church, constructed in the fourteenth century, was being slowly cleaned, the years of grime painted over. When the Russian troops descended on the region, their commanders had nailed the front door shut and used the side entrances, first as a horse livery and then as the local garbage dump. They had cut a hole in the roof to let the stench out and allow the rain, snow, and sleet in.

When we left the town after a few hours of looking around, my husband joked bitterly, "Well, darling, I hope you agree we've been here twice — the first and the last time."

AFTER THAT VISIT, I tried to shut the place out of my mind and could never have imagined writing this story until I met Chaviva Hosek's uncle, Sandor Weisz. He had also been born there and, through his eyes, I learned once again to appreciate the incredibly interesting lives and relationships that had unfolded there.

In March 1944, the Germans occupied Hungary and Adolf Eichmann himself moved to Budapest to supervise the "Final Solution." By April, the ten thousand Jews of Ugocsa County had been placed in a ghetto in Nagyszollos. Between May and June, some 100,000 Karpataljan Jews were deported to the death camps in Auschwitz-Birkenau. Sandor Weisz, his sisters, and his father were among them. Most never returned.

Sandor Weisz went to Palestine after being liberated from Mauthausen in the spring of 1945, determined to leave the damn continent of Europe behind him forever. He denied his Hungarian past, refusing to utter a single word in Hungarian for over thirty years. It was too painful.

His family were Hungarian Jews, immersed in the Hungarian language and culture, who had been living in Hungary since the 1700s. He became a Zionist and changed his name to Yitzhak Livnat.

But, in the mid-1970s, Yitzhak Livnat grew tired of denial, tired of rejecting his past, his mother tongue, the culture, and the world he was raised in. Today, Yitzhak Livnat, known by his childhood nickname of Suti, spends his time scouring the village records and archives of the towns where his ancestors once lived, pulling together the fragments of his own and his family's past, documenting their lives and coming to terms with what happened to them over sixty years ago.

While I had heard and read much about the Holocaust, hearing about and experiencing the story of this one family changed my outlook forever. The saga of their suffering is overwhelming.

I also found out, bit by bit, the details of a mysterious love affair between a Christian man, Tibor Schroeder, and a Jewish girl, Hedy Weisz, who fell in love at a time when such a relationship was against the law, defined as a "defamation of race." This love affair and the time in which it occurred are the core of this book.

The Schroeder-Aykler residence on the hill overlooking Nagyszollos.

Since delving into their history, I have come to appreciate how unusual this story is and what an enormous amount of courage it took for Tibor to try to save Hedy. The story, I think, is unprecedented.

While many stories have been told about how individuals survived the Holocaust, this story is very different. It is the story of the human interconnectedness of two individuals from very different backgrounds, their love for each other, and their vow to stay true to one another despite what human conventions or historical situations demanded of them. It is the story of tremendous courage and passion, the enduring nature of hope, and belief in the goodness of the human heart.

All the events are true.

Tibor passed away in January 1982 but left detailed documentation, letters, and diaries of his life. I am indebted to my now-deceased mother-in-law, Karola Aykler — Tibor, Bela, and Picke's mother — who wrote extensive diaries of her early life in Nagyszollos, where this story begins.

This book is their story, a tribute and a legacy to them.

chapter 1 | 1928

As the horse-drawn carriage pulled up to the construction site that would soon be their new family home, Karola realized she had never felt such happiness, such pure contentment, before in her life. Karola's first marriage had disintegrated, leaving her alone with two sons, but she was recently remarried and pregnant again. This house symbolized a new beginning, a fresh start for all of them. She stepped out of the carriage, very elegant in her beige wool coat, her long brown hair pinned up under a matching hat. She adjusted her cashmere scarf more snugly around her neck and pulled on her gloves. It was February and, in this region surrounded by the foothills of the Carpathian Mountains, the winter cold crept into one's bones. Karola gazed out at the land owned by her family and the vineyards that stretched as far as the eye could see up the hill and beyond. The vineyards in this area were renowned for producing particularly good wine because of the rich volcanic soil on the terraced hillsides. Her father had amalgamated all their properties to build this dream house and she was amazed at how the massive structure that would soon be an integral part of their lives became more remarkable, more a distinct entity each time they visited. The two storeys were already under roof now and carpenters were busy laying the oak parquet floors onto the unfinished concrete.

With her new husband, her father, and her son, Tibor, by her side, she walked up the long pathway that ascended to the house. It sat perched on the side of a prominent hill. They stepped gingerly into the front hall atrium. The entranceway had turned out to be far more impressive than even she had imagined. She breathed in deeply the delicate scent of wood shavings that emanated from the front hall. The house was swarming with workers, each focussed on his particular task. A team of carpenters was just finishing lining the two-storey atrium with rows of floor-to-ceiling handcrafted oak bookshelves. She marvelled at the honeyed hue of the wood that exuded warmth throughout the entrance and stopped to admire the fine craftsmanship. Her husband, Domokos, shared her sense of excitement and, as he stood next to her, he reached for her hand and squeezed it gently.

Herman, the master carpenter who had been brought in from the Black Forest region of southern Germany to oversee the construction, seemingly held his breath as he gave them all a chance to take a good look at his work. Karola's father, Janos, was a man of few words but when the distinguished-looking man with the thick moustache spoke, his words carried a weight that prompted people to listen. Without his financial backing and assistance, this home could not have come to fruition.

"Herman, you have outdone yourself," Janos beamed. "I never imagined it would turn out this well." Herman nodded his appreciation of the praise.

While his parents spoke to Herman, seven-year-old Tibor wandered off, enticed by the activity going on around him. He always insisted on coming with them when they scheduled such house inspections. Before they left home he would proudly put on the toy toolbelt his grandfather had brought back for him from Vienna when he was five. It was his most prized possession. He walked around studying the workmen and watching with fascination as they hammered and sawed, built the wooden frame, mixed and lay concrete, and bore holes to insert the plumbing pipes. On the site and off, Tibor had come to be known as "the little working man."

As he walked around, Tibor noticed one obscure nail that stood out from a baseboard at the bottom of the circular oak library. While the adults were all admiring the empty shelves, Tibor began pounding away at the loose nail with his toy wooden hammer. When Karola heard the noise, she rushed to the child.

"What are you doing, my darling?" she asked as she put her hand out to stop him from hammering.

The dark-eyed child looked sternly at his mother and explained as patiently as he could, "I'm fixing a nail that the workmen left to me to fix."

Karola bent down, putting her arm around her son, and looked at the baseboard. There was indeed a nail sticking out, hanging halfway out of the wall — a nail that could be dangerous to someone walking by.

Herman hurried to their side and crouched beside them. "You are right, young man," he said. "Let me give you a hand." With a quick motion, he hammered in the unfinished nail. Then he turned to Tibor. "Thank you for noticing our mistake, Tibor. You will make a fine master craftsman someday."

Tibor's dark eyes beamed with pride as he tucked his toy hammer back into his belt and rubbed a bit of sawdust off his hands. Karola watched her son. He'd been such a calm, contended little human almost from the moment of his birth. A deep sense of serenity had enfolded Karola the day Tibor was born for she felt this baby would herald a new beginning in her life. She felt instinctively that as the Great War finally ended, so would her marriage. She couldn't tolerate living with her volatile husband much longer. Their married life had been dominated by his toxic bouts of depression, followed by fits of uncontrolled anger. Karola never knew what to expect. How could she have known when she met him what he was really like? As a first lieutenant, Istvan Schroeder had made such a fine impression on Karola and her family. But once they were married, he became unrecognizable. The only valuable legacies left from the bitterly unhappy marriage were her two fine sons: Istvan, the firstborn, and Tibor.

The town of Nagyszollos had also gone through much dislocation and turmoil since the end of the Great War. Nagyszollos was part of a region known as Karpatalja that had always been part of Hungary but, after the war, the victorious powers, particularly France and England, were cruel when they dismembered the vanquished Austro-Hungarian monarchy. Two-thirds of Hungary's historic territory and one-third of her population were forced to become part of newly created foreign countries such as Czechoslovakia and Yugoslavia. Romania became greatly enlarged. In 1920, a new border was dictated and most of Karpatalja — along with Karola, her family, and their lands — would be partitioned to the newly created state of Czechoslovakia.

The new borders brought dislocation, chaos, and unemployment to the region. Nagyszollos was renamed Sevljus, but the only thing that was Czech about the town was its new name. There were hardly a handful of Czech residents — mainly the recently arrived civil servants and administrators. The new regime in Prague didn't want the international community to discover they had misrepresented the ethnic makeup of the population of Karpatalja at the Paris Peace talks, so one of the first declarations of the new government was to demand a certificate of citizenship in communities where practically no one had such a certificate. Karola and her family were directly affected by the cruel decree. She was *persona non grata* in the new state. She and her children were denied citizenship, as was her father, even though he was a landowner and taxpayer. She was informed that if she left the new country for any length of time, she might not be allowed to return. Furthermore, her children could not be enrolled in school. Without citizenship, they were stripped of any rights. She would have to secure a private tutor for them.

Karola was incensed by the injustices she witnessed around her — the unemployed, the disenfranchisement, the hardships of the elderly she saw daily as she walked down the main street of Nagyszollos. The tragic events, the collapse of her homeland, had hardened her. Beggars, many of them pensioners, lined the streets trying to sell their last possessions in order to buy food. The only things that kept her going were her family and the land — the vineyards that had given them all so much sustenance and prosperity for so many years.

Her parents had found Nagyszollos a wonderfully entertaining place to live, so different from the stuffy, self-important social circles they had left behind in the capital. The townspeople were of varied backgrounds and religions — a dozen different churches and synagogues lined or were just off the main street, Verboczy ut. While strolling the main street on any day of the week you could hear many languages: Hungarian, Yiddish,

Rusyn, Slovak, and German. The Rusyns, a proud but poor Slavic people, spoke a language distinct from Ukrainian and Russian. Those who lived in the mountain regions were known as Huculs: rugged, independent people who kept mostly to themselves.

About one-third of the townspeople were Jews. Skilled craftsmen, they operated many of the small shops along the main street. On Fridays, at sundown, many of the stores in town closed and the streets became eerily quiet as Jewish families went home to light candles and celebrate the start of the Sabbath. Everyone seemed to know about and respect each other's dress, customs, and holidays.

Karola sighed as she looked around her. Through the openings in the construction she could see the breathtaking view into the vineyards and the mountains beyond. She couldn't imagine a more colourful place to live.

Upstairs now, Karola and her husband were admiring the size of the bedrooms — recently installed large windows filled the rooms with light, stunning vistas, and a feeling of expansiveness.

Five in all, room for all of them: her father, her boys from her previous marriage, and their new baby. Even Domokos's son by his first marriage would have a guest room when he came to visit.

"This switch will be installed in each and every room, right by the door," Tamas Vag, the electrician, explained as he clicked the main hall chandelier on and off. They marvelled. Their home would be the first fully electrified house in Nagyszollos.

As they stood admiring the work of the electrician, Tibor zipped up the stairs, making a beeline straight to his mother, grabbing her hand, pulling. "Come see, Mother! You will never believe it!"

The excitement of the child was contagious. Everyone smiled as Karola asked: "What is it darling?"

"Mother," Tibor exclaimed, "there are railway tracks going into our basement! Come see!" The child said it with reverence and caution, as if it was too bizarre to be believed, yet it was so amazing and exciting! Imagine ... Train tracks leading into their basement!

"Yes, sweetheart, I know," said Karola. "Your grandfather saw that many other wine producers were bringing in their crop utilizing mini

Tibor Schroeder as a young boy with his younger sister, Picke, and brother, Bela, in pram, 1930.

railway cars. Grapes are very heavy when harvested. To move the bushels of harvested grapes for any significant distance takes a lot of men working long hours. These lines and cars will make it much easier to bring the grapes into the pressing facility, which will be built into our basement."

Domokos, to further encourage the child's delight, leaned down to his stepson and asked, "Why don't you show me where the lines come into the basement?"

Tibor took his hand and led them all down the stairs. Domokos smiled broadly at his wife, sharing her enthusiasm. It seemed God had blessed them so abundantly.

DOMOKOS AYKLER HAD BEEN the postmaster of this town before the war and was one of the few fortunate individuals who were able to resume their jobs when the war ended. Karola met Domokos socially when he had come to call on her father concerning a business matter. A number of their friends were over for tea, and they invited Domokos Aykler to join them.

When she met him again, after the war, Karola was surprised by her own reaction. She was very pleased to see him again and stammered a bit as she greeted him. He smiled tentatively but his eyes reflected warmth and tenderness as he returned the greeting. He was handsome, not particularly tall, but muscular with strong but gentle eyes. He had a long beard and distinctive facial features that caused people to sometimes mistake him for a Jew. Later she would learn that one part of his family had Armenian roots.

Istvan and Tibor were upstairs with the tutor and her father wasn't at home, but she invited Domokos into the parlour and reminded him of that significant day they had first met — the day the Austrian heir to the throne was assassinated in Sarajevo. Her friends, all civilians, had speculated excitedly about what would happen next. They had predicted that the Empire would crush its enemies. Looking back, Karola realized Domokos had been the sole voice of reason and the only one who had realized the gravity of what was to come. She remembered how sad his eyes looked as he stated unambiguously, "This will lead to war."

Now she offered him tea and they sat and talked at length about all that had enfolded in their lives since the last time they met. There was fire in his eyes when he spoke of the suffering of the people since Karpatalja had been annexed to Czechoslovakia.

"This state of affairs cannot continue," Domokos said, quoting the great American president Abraham Lincoln. "Nothing is settled finally, unless it is settled justly."

He told her about all that had happened to him and Karola realized that, as a captain in the Austro-Hungarian army, Domokos had been through his own incredible, soul-annihilating experiences. He had fought on the eastern front, had been captured and been a prisoner of war in Russia where he was condemned to death on several occasions. Once he managed to escape from a forced labour camp by pretending to be insane. She sat mesmerized as he related his experiences. He spoke calmly, without embellishment, radiating an inner strength that captivated her. She was impressed that, despite all he had gone through and survived, he still sat across from her undaunted, unbroken, a strong and determined man. But at the same time, she realized, there was still so much kindness in this man.

By the time their long conversation ended, Karola realized that she was drawn to this determined man sitting across from her. From that day forward, she invited Domokos to meals on the terrace of their home more and more frequently. They shared the same opinion on so many topics and discussed everything from world politics, inflation, and history to the education of Karola's sons, poetry, and the grape harvest. Their long conversations often extended into the early hours of the morning. They seemed oblivious to everything around them as they took long walks in the vineyard. In the small town of Nagyszollos, or Sevljus, their romance was the topic of much speculation and gossip. Even though Domokos was married and had a son, his marriage had also disintegrated, just as hers had.

After a whirlwind but discrete courtship, Karola Schroeder married Domokos Aykler in a quiet ceremony in 1924.

Their first child, a daughter named Karola, was born in March of 1925. Just a few pounds at birth, Karola and Domokos endeared her with the name of "Picke," or "tiny one."

Istvan Schroeder, Karola's first husband, died at the age of forty in a sanatorium where he was still recovering from "nerve damage" suffered during the war. Many speculated that he had taken his own life but the official reason for his death was listed on the death certificate as "heart failure." The body was found several hours after rigor mortis had set in. In his tightly clenched fist they found his wedding band.

The family didn't move into the stately house on the hill until 1929 when Karola was pregnant again. She was still overseeing the installation of draperies, upholstery, wallpaper, and finishing touches to the house when, in the spring of 1929, she gave birth, upstairs in their bedroom overlooking the vineyards, to their youngest, a baby boy named Bela.

View of Nagyszollos, circa 1930. The town was renamed Sevjlus when it became part of Czechoslovakia in 1920.

chapter 2 | 1933

BY THE TIME TIBOR was a teenager, he was acutely aware of the political realities of the day and curious about the turmoil in the world. He was eager to understand what was happening around him and realized there were only two individuals with whom he could discuss politics, economics, and the opposite sex. One was his older brother, Istvan. There was a natural bond between the two siblings despite the four-year age difference. They were very young when their parents separated and, once their mother remarried, they never saw their biological father again. Whenever they asked their mother questions about their father, she dealt with them curtly.

"He contracted a little-known disease after the war and became very unstable," she told them. When they learned he had passed away, they speculated about what a brave and handsome officer he must have been.

Istvan and Tibor respected and grew to love their stepfather, Domokos. After all, he was the only father they knew. As their family grew, with the birth of their younger sister, Picke and, later, brother Bela, the two boys became enamoured with them. Their mother made very sure that no distinctions were made between the two sets of siblings and they were all treated as "our" children.

The other person Tibor trusted implicitly was Marton Kadar, his tutor for many years who later became a friend. Tibor felt he could get straight answers and a keener insight into the ever-changing socio-political state of the world from him than from anyone else.

Marton Kadar had been fired from his teaching position at the secondary school when the region was annexed by Czechoslovakia.

The new regime demanded that teachers sign an oath to the new state. Being a specialist in the history and geography of central Europe and understanding that under the new regime the history of Hungary was a taboo subject in the schools, Marton knew that he could not possibly teach the history of the region while ignoring the history of the neighbouring country. He refused to sign the oath, and was terminated.

Karola was aware that Marton Kadar was an excellent teacher and when she learned that he was available as a tutor, she knew he would be ideal for her sons. At first, Tibor and Istvan were intimidated by the serious-looking tutor. Marton's stature was not particularly overwhelming — he was of medium height and build. But his deep brown eyes looked straight and unflinchingly at them and the boys felt instinctively that he would demand the best of them. He was also a meticulous dresser, and his hands were always well-manicured and his shoes always polished. Would he expect them also to look so perfect?

In time, however, Istvan and Tibor realized they could ask this man practically anything. The surprise came on a day when the boys were waiting for Marton to arrive. Istvan had acquired a package of condoms. Tibor wasn't exactly clear on what they were for, but Istvan wouldn't tell his younger brother where he got them or from whom. By themselves in the study, the teenagers were filling the condoms with water, tying the ends and throwing them onto the top of a bookcase. Istvan called it a "quality control test." He wanted to see if they would burst from the weight of the water or from the crash landing. They could barely contain their laughter as they flung the condoms onto the top of the bookcase, watching as they sometimes bounced right off and back onto the carpet below.

It was at just such a moment that Marton walked into the room, catching the boys squealing with laughter. Tibor thought he would die of embarrassment. There he stood, the front of his pants splashed with water, a water-filled condom in his hand. Both boys turned crimson as they watched their tutor calmly go to his desk, put his briefcase on the floor in front of him, and ask them what they were doing. Istvan opened his mouth and started stammering. Marton looked from one to the other and asked Tibor if he knew what a condom was for. Tibor quietly replied that he didn't. Marton told him.

As growing boys, they were curious about their own bodies and wanted details that were difficult to obtain. Initially, it took a lot of courage for them to ask the things they really wanted to know, but the incident with the condoms taught them that Marton would certainly not scold them for their questions. He made it clear that there was no such thing as a stupid or bad question and assured the boys that if he knew the answer he would tell them and, if he didn't know, he would find out.

Also, they had discovered that Marton was single and in love with a particular woman. That fact made him seem a little more human and approachable. Istvan deduced that he was probably in love with a married woman and speculated about it endlessly, imagining how they arranged secret rendezvous without her husband finding out about them. But Tibor wouldn't believe any of it. Infidelity in Nagyszollos? Impossible!

Marton realized early on that, if he was to keep the rapt attention of the two boys, he would have to submit to questions that interested them as well. The questions began innocently enough. Would masturbation truly cause them to go blind? Why did the urge for sex come upon them while they slept? As the years passed, though, the students became more comfortable with their teacher and the questions became more complicated. They wanted to know things like how babies were made in the womb of a woman. Marton answered their questions matter-of-factly and never scolded them for or appeared embarrassed by their questions, even though he was sometimes taken aback by how little the teenagers knew about their own biological urges, desires and processes.

So, when Marton began to discuss the topic of history or economics or geography, Tibor and his brother learned they could interject with a question on the topic that really fascinated them. By the time Istvan went away to school in 1932, Tibor had turned thirteen and had Marton completely to himself. Tibor enjoyed learning and soon realized that, through his tutor, he was gaining a much wider, more comprehensive view of world events than he ever would have otherwise. Marton brought immediacy to his lessons with visual aids. He had dozens of maps of the world: maps of the United States, Canada, Central and South America, and, of course, hidden among the ones of the newly organized post-1920 Europe, there was a map of Europe prior to the Great War. He taught Tibor about the French Revolution and the theories of Alexander de Tocqueville. He also talked about the United States and they discussed how democracy and government worked there. Tibor became more and more fascinated with the history of the United States, a country that he began to see as a beacon of freedom and opportunity in the world — one that all nations should emulate.

"Myopic" was the word Marton used to describe so many of the false political theories and beliefs that were widely accepted at that time. He spent a considerable amount of time talking to Tibor about the question of how the mentality of the Hungarian nation had changed since the collapse of the Austro-Hungarian Empire. In the 1920s and 30s, Marton told him, the rallying cry for the Hungarian nation had become *"Nem, Nem. Soha!"* ("No, No, Never!"), named after a poem of same title by the brilliant Hungarian poet Jozsef Attila. Never would the country and its citizens accept the injustices of the Treaty of Trianon. Hungary had been a multicultural, multilingual nation. All that had changed with the Treaty of Trianon when territories that historically had belonged to Hungary were carved up. "Hungarians became insular, self-absorbed and angry," Marton told Tibor.

Tibor learned that there were one million Jews living in Hungary — almost five percent of the population before Trianon. Marton spoke to Tibor about the loyalty of these Jews who had remained ardent Hungarians and had retained the Hungarian language and culture even after the territory where they lived had been partitioned off to the successor states.

"Yet, who did the Hungarians blame after their country was dismembered?" Marton asked Tibor.

"The Jews," Tibor replied.

"Why?" Marton asked. Tibor looked at his tutor and waited. "Scapegoats," Marton said. "The Hungarians made them into scapegoats for all that was wrong."

Marton explained to Tibor why this had happened. The short-lived, 1919 communist takeover of Hungary occurred just as the peace talks after the First World War were taking place in Paris. This communist regime, organized and led by Bela Kun and his henchmen, created widespread fear of Hungary in the West. Kun was Jewish, as were some of his deputies, and, looking back, it seemed that Hungarians were convinced it was this takeover of the country by Kun that had fuelled the vitriolic hatred of Hungary at the peace talks. In a short time, the Romanians, Czechs, Slovaks, Serbs, and Croats had convinced the major victorious powers that they would wipe Hungary clean of the communist scum, if only they were granted more territory.

This conviction led to the first of a series of "*Numerus Clausus*"—laws enacted in 1920 that limited the number of Jews allowed to participate in education and business.

"History continues to affect us in countless ways," Marton lectured Tibor. "Trauma inflicted by history will haunt future generations. That is why we should study history and learn from it. Otherwise, we will continue to make the same mistakes over and over again. What is the great lesson

The Aykler distillery.

in this all? We must continue to learn. It is a crime to prevent the study of the history of any people or nation."

As he tutored his willing student, Marton placed special emphasis on how economic factors played such a critical role in history. Following the Great War, he explained, the three countries surrounding Hungary (Czechoslovakia, Yugoslavia, and Romania) formed an economic and trade union called the Little Entente. This alliance was supported in large part by France and provided the evidence Hungarians needed that a conspiracy existed to strangle the country economically and destroy any hope they had of rebuilding their crippled country.

"What has the Little Entente achieved?" Marton queried Tibor.

"It has driven Hungary into Germany's sphere of influence again," he answered. The fourteen-year-old Tibor was enthralled and excited by the thinking process his teacher encouraged in him. "Because Hungary was excluded from the Little Entente," he went on, "it had to find other trading partners. This drew her close to Germany who became, once again, her largest trading partner."

Marton nodded. He was pleased with Tibor's ability to grasp what he taught him.

"Now," Marton continued, jabbing his finger into the air, "the world is witnessing the meteoric rise of a politician named Hitler. His new German regime promises territorial revision to the government of Hungary in return for its alliance."

Tibor continued to seek out Marton for long discussions about how this situation would affect them all. So much was happening so quickly. Hungary was still a kingdom, although without a king. The government was headed by Regent Miklos Horthy, an admiral of the former Austro-Hungarian Navy. Hungary no longer had a navy or access to a seacoast, however, the former naval admiral impressed Hungarians with his demeanour and right-wing politics and Horthy promised to bring stability to the much-diminished country and to work for territorial revision.

Meanwhile, his own father, Domokos Aykler, was in a Czech prison being tortured and detained for speaking out against injustice. Tibor was incensed and struggled to understand what possessed people to be so cruel.

chapter 3 | 1936

VILMOS WEISZ THOUGHT HE was hallucinating. He stopped in front of their house, staring at the top of the chimney stack of the distillery. He distinctly saw the head and upper torso of his older son, Bandi, pop out of the top of the chimney. Bandi was examining the lightning rod just outside the outside apex of the chimney. The lightning rod was a source of constant fascination for the boys. Suddenly Bandi glanced around and saw his father as well. Vilmos withdrew back into the house, barely able to breathe — the clatter of children's voices echoing inside the tall chimney filled him with dread and foreboding. As supervisor of the distillery, he would be held responsible if anyone was injured or killed on this site, even if he had been completely unaware of the accident. His own children had been repeatedly warned about the dangers of being near the chimney, let alone inside it.

He looked up warily at the thirty-metre chimney looming above him. His son wasn't there anymore. Vilmos stepped closer, tilting his head, his ear directly in line with the resonance. He was close enough now to the structure to distinctly hear two voices and he listened intently. As he crooked his head closer still, he heard the soft sound of small footsteps clambering down the ladder. In a few seconds, his youngest son, Suti, popped out, enveloped from head to toe in black soot. Vilmos couldn't even make out the colour of the child's hair.

When Suti saw him, he stopped abruptly and his eyes opened wide as tears began streaming down his face. Suti stretched out his small arm, pointing behind him, and cried out in a plaintive voice, "I only went up half way!"

Vilmos had to concentrate on maintaining his serious, irate expression, but the boy's appearance was so comical he wanted to laugh. The white orbs of his eyes were the only part of him that weren't jet black.

"What are you pointing to?" Vilmos said, feigning anger. He assumed the boy's older brother, Bandi, was still inside the chimney.

Not knowing whether to laugh or cry, so relieved to see that his sons were unharmed, Vilmos called out to his wife. "Terike, come quickly. I can't tell if this is our child but, whoever he is, he needs a bath."

Terez came running toward her husband, wiping her hands on her apron. She stopped short when she saw Suti, laughter welling up in her throat. The poor child was crying so bitterly it broke her heart just to listen to him.

"Where's your brother?" she said as she took his hand. Suti pointed to the tower. "I'm sure Bandi will be coming down immediately, if not sooner," she scolded as she led the child home to bathe. "And your father will deal with him." She bit her lip to hold back a smile.

As she began to scrub the black soot off her son, Terez looked around at her home with pride. She, her husband, and their five children lived in a one-storey house with five rooms near the distillery of Baron Perenyi. A deep well with fresh, cold water supplied their household throughout the year and she considered herself lucky that she could bathe the children and wash their hair whenever she wanted to. A specialized heating element at the distillery gave them constant warm water and the children considered it their private little swimming pool.

Suti sat in the bath, relishing the warm water and his mother's soft, gentle hands on his body. Even as an eight-year-old, he knew instinctively that he lived in a paradise. His family lived on the grand acres of the Perenyi Estate, where his father was not only responsible for running the distillery, but also for harvesting and bringing in the crops needed to operate it. This entailed hiring the workers, organizing the farm machinery, and ensuring that everything was completed in a timely, efficient manner.

When his friends weren't around, Suti had his siblings, his dogs Buksi and Medi, and the cat Pityur to play with. Aliz and Bandi were much older but Suti felt comfortably cushioned between his middle sister, Hedy, and Icuka, the youngest in the family, who was a year and a half younger than Suti and always around. Hedy and Icuka were also his best friends, although he wouldn't tell them that directly.

He adored spending time with Hedy. They were constantly laughing, inventing riddles and word games. The days were never boring when Hedy was around; she was smart and he learned a lot from her.

Their town had an entertainment centre called the Casino, a hall where dances and social gatherings were held. On rare occasions, it was even transformed into a cinema and it was where Suti saw his first movie, *The Thief of Baghdad*. He was mesmerized by it. Hedy explained to him beforehand that those weren't real people on the big screen, they were actors who were acting, and it was all recorded with a camera and film. But, to Suti, it all seemed so real. During one particularly hair-raising scene when the evil magician Veidt was ready to kill the native boy Sabu, Suti couldn't stand the tension. He stood up, pointed at the screen, and yelled, "Look behind you! He has a knife!" Hedy wouldn't speak to him for a week after they were ejected from the theatre because of his outburst.

Hedy was Icuka's role model and told everyone that when she grew up she would be just like her picture-perfect older sister. When Hedy was getting ready to go out to meet her friends, Icuka would sit on a footstool next to her sister and imitate her every move as Hedy primped in front of the mirror, combing her hair, brushing her teeth, and applying a bit of imaginary blush.

Icuka, being a year and a half younger than Suti, followed him around everywhere. Suti didn't really mind and he had fun with her even though she was younger. There was something about his younger sister that was irresistible. Icuka had chestnut-coloured brown eyes that matched her deep brown hair and she had a warm, loving nature, a quick wit, and a delightful smile.

As soon as she could walk and talk, everyone in the family noticed how clever she was. When Suti read a book, even as a toddler, she would sit next to him and pretend to read. She imitated his every intonation. One day, as she was telling a story from a book she had heard Suti read dozens of times, she completely skipped a page but kept turning the pages and telling the story. The family knew she didn't know how to read and had just memorized the entire book, which she recited from memory.

Suti smiled now, remembering how funny it was. He closed his eyes and relaxed into his mother's arms, swaying back and forth as she scrubbed the black soot off his back. His mother was the true centre of his life. He knew she was the centre of all their lives, but Suti liked to think that, in some ways, she belonged exclusively to him. He could not imagine anyone more beautiful than his mother, and it fascinated him that whenever he asked her anything, she always knew the right answer. How could anyone be so smart? When he was at home, he just wanted to be near her comforting presence.

Suti knew instinctively that it was because of her that they all felt so safe. She had established a routine to their lives that never varied. Monday was wash day when Suti and Icuka squealed with joy as they played hide-and-seek between the freshly washed sheets drying stiffly on the line. Tuesday was ironing and Wednesday was cleaning day. His mother, who had a melodious, captivating voice, often sang while she worked and Suti learned the lyrics to almost every song she sang.

The children always knew when it was Thursday because of the wonderful smell of freshly baked bread that filled the house. His favourite, though, was *kakaos kifli* (cinnamon-and-cocoa-filled buns) that she would bake to his great delight. Sometimes she even filled the buns with poppy-seed filling. It seemed that whenever Suti and Icuka started to argue over something, Mother was always there with the cinnamon-and-cocoa-filled buns and milk to settle them down. Mother was also a wonderful cook. She made the best *toltott kaposzta* (cabbage rolls) Suti had ever tasted and wonderful soups and stews. There was always a delicious aroma wafting through the house when she cooked. But there were certain foods, like garlic and cornbread, that she strictly kept out of their home.

On high holidays, Father took the family to the synagogue, but it was Mother who kept a kosher household and lit candles on Friday night. She told her children about Jewish traditions and dreamed of someday making *aliyah* — settling in Palestine, the Jewish homeland.

She was proud that her children would go to Hebrew elementary school before they transferred to the *polgari* (middle school).

Terez smiled down at her son now as Suti stood on the floor and she rubbed him dry with a towel. The young wife and mother knew she was the central focus of the family — the one who kept them all going. They relied on her for practically everything and she, in turn, realized her life would be pointless without her loving husband and children. She was content and loved the rhythm, the steady, predictable flow of their structured lives. Spring came slowly to this region, being so close of the mountains, and April was frequently rainy and cool. But once the lilacs came into bloom, Terez knew that her days would soon be filled with vital tasks until winter. In the spring, Terez planted and tended her garden. The rich soil of Karpatalja produced a bountiful crop of vegetables and, as she weeded and cultivated her plants, she could keep a watchful eye on the children as they played. Then there was the fruit orchard which needed nurturing all summer. The acacia trees, which lent their sweetness to the honey the bees made in the region, also needed attention. When summer ended and the leaves began to transform into rich auburns, yellows, and oranges, Terez set to

The Weisz family. Back row (left to right): Bandi, Hedy, and Aliz. Front row (left to right): Terez, Suti, Icuka, and Vilmos.

work harvesting, pickling, and storing the vegetables she had grown all summer. She cooked vats of jam with the fruit from the abundant plum, peach, and apricot trees. In this cycle of abundance, their household was practically self-contained and the few things they didn't produce they acquired by barter or purchase. The family's every need was in close proximity to their home.

Terez considered herself fortunate. Her family lived a protected, privileged life and her husband, Vilmos, was well-respected in the small community of Nagyszollos, not only because of his close relationship with Baron Perenyi but also because he was straightforward and led an honest life. She remembered the day when the handsome Vilmos Weisz had come calling. He was a proper young man from a good Jewish family and had recently returned from serving in the Austro-Hungarian army with distinction in the First World War. Although the courtship didn't last long — they really didn't know each other very well before they got married — Terez was excited by the possibility of sharing her life with this determined young man.

Vilmos Weisz and Terez Leizerovics were married in a traditional Jewish ceremony on March 13, 1921. Their first child — a daughter they named Aliz — was born in Ordarma, near Ungvar, where they lived. She was soon followed by a son, Bandi. In 1924, Vilmos was invited by Baron Perenyi to take charge of his distillery in Nagyszollos and that year Vilmos, his young wife, Terez, and their two children, Aliz and Bandi, moved to the baron's estate in Nagyszollos where their family settled in and where three more children, Hedy, Sandor (nicknamed "Suti") and Icuka were born.

Vilmos was the love of Terez's life. She loved her husband's tenderness and knew Vilmos was devoted to her and the children. He showed her he loved her every day in all kinds of little ways. He had a good sense of humour and there was always laughter in their home. In the evenings, when they gathered as a family, he played Hungarian folk songs on his violin with zest, feeling the emotional lyrics of the tragic songs. One of their favourite songs was *"A Ven Cigany"* ("The Old Gypsy"). It told the story of an aging gypsy whose songs are no longer wanted by anyone at the tavern where he has played all his life. At the end of the song, the gypsy's wife comes to collect her husband from the tavern and expresses thanks to the tavern-goers as she says good night. But they hardly notice her. By the time Vilmos got to the last notes of this particular song, tears were usually streaming down his face.

Terez loved the fact that he could show his emotions, unlike so many men of his generation. In his heart, Vilmos was a proud Hungarian and even though Nagyszollos hadn't been part of Hungary since 1920, he empathized with the Hungarian minority in Karpatalja.

After she helped Suti dress and sent him back outside with a gentle slap on the behind, she settled down to read a little before the family congregated for dinner. When she had a little time to herself, Terez always read. She was very young when she married Vilmos and naïve in the ways of the world, so she immersed herself in history books, current events, and the lives of the characters in books that transported her out of this relatively small town, if only for a short time. She scoured the town's small library for books she hadn't yet read, establishing a network of like-minded women with whom she formed a book exchange, a sort of informal lending library. Cultural magazines such as the monthly magazine *Szinhazi Elet*, about news in the world of theatre, came regularly to the house from Budapest. She also perused the latest fashion magazines and sewed well-tailored, *au courant* dresses and outfits for herself and the children. Whenever she went out, she proudly wore a hat and the stylish outfits she had made herself.

But it was when Bandi, Aliz, and Hedy were at school and the two little ones had settled down for a nap in the afternoon that she settled down to read the serious articles in the Zionist periodical *Mult es Jovo* (*Past and Future*). From a series published by that periodical, she learned much about the history of the Jews in the region where she lived, who had lived in the Carpathian Basin almost without interruption for over one thousand years. The Jewish population in Hungary was eighty thousand in 1787 and their numbers tripled to 238,000 by 1840. At that time, larger numbers of Jews who were fleeing from pogroms and political instability in what is present day Ukraine and Russia began to arrive in the northeastern part of the Hungarian Kingdom from Galicia, north of the Carpathians.

In 1895, the legal status of the Jews was sealed with the admission of Judaism into the legally recognized religions of Hungary (*recepcio*). The ramifications of this, as Terez learned from her readings, were that the Jews no longer had to be identified as a separate ethnic group. By 1910, their numbers reached nearly one million. More importantly, seventy-five percent of Jews — about 705,000 — declared Hungarian to be their mother tongue. By 1930, fourteen percent of the population in Karpatalja — or 102,500 people — were Jewish. In towns such as Nagyszollos, whose total population was fifteen thousand, the Jewish numbers reached one-third of the population.

Once Terez understood the history, she knew why her family had stayed in Hungary. As far back as she could remember, her family had lived in the Kingdom of Hungary and she could trace her ancestral lineage back to the late 1700s. It was then that landowners were required to register the size of their holdings and her grandfather's brother, Jozsef Leizerovics, was registered as a landowner in the village of Ladmoc in Zemplen County in northern Hungary in the second half of the nineteenth century. Her own grandfather, Jakab, had owned and operated a lime kiln (*meszegeto*).

The periodical wrote at length about history and current events, and detailed the shocking reality of life for German Jews who, by 1936, had been stripped of all their economic power. She read how over 250,000 of them had been forced to leave the country, many immigrating to Palestine. Terez had to read and reread the reports on *Kristallnacht*. It seemed incomprehensible to her that 191 synagogues had been destroyed with axes and hammers by incensed mobs. *Mult es Jovo* also published first-hand accounts of the widespread rioting in Palestine and, later, explained how the British commissioned a white paper to set up a quota system limiting Jewish immigration to twelve thousand people per year to appease the Arabs in the British Colonies.

The more she read, the more dread filled her heart as she realized that the political situation in Germany was spilling over into other countries as well. When neighbouring Romania joined Hitler's Germany, the periodical provided the first detailed reports of the terror tactics of the Iron Guard in Romania and the bombing of a Jewish theatre in Timisoara (*Temesvar*).

Sometimes Terez became so distraught after reading *Mult es Jovo* that she had to put it away and couldn't pick it up again for days. The stories of what was happening to Jews in other areas filled her with horror at what might happen at home. One evening, as they made their way home after dark, Vilmos and Terez saw two men come stumbling out of a local bar. They were obviously drunk. Still a bit of a distance from them, they overheard one of the men say to the other, "Hey Joska, now that we're feeling no pain, let's go beat up the next person we see."

"Good idea," replied the other.

Terez put her hand on her husband's arm and whispered to him, "Let's go home another way, Vilmos."

"Nonsense," Vilmos responded as he purposefully walked toward the inebriated men. When they approached, Joska stopped for a moment then recognized the couple. He lifted his hat with his hand, put it to his chest in a swooping motion, and said, "*Jo estet Weisz ur!*" ("Good evening, Mr. Weisz!")

Still, her world was safe and the rhythm of their lives continued unchanged. She was determined to teach her children about the wonderful world of books and, before bed, after all the children were changed into their pyjamas and had washed and brushed their hair, Terez read aloud to them. Every evening, she gathered her children around her and read poetry to them with the youngest, Icuka, curled up on her lap. She knew much poetry by heart and recited her favourites, particularly the poetry of her favourite poet, Sandor Petofi.

One evening, as she read Petofi's "*Egy Telem Debrecenben*" ("One of My Winters in Debrecen"), she told the children that Petofi had been poor and talked to them about the misery of poverty and hunger. By the time she finished reading the poem, all the children had tears in their eyes.

"Mother," Bandi asked, turning to his mother, "are we rich?"

"Why do you ask, my son?" Terez asked, surprised by the question.

"Maybe we could send a hundred korona to Petofi," Bandi replied, pleading a little.

Terez was proud of her son, proud of his generous heart, and had to explain to him that Petofi had died a long time ago.

chapter 4 | 1937

WHEN BELA AYKLER WAS three, he wouldn't go to sleep unless his *pesztonka*, his sixteen-year-old babysitter, lay down next to him. He loved the smell of her hair, the softness of her skin, and he would wrap his fingers around her plump, blond ringlets and put his face right next to hers until he fell asleep. As the baby of the family, his mother, Karola, doted on him. Little Bela's world was full of fascination and discovery, and his bedroom had shelf upon shelf of children's books he could explore. But very quickly he learned to pass over the stories of gnomes, witches, princesses, and dragons and went directly to the stories of great battles and conflicts. He loved military history from an early age, whether tales of Roman legionnaires or Napoleon's conquests, and dreamt of knights and great battles of valour and glory.

He would plead with his mother to tell and retell the story of one of his great, great, great granduncles who had helped to defend the fortress of Szigetvar against the Turks. Over and over she read to him about the siege that lasted for years and the endless onslaught of fierce, turbaned warriors with black eyes who clashed with the brave Magyar officers and their men defending the fortress. When they ran out of cannonballs, his mother told him, the Magyars poured vats of boiling tar and water on the heads of their enemies. The Turks, in turn, formed a human tourniquet around the fortress and blockaded anyone or anything from getting in or out. Eventually, the defenders ran out of ammunition and were being slowly starved to death. When it became impossible to continue, the warriors who remained inside the fortress made a pact. Instead of waiting for the inevitable surrender or slaughter, they rode out

Tibor Schroeder as a young man.

of the fortress in a blaze of glory, knowing they were facing imminent but mercifully quick death.

Bela's brown eyes would open wide as he listened, rapt with emotion, to his mother's story. His ancestor had been one of those brave warriors, a captain who rode out alongside the fortress commander Miklos Zrinyi on that final day. He never grew tired of this tale and knew that, one day, he would follow in the footsteps of his father, grandfather, and great-great-great-granduncle and would become a professional soldier, a great warrior, as many generations of his family had been before him since 1525 in Bavaria.

When he turned six and could read for himself, his favourite stories were of the Wild West — stories by Karl May about Winnetou, the wise Chief of the Apache Tribe, and Old Shatterhand his white blood-brother. By the age of eight, he had begun organizing the neighbourhood boys into elaborate games of cowboys and Indians. Bela always wanted to be an Indian. He made a deliberate decision to be on the side of the underdogs because he identified with them. He felt a great affinity with the side that was outnumbered, outgunned, squeezed out of their native land, and living in a country where they were not welcome because they were part of a different tribe.

When two local bullies, the Balsai boys, pummelled his best friend Istvan Hokky and split his upper lip, Bela vowed revenge. Istvan was skinny, wore glasses, and was often sick with earaches and nosebleeds. Bela, on the other hand, was pudgy and strong, even as a young boy. He was incensed that the two bullies would attack his weak friend and knew in his heart they wouldn't have dared touch Istvan if he had been around.

The Balsai boys often used a path that went through his family's vine-yard to get to their summer house. Bela devised an elaborate plan to pay back the bullies. He organized all his friends, luring them over to his house in the afternoons after school to play cowboys and Indians, and waited. On a particularly bright and crisp fall afternoon, the Balsai brothers final-ly came walking through and were ambushed by a half dozen of Bela's "army" who tied them by the arms to a branch of a tree and left them there with their feet dangling. By the time the overseer, Mihaly bacsi, heard the blood-curdling screams of the captives and came to their rescue, the fire Bela and the gang had set underneath them was already smoking their feet.

Bela wasn't intimidated by the punishment he would receive. The satisfaction of knowing he had evened the score for his friend Istvan made it all worthwhile. They had succeeded in smoking out the enemy by exactly the same methods the Indians utilized on the white men who massacred Indians or encroached on their land. He knew the Balsai boys would never intimidate them again.

Bela lived with his parents, his older brothers, Istvan and Tibor, and older sister, Picke, in a big house on the side of a hill, their vineyards extending in every direction. For Bela, their home was an amazing place and their land was magnificent with its own streams and forest. The property bordered on the ruin of the fourteenth-century Kanko Castle, whose stone foundation and partial remnants were owned by the Perenyi family. Bela considered it his own private haunted fiefdom, where he and his friends, or the "army of liberation" as they liked to call themselves, played in the old ruins and re-enacted the many stories and legends they heard about the place. According to local lore, a famous Franciscan monk was buried there, a priest who had led the charge against the Turks in a place called Nandorfehervar. When he died, his supporters had smuggled his body back here for safe burial. Another local legend claimed that a few renegade Franciscans had once kidnapped a beautiful young Perenyi girl from the baron's estate and held her captive in the castle.

Bela's grandfather and mother ran the winery and he knew from a very early age that growing grapes was a meticulous, time-consuming occupation. At various times of the year there were hundreds of workers who arrived from the surrounding hillside districts to help in the planting, separating, covering up, weeding, and harvesting of the grapes. Young Bela looked up to his tall, distinguished-looking grandfather and would follow him along as he directed the work to be done in the vineyards. He loved the sound of Grandfather's melodious, calm voice as he provided direction and inquired about the progress of the work.

When merchants arrived at the house wanting to buy grapes or wine, Bela knew that if he wanted to stay in the room, he had to be very quiet. He sat patiently, not uttering a word, bewitched by the way his grandfather firmly and quietly negotiated with the purchasers. The most interesting buyers were men who Grandfather called *Ortodox Zsidok* (Orthodox Jews). They had long beards like Bela's father but curly sideburns as well. The Jews not only bought the grapes but insisted on pressing them the old-fashioned way: by foot. Bela always sat close by and watched the rhythm of their movements, listening as they sang their fascinating songs. They would come in threes and the men would roll up their loose pant legs and get into the vat full of grapes. They held on to each other's shoulders and sang in a language that Grandfather said was called Hebrew as they crushed the grapes to make their special kosher wine. Grandfather told Bela that although their religion was different, these Jews were Hungarians and had stayed loyal to Hungary, even after the borders were changed. At Easter time, Jewish women brought freshly baked sheets of *paszka* (matzo) to the house as gifts for his grandfather. Bela loved to bite into the crispy treats.

But Bela only realized how many people loved his grandfather when he passed away. The wake was held at the house and Bela, barely four years old, sat perched at the top of the staircase watching as long rows of neighbours and friends came to pay their respects. It seemed the lines lasted days. When they took the coffin away to the cemetery in a fancy horse-drawn carriage, Bela was allowed to sit in the front with the coachman. The seat was high and he was amazed at how much he could see from above. He felt very important sitting up there, not quite realizing at such a young age what it was all about.

After his grandfather died, the full house he was used to as a child began to change. First, his dearly loved older brother, Tibor, went away to high school in nearby Kassa. There were ten years between them. Although Tibor was already a teenager when Bela was growing up, he always made time for his little brother. Tibor pursued hobbies that were out of the ordinary, like photography and assembling ham radio receivers. Everything Tibor did fascinated Bela. Tibor owned an attention-grabbing motorcycle and taught himself how to disassemble and reassemble the motor. Bela swooned at the chance to grab a ride on the motorbike with his brother. Bela sat behind Tibor, wore a special safety helmet, and hung on to his brother's waist for exhilarating rides in the countryside.

Tibor also dated the best-looking girls. The estate had a guest bungalow more than a kilometre up from the main house, a cozy place with sleeping accommodations in three bedrooms and an expansive patio balcony. Tibor frequently took young ladies up to the guest house. Bela wasn't sure what they were doing up there, but Tibor made his little brother promise not to tell their mother about the mysterious female guests and vowed to make earlier and more frequent payments in ice cream.

When Bela's older sister, Picke, turned thirteen, she went away to school as well, first in Beregszasz, and then later in Munkacs. Bela was seven at the time and was attending a primary school in Nagyszollos at the Catholic elementary school. He really missed her when she left. She was closest to him in age, just four years older, and they got along well except when he teased her about her blossoming breasts and boyfriends — always in front of her friends, of course.

His father, Domokos, was also rarely at home. Bela felt instinctively, as a child does, that there was something wrong. Bela saw that his mother often wiped away tears when he asked where his father was. He knew it had something to do with the Czechs. He hadn't actually met any Czech children — there were none in the Catholic and later Polgari school he attended or among the Rusyn boys he played with. The only contact he had with Czechs was with the stern detectives who sometimes came to search the house. His mother told him they were looking for guns and ammunition. Then the Czech detectives took his father away for interrogations and Mother said they did this because the family was Hungarian.

After they took Father away, the house searches became more frequent. Sometimes as many as twenty detectives descended on the house. They would rummage around the house, two searching each room, emptying drawers, desks, armoires, closets, and trunks, often overturning mattresses, tossing everything on the floor. Once, Bela came home to find all of the storybooks in his bedroom scattered on the floor. Sometimes the searches went on relentlessly all day, sometimes they lasted just for a few hours. The detectives searched the packing houses and stables as well, and ordering all the employees out of the distillery while they rummaged through each nook and cranny of the buildings. While the house and grounds were being searched, his mother was taken away to a separate room and questioned for hours by two or three detectives.

One rainy afternoon, Bela arrived home from school to find the front door bolted from the inside. Several Tatra cars were parked ominously in front and he knew the detectives were inside conducting their searches again. His mother had locked the front door from the inside as a pre-arranged signal. It meant that Bela should go to the neighbours' house until the search was over. But Bela's curiosity got the better of him and he thought maybe he could distract the detectives by being inside the house, so he crawled in through the lower-level bathroom window. This was something he did quite often, especially when he forgot to take his key. But it was a rare occasion that no one was at home. Usually Mother or Anna neni, the cook, would be waiting for him with a glass of milk and a freshly baked *fank* (donut) or *kalacs* (cinnamon bun).

Once inside, he inched his way toward the main front entranceway and, without making a sound, crept into the living room where two detectives were scouring the drawers and bookcases. One of them had taken a particular interest in Bela's toy soldier collection, which Mother had let him set up in one corner of the living room so that he could be near her when he played. Bela looked sadly now at the elaborate battlefield he had created with hundreds of toy soldiers, bridges, barricades, cannons, horses, and a fortress. One of the detectives, whose wire-rimmed glasses sat on the rim of his very straight nose, was examining the battlefield intently. The detective picked up a toy soldier — a flag bearer who was a particular favourite of Bela's — and was studying the flag held by the miniature figure. Bela had painted the flag red, white, and green, using toothpicks to put the tiny bits of colour on the rubber flag. He knew it was forbidden by law to display the Hungarian tricolour in Czechoslovakia, but the toy soldier was small, only about three centimetres tall, so the flag was tiny.

When the detective spotted Bela, he turned to him and asked the obvious: "And whose toy soldiers are these?"

Bela scanned the meticulously assembled battlefield and exclaimed proudly, "They're mine!"

Suddenly, the detective's face turned red with anger. Still holding the toy soldier in one hand, he raised his other hand and slapped Bela across the face with such force that the eight-year-old flew across the room, landing at the edge of a chaise-lounge and hitting his head. The pain of the slap was searing into his face, his head was pounding from the blow, the shock of it all was already stinging his eyes, but despite all, Bela was determined not to cry or yell out. As he instinctively put his hand up to the spot on the side of his head where he hit the furniture, he felt a bit of blood. The phrase "Never let the enemy know how much they have injured you" popped into his brain. He remembered it from one of his books. He conjured up the most hateful look he could muster and glowered at the detective in anger, determined that someday, when he grew up, he would repay this horrible man.

The detective studied the boy's contorted face and, in broken Hungarian, growled at him, "You could kill me, couldn't you, you little shit?"

At that moment, the senior detective entered the room with Karola, asking her questions as they walked. They both stopped and stared at the child fighting back tears on the floor, a red welt streaked across his face. The embarrassed detective noticed them and hurriedly placed the toy soldier back with the others. The head of the search team made a show of looking around but ignored the incident and kept talking to Karola as if nothing had happened. She, however, turned white when she saw Bela and clasped her hands together, heading straight to the child.

"What happened to your face, darling?" she exclaimed.

The head detective grabbed her by the elbow and kept talking, hoping that what she had seen would frighten her into telling them what they wanted her to confess. But she had stopped listening. She seemed to shut down as she stared at her young son, both of them silent and passive, frozen to the spot. The head detective finally ordered the group to leave, seeing that no confessions would be forthcoming today from the wife of the man they wanted to indict. When they left, Karola gathered her son in her arms and they sat huddled together on the carpet, each crying bitter tears and comforting one another.

chapter 5 | 1938

BY MARCH 1938, HITLER'S armies were being welcomed by cheering and flower-waving crowds in cities across Austria. Soon the Anschluss, the reunification of the two German-speaking countries of Germany and Austria, was complete and Hitler was jubilantly welcomed at his glorious homecoming to his place of birth.

In June of 1938, Tibor graduated with a degree in Engineering Technology from the Royal Hungarian Industrial Technical College in Kassa. His grades were outstanding. The graduation ceremony was a muted affair since the war was looming just beyond their borders. Despite this, Vilmos Koch, Director of the College, made a point of congratulating Karola on Tibor's ranking.

"Tibor has excelled in the fields of electrical, mechanical engineering, and drafting," the wiry little man began. "During the two-year course, he has hardly missed a few days of class." Koch looked over his spectacles at Karola. "I am confident that, with his new technical education and skills, Tibor will be able to find work practically anywhere."

Karola shook the distinguished man's hand and thanked him for his kind words. She was secretly hoping that Tibor would come home to help run the family business. Each time he returned home, though, Tibor was anxious only to talk to his tutor Marton, to discuss and debate, to question and learn more about the complicated state of geopolitical events around them.

By September, Hitler had managed to convince the British, French, and Italian leaders of Germany's right to the part of Czechoslovakia known as Sudetenland. The Great Powers met in Munich to accept the reversal of their previous agreement with the Czechs. They handed the Sudetenland back to the Germans and, without firing a shot, the German army occupied the Sudetenland.

This agreement also included a clause that granted immediate amnesty and release for all political prisoners being held in Czechoslovakia. Domokos Aykler was one of the thousands released. His clothes and the original amount of money taken away from him upon his imprisonment were returned and he was free to go. After months of interrogation and torture, he was a shadow of his former self. He had lived for so long on thin gruel and stale bread that he found it painful to swallow anything but liquids and, although he was bone-tired, Domokos was unable to sleep, afraid of what he would dream.

Once he was on the departing train, though, and the train pulled out of the station heading east, he dozed off. Floating in and out of consciousness, Domokos imagined himself back in custody. The method of torture they had used on him was referred to as "The Spanish Boots." He was forced to wear extremely tight rubber boots that cut off all circulation to his legs, and the detectives beat his feet with rubber

Lunch on the back terrace overlooking the vineyards.

truncheons until he was paralyzed with pain. Afterward, Domokos was hardly able to walk without assistance. It was a popular form of torture because, due to the rubber constriction, there was little bruising.

On the train, he was suddenly awoken again by someone yanking on his long beard. "Dirty Jew" is all he heard in his semi-conscious state as he was pulled off the bench. Domokos had no strength to fight back and couldn't comprehend what this man wanted from him. The man in civilian clothing lifted the barrel of his machine gun. Domokos closed his eyes and raised his hands to protect his face when he heard, "Stop! That's Domokos Aykler. Don't you know him? He's the leader of the underground resistance and was just released from prison."

As suddenly as he had been assaulted, the men lifted him back onto his seat, apologized, and departed.

Conscious, Domokos peered through the window trying to make out the place name of the station, then realized the train wasn't moving. He saw the station name, "Bene Borsova," and heard yelling all around them. Then he noticed that the train next to them — the train going westbound — was under some sort of military siege. Civilians with machine guns were ordering hundreds of soldiers to disembark and strip. All their clothing and equipment (boots, socks, undershirts, side arms, guns) were put into one enormous pile. Domokos recognized the Czech uniforms. As his train lurched forward again, Domokos took one last look and saw gasoline being poured on the pile. He watched as a match was lit and thrown. He could see the enormous bonfire for miles as his train headed eastward.

WHEN THE TRAIN PULLED into Nagyszollos, Tibor was there, waiting for him. News of the amnesty had travelled fast and Tibor reassured his mother that he would go every day to wait for the train that arrived once a day from Kassa. Karola had prayed each day and waited anxiously for her husband's safe return home. Now, when she heard the horse-drawn carriage arrive at the front of the house, she flew to the front door.

Susan M. Papp

Tibor and Istvan Schroeder at the vineyards.

Istvan Schroeder's wedding.

Karola abruptly stopped running when she saw Tibor extend a hand to assist his stepfather stepping down from the carriage. She was stunned and walked more slowly down the long stairs leading out of the house. Fighting back tears, she willed herself to stay calm and strong for him.

Domokos, with Tibor by his side supporting him, saw his wife coming toward him and tried to stand straighter, pulling his shoulders out. When she reached him, they melted into each others arms. Sobbing softly, she repeated over and over again, "I'm so glad you're home. Thank God you're home. I will never let you go away again." She looked up at her thin, pale husband, gently stoked his cheek, and smiled. "We've prepared your favourite meal, Domokos." She glanced at her son and saw that he was choking back tears as well.

With his wife on one side and Tibor supporting him on the other, Domokos made his way slowly up the stairs to the house. Their daughter was away at boarding school in the nearby town of Beregszasz and their younger son, Bela, hadn't yet come home from school. Karola was grateful for their absence.

After soaking his battered feet in a gentle, saltwater solution, Domokos lay down in his clean, comfortable bed and slept soundly for the first time in many months. Karola lay next to him, gently wrapping her arms around him.

The next morning, Bela knocked on their door as soon as he woke up, anxious to see his father again. Karola calmed her son. "Your father will be dressed and down for breakfast soon, darling. Just be patient."

When Domokos did come down for breakfast, Bela simply ran to his father, burying his head in his lap. A single tear slipped out of Domokos's eye as he gently stroked Bela's hair.

News of Domokos's return spread quickly through the town and, by ten o'clock the next morning, a long line of people wove its way down the lengthy driveway on Kaplincka ulica. The local residents waited patiently to speak to Domokos Aykler. In their eyes, he was still the man who could take care of local problems in Nagyszollos, even if he had just been released from a Czech prison. Karola was frantic when she saw the lineup and begged him not to go out of the house.

Domokos smiled at his wife and patted her hand. "The entire town knows what I have been through and where I have been. It is important that I make an appearance. People need to see that the Czechs have not succeeded in breaking me."

She knew she would not deter him in this, as she had not been able to influence him in any of his political activities. "At least sit on the terrace to receive them."

Domokos knew he wouldn't have the strength to deal with all of these people individually and decided to address them as a group and speak for a few minutes. He inhaled deeply and pulled himself out of the armchair. The crowd grew silent as soon as he appeared and they pressed closer.

"I speak to you today as a free man," he began. From the corner of his eye, Domokos caught a glimpse of Karola, her forehead wrinkled with worry. "My wife is worried about me. You know the way wives are …." There was a smattering of laughter in the crowd. "I stand before you as a man who has been charged with treason in this country and has been condemned to death." An audible gasp went up from the crowd. Domokos raised an arm to calm them and continued. "Yet, here I am in front of you today. I am not worried and want you to stay calm too, to be patient." He paused and chose his next words very carefully. Raising his right arm high into the air, he cried out, summoning all the strength he could, "Our sufferings as a minority in this country will be over soon." With that, Domokos turned and started for the house, nearly collapsing before he made it to the nearest chair.

People continued milling about outside until noon, and then everyone was told to go home. Later that evening, Senator Karoly Hokky, a close family friend, came to visit. He didn't call ahead as he usually did, and apologized to Karola for arriving unannounced. He asked to speak to Domokos in private and had a request. He asked if one of the maids could put a few logs in the fire. The fall evenings were starting to get cool, he told her, and he had caught a bit of a chill coming over. Karola nodded her head and led him into the drawing room where Domokos was sitting.

The men sat quietly as the maid brought in the logs and lit the fire. When she left, Domokos began to talk but Karoly Hokky put his finger to his lips, directing the conversation to the weather. As he spoke, he walked over to the wireless radio, turned it on, and tuned it to a Czech station where the news was just being read. He turned the volume up as Domokos watched him intently. Then Karoly Hokky opened the desk that sat in the corner and pulled out a handful of stationery, drawing his pen out of his waistcoat pocket. He began to write something and handed the note to Domokos.

"This house is probably bugged," the note began. "Detectives have searched your home many times while you were away. They could easily have planted listening devices at any time. I have warned your wife of this as well."

Domokos read the note and nodded his understanding. He handed the note back to Hokky who threw it into the fire and pulled out a fresh piece of paper. Then he continued writing. "They have probably already issued a warrant for your re-arrest. This time they will undoubtedly not postpone the sentence." The senator handed the note back to Domokos and looked gravely at his dear friend. When Domokos gave him the paper back, he smiled sadly. Hokky continued. "Yesterday, a group of *Rongyos Garda* (Ragged Guard) sabotaged a train and ordered some three hundred Czech soldiers off. They burned their equipment and uniforms."

Domokos nodded knowingly as Hokky crumpled up the paper and threw it also into the fire. Domokos motioned to his friend to give him a piece of paper. "Was anyone killed?" he wrote.

"Only the station master," Hokky wrote back. "He happened to be an ethnic Hungarian." Hokky looked up at his friend and continued to write. "These groups worry me, Domokos."

Domokos read what he had written and nodded. "They nearly killed me yesterday," he wrote back. "They thought I was a Jew."

Finally, Hokky put his pen to a final sheet of paper. "I want to take you to the western part of the country tomorrow afternoon. Tell no one where you are going. I think it best you tell your wife you are going to Prague to appeal your case. We will cross the border at an obscure border

Karola Aykler and Domokos Aykler in the vineyard, circa 1937.

crossing and you will be hidden in my car. My diplomatic immunity will prevent them from searching the car at the border." Domokos lifted his tear-filled eyes from the sheet of paper and nodded.

Hokky flung the final page into the fire and, as they watched their conversation go up in flames, erasing the evidence of their discussion, both men sat in silence as the edges of the pages curled up and were sucked into the fire. When Karola came into the room with a tray of tea and pastries, she immediately sensed that something wasn't right. The radio was blaring and the fire was ablaze, even though it wasn't cold. Before she had even put the tray down, the senator stood up, bowed from the waist, and told Karola his wife sent her love. He shook hands with Domokos and said good night to both of them. Without another word, he left the house.

Karola knelt at her husband's chair and put her head on his lap. Domokos took his wife's hand, kissed it, and helped her up. Then he led her out of the parlour and out onto the back terrace where they both sat down on a bench. He closed his eyes, enjoying the cool, autumn air of home. There is just enough of a breeze, Domokos thought, so that we can talk freely. He put his lips into her hair and whispered to her. "Our friend fears for my safety. He thinks the Czechs will probably re-arrest me in a few days. I must go away tomorrow." Even with just the soft glow of moonlight casting light on her face, Domokos could see the look of utter desolation on his wife's face. "We will be together soon, my darling. I promise you that." Karola took a breath, ready with the next question. "It's best you don't know where I am going," Domokos continued, cutting her off. "I will send for you and the children as soon as I am safe. Should anyone ask you, I've gone to Prague to appeal my sentence."

The next day he was gone and Karola Aykler was again left alone to manage the vineyards and raise her children.

chapter 6 | early march 1939

THE FIRST GREYS OF dawn spread slowly into the hills and valleys of the region, followed by streaks of magenta as the first rays of the sun pushed their way into the sky from the east. Officially on a covert military operation, the soldiers were in civilian clothing. They had been out all night surreptitiously criss-crossing the border region with Czechoslovakia. Scouts moved unnoticed on bicycles and mopeds, traversing with ease between villages and towns, in many locations, aided by the local population. Their mission was to destabilize the border region, but the border was porous by then. Part of the region had already been re-annexed to Hungary as part of the First Vienna Accords.

The men were exhausted but elated. They could hardly wait to report to their commanding officer. "The border guards are gone, sir," one of the five announced, saluting, barely able to contain his excitement. "The Czechs have withdrawn from the region."

Domokos Aykler, the commander of this small detachment, saluted back and smiled. He had been notified some days earlier by top-secret military messenger that March 15, 1939 would be the fateful day when the rest of Karpatalja, including Nagyszollos, would be reoccupied by the Hungarian military. He was very well aware that on the same day less than one hundred years ago, in 1848, the Hungarians, led by Lajos Kossuth, declared their independence from the Hapsburgs. The day had enormous historical significance for Hungarians. It was an amazing coincidence that the liberation of their hometown and district was to take place on the same day!

One week before this military action, his men had reported little resistance in the district and Domokos calculated that there was minimal risk of danger to his family. He sent for his wife and son, Bela (the other children were away at school). Domokos wanted his loved ones by his side as the Hungarians reoccupied the region.

On March 15, 1939, the German army occupied Bohemia and Moravia, the two western provinces of Czechoslovakia. As soon as they did, Slovakia ceded from Czechoslovakia and created its own independent, fascist state under the protection of the Third Reich. That same day, the Hungarian army reoccupied Nagyszollos and, within three days, it took all of Karpatalja without much resistance.

Following behind the tanks and lines of infantrymen that rolled into Nagyszollos, Domokos sat in front of a black Tatra sedan with his wife and son in the back seat. The main street, Verboczy ut, was lined on both sides with ecstatic, cheering crowds. Women were dashing in among the troops, thrusting red and white carnations into their hands and lapel buttons, planting random kisses of welcome on the cheeks of soldiers. Many people along the route had tears of joy in their eyes.

Bela felt he would burst with pride. His father was the commander of the troops marching into Nagyszollos, and he, Bela, was sitting in the back seat of the command vehicle! The red, white, and green Hungarian flags that had been forbidden until then were popping up everywhere in windows and doorways and flying from balconies and rooftops. Each time the familiar tricolour was pushed through a second-storey window of a house or shop window, Bela would yell, "Look, Father, another flag! And another. Look, Mother! It's unbelievable!"

Along with the thousands of residents lining the streets that day was Suti Weisz who, together with his father, Vilmos, stood proudly waving a red, white, and green tricolour and yelling patriotic slogans. "Our people are back," he chanted. "We are part of Hungary again!"

Karola, dressed in an elegant beige linen suit with matching hat, watched her excited son and couldn't stop the tears of joy from streaming down her face. She was so proud of Domokos. She could barely believe that her husband was home again, that there were no more borders to contend with, no more searches, no more intimidations. They would no longer be made to feel like second-class citizens in their own homes.

WITHIN TWO MONTHS, THE government of Hungary appointed five parliamentarians, including Karoly Hokky, who had formerly represented the region in the Prague parliament, and they were invested and welcomed into the parliament in Budapest. Baron Zsigmond Perenyi was appointed governor of the region. The Weisz family was particularly proud when they learned the news.

Karola Aykler felt as if she were living in a state of euphoria. For so many years they had been living in perpetual fear of and intimidation by the authorities. Now she could finally breathe. The timing of the political changes was a godsend for the family economically. They had mortgaged the house, the businesses, and the vineyards to stay afloat and if they had remained part of Czechoslovakia, they would have eventually lost everything. Now, new markets were opening up for Hungary. The distillery was working in two shifts to keep up with the new demand for pear, peach, and plum brandy. Wine merchants came in a steady stream to taste and order wine from Nagyszollos; for most, the Spolarich-Aykler winery was the first stop on their visit.

Because they were an influential family that had obviously suffered as ethnic Hungarians under the Czech regime, they were rewarded for their loyalty in economic benefits. The family received lucrative state contracts and concessions. In addition, the Hungarians needed reliable local individuals to keep critical businesses working well. Both Istvan and Tibor, who now had engineering degrees, were awarded businesses.

Istvan and his partner, Bela Friedmann Farago, were appointed managers of Futura, the largest grain wholesaler and distribution centre in the region.

Tibor and his partner, Jaszli Berliner, operated another state-controlled business in town. It was basically an administrative centre where the paperwork was filled out for residents wishing to requisition radio parts, rubber products, and yeast products. Once the administrative paperwork was completed and approved, the purchased items were delivered from distribution centres off-site.

Tibor and Istvan were very close. In Tibor's eyes, Istvan was worldly. In addition to politics and history, Tibor felt he could discuss anything with his older brother. He often spoke to Istvan about the gentleman's code of ethics, behaviour, and dress. Most importantly, his older brother coached him on how to court women. When Tibor graduated, Istvan took him to Kassa and introduced him to a voluptuous blonde named Mancika, who taught Tibor the secrets of making love to a woman. Tibor had never seen such sexy long legs. He was mesmerized by her perfectly sculpted breasts, overwhelmed by her sexual prowess, and simply wanted to stay in her arms forever. Tibor returned several more times without telling his brother. Istvan finally enlightened him as to what a prostitute does and explained to Tibor that making a habit of visiting a brothel is not something that a gentleman should cultivate.

Still, Tibor was eternally grateful to Istvan for enlightening him about the realities of life. His experience with Mancika gave him a real self-confidence around women and he realized he enjoyed their company to a much greater degree than the company of men. Now that Istvan was married and both brothers had steady incomes, Tibor accompanied Istvan to Budapest as often as they could on business and shopping trips. They set up meetings with prospective business clients and found time to visit the finest tailor shops where they ordered stylish custom-made suits and shirts. Tibor made it a habit to get his hair cut and styled at a barber in Budapest. He had begun to notice that the barbers in Nagyszollos provided the same uniform haircut for everyone. He even treated himself to the luxury of a manicure.

As his experience of the world grew, Tibor cultivated a real passion for music. There were so many enthralling sounds of jazz and big-band swing coming out of the United States: Tommy Dorsey and his Orchestra, Duke Ellington, Benny Goodman, and Glenn Miller. He absolutely had to have the newest recordings by singers such as Bing Crosby and such sultry female vocalists as Ella Fitzgerald and Marlene Dietrich. With each trip to Budapest, he expanded his record collection. In school, he had been taught the basic steps of ballroom dancing and now, as an adult, Tibor hired a dance instructor to help him become adept at dancing to big-band swing, the tango, and the cha-cha.

The cafés of Budapest were overflowing with patrons eager to eat and drink until the small hours of the morning. Music and laughter spilled out onto the corso of the Danube that was lined with cafés and restaurants night after night. The citizens were apparently oblivious or didn't want to hear about the war that seemed to be just beyond Hungary's borders.

For Tibor, such outings to Budapest meant the ultimate escape and each time he returned to their sleepy provincial town, he became determined to bring back a bit of the sophistication and culture of the capital. He joined a cultural group that regularly invited visiting acting troupes to Karpatalja, insisting that these tours include Nagyszollos and providing the financial incentives to make this happen. Following performances at the Casino, Tibor would invite the troupe back to the house up in the vineyard for late-night parties. Eventually, Tibor Schroeder earned a reputation as an incredibly attentive and generous host to the visiting artists. He, in turn, prided himself on his friendship with some of the more famous actors and actresses of the time.

To Istvan and Tibor, it was inconsequential that their business partners were Jewish. Istvan and Bela Farago Friedmann had served together in the Rongyos Garda and Istvan could think of no one else who would be a better partner than his friend and comrade-in-arms. Jaszli was Tibor's friend and an integral part of the business. But events that affected Karpatalja were taking place at an incredible pace — faster than most residents could absorb. When the second anti-Jewish legislation was enacted in May, 1939 limiting Jewish ownership of businesses, nothing changed in the day-to-day operations, profit distribution, or ownership of their businesses. But, just in case proof of the non-Jewish ownership of the business was required, all the necessary superficial documents were prepared and ready.

The reintegration of the region into Hungary also brought many other changes. Hungary now shared a common border with Poland, a cause for celebration as Hungarians had always cherished their close relationship with the Polish people. Throughout history, Poles and Hungarians had, at times, shared common kings and queens and they had been on the same side through many tumultuous upheavals and wars. The celebrations of this mutual border were widespread and heartfelt since many of the region's families had Polish ancestry and relatives.

Yet in September 1939, only a few months after Karpatalja became part of Hungary again, the German blitzkrieg invaded Poland from the west while the Russians invaded from the east, crushing the army of the country and scattering its people. Over one hundred thousand Poles fled south into Hungary. Some loaded themselves onto horse-drawn carriages while others came in trucks. But most of them came on foot, often carrying nothing but the children in their arms or on their backs, many of them still in shock caused by the brutality of the invasion they had witnessed. Starved and parched from days of walking, the devastated stragglers came to the door with empty stares.

In many regions of Karpatalja, the residents lined the streets in sympathy, hoping to offer solace through demonstrating solidarity, offering bread, water, and whatever they could. The procession of dazed refugees continued for weeks. It was seemingly never-ending. The municipal governments of the main cities in Karpatalja (Ungvar, Kassa, and Nagyszollos) voted to set aside resources for the accommodation and food for the refugees. Karola ordered cartfuls of grapes and freshly baked bread to be sent to the road leading through town. She sent the overseer and her own young children, Picke and Bela, to distribute the food to the refugees as they walked by. Many other residents offered similar acts of kindness. The Poles slept by the roadside and continued their journey aimlessly south, trying to get as far away from the fighting as possible.

At the same time, the refugees raised thorny questions that Hungarians were not prepared to deal with. How could a regime that had promised to undo the injustices of the Treaty of Trianon destroy the homeland of their best-loved neighbour? Hungary hadn't yet declared war on anyone, yet the consequences of war were thrusting themselves upon the consciousness of the Hungarian people.

It broke Tibor's heart to watch the Polish refugees as they came through Nagyszollos. He felt it was an ominous sign of things to come. Although he came from a family with a strong military tradition, his feelings toward all things military and to war itself secretly filled him with dread. The only person with whom he could share these feelings was his older brother, Istvan.

Istvan had served in the Czech army and presented a view of the Czechs that was completely different from what the local populace knew of them. Istvan believed that the Czechs were more adept administrators and much more clever at the game of politics than the Hungarians were.

"We lived in a democracy in Czechoslovakia," asserted Istvan. "They had to listen to our grievances in Prague, whether they liked us or not. I'm not so sure they will be listening to us in Budapest now that we are part of Hungary again."

Following the invasion of Poland, Britain and France declared war on Germany. Still the German victories spread. They took Norway, Denmark, Belgium, and the Netherlands in May. By June 1940, German troops were marching down the Champs-Elysées. Paris had fallen.

As these unbelievable events occurred, Tibor looked to his older brother for direction and guidance. They spent hours discussing the news of the day, the disastrous war just beyond their borders, the poverty of the hard-working Rusyns in their community, and the increasing number of discriminatory laws against their Jewish neighbours. In general, their homeland was in a sad state of affairs.

In August 1940, the Second Vienna Award resulted in more territorial revision. Northern Transylvania (Erdely) and the Szekely region were regained from Romania. The newsreels showed the wildly joyous welcoming crowds who offered the soldiers flowers with tears of joy and celebrated for days in the villages and towns of northern Transylvania.

The celebrations were short-lived. On June 22, 1941, Germany launched its attack on the Soviet Union. A few days later, on June 26, unmarked planes bombed the city of Kassa. Hungary reacted by declaring war on the Soviet Union, officially joining the war.

chapter 7 | summer 1941

SUTI HAD BECOME WHOLLY focussed on the little bee that had somehow wound its way into the classroom. Every once in a while, a stern buzzing noise emanated from the creature's tiny wings as it pushed itself away from the wall only to bounce back a short distance later. With each attempt to find an exit to freedom, the circles it made became smaller in length and shorter in distance and its buzzing noise diminished. Suti watched it anxiously, realizing that it had probably been trapped inside for some time now.

He was mesmerized by the bee's struggle despite the fact that his beloved teacher, Victor Ortutay, was telling them a tale — "The Legend of the White Stag" — that never failed to fascinate him. Suti's mother had read the story of how the Magyar tribes arrived at the Carpathian Basin to him many times and he knew it by heart. He listened with one ear as his teacher told the class that, while hunting, the two brothers, Hunor and Magyar, had come across a rare white stag so majestic and stunning that they became determined to follow it. Taking their wives, families, and their entire tribe with them, they followed the amazing stag for days that stretched into weeks. Each time they got close enough to shoot it with their bows and arrows, the stag mysteriously melted away into the forest. Finally, after weeks of pursuit, the stag led them to a land of plenty where the forests were full of wildlife and game and the crystal-pure waterfalls and rivers teemed with fish.

Suti had just turned eleven a month earlier or, as he preferred to say, had recently "stepped into his twelfth year." Now that he was older, he felt he understood the world so much better and, this afternoon, the story seemed secondary. He simply couldn't take his eyes off the little bee caught in what he viewed as a life and death struggle to find his way to freedom.

His daydreams on this particularly warm day in April were interrupted by the principal, who bounded through the door quite suddenly. He spoke a few quiet words with his teacher, turned, and scanned the classroom.

"Sandor Weisz," he said loudly. Suddenly shaken back into reality, Suti felt as if the little bee was buzzing right inside his head. He stood up. He was embarrassed at being singled out and was painfully aware of the blood rushing to his neck as he followed the principal out the door.

But as he sat across the desk from the principal in his office, his fears quickly abated. The principal, no doubt with some advice from his teacher, had chosen Suti to help in the town's library. The chief librarian had signed up for military service, the principal told him, and it was the school's responsibility to keep the library operating with the help of young volunteers. About half a dozen students had been recruited to work a few hours after school every other day in rotating shifts, and Suti was among them. There had only been one requirement: all the students had to share in the love of books. Suti realized that it was a great privilege to be chosen. He felt there was no place of greater importance than the local library, where he was surrounded by so many stories about faraway places and fascinating individuals.

Hedy noticed changes in her little brother as soon as he started working in the library. He would arrive home and talk incessantly and proudly about his after-school job. Suti was her cream-faced, darling younger brother who was unabashedly loyal to his sisters and older brother. She dearly loved the way his deep brown eyes became rounder and more pronounced when he launched into one of his stories.

Although he didn't say one word about his secret admiration for the librarian, Krisztina, anyone who saw Suti as he followed her around in awe could easily spot the utter devotion the young boy had for the older woman.

Suti was in love for the first time in his life. Thoroughly enamoured from the first time he saw her, he was attracted to Krisztina's delicate face and hands and her sensitive, warm personality. He had never experienced this feeling before and didn't want to admit to himself, or anyone else for that matter, that when she smiled at him, he felt his heart pounding loudly in his chest. Around her, he felt as if his feet didn't quite tread on the ground. Spending every bit of free time he had at the library just to be near her, Suti was determined that someday he would marry her. There was only one slight hitch: Krisztina was a number of years older than Suti and was already married to a Greek Catholic priest. But Suti pushed those details away from his mind. It simply didn't matter. She was the one. He would just have to be patient and wait a few years.

Hedy knew what Suti was feeling but felt that, with time, this infatuation would pass. She didn't say anything to him about it even though, with his new maturity and sensitivity, they had become even closer and confided in each other. Especially regarding her own love life, Hedy's younger brother had very definite and often pointed opinions on the many teenagers who came to court her. Hedy had come to realize that Suti was wise and pragmatic for his young years. He usually let Hedy come to her own realization about the prospective suitors but told her, well in advance, that David Klein was not smart enough for her despite the fact that his family was quite well off. Mor Rothmann was a genius in math but, according to Suti, he just wanted to win the heart of a stunning young woman like Hedy to offset his unappealing looks. The Steinmetz twins came to court Hedy together. When they came, Suti was the one Hedy entrusted to go and make excuses as to why she wasn't available. He would come back shaking his head. "There is something weird about the twins," Suti told her laughingly. "They probably want to share you as a common wife for both of them."

Hedy hugged her brother close at those times and sighed heavily. She loved Suti and couldn't help but feel a coldness grip her heart as she breathed in the scent of soap in his hair. Sometimes she felt as if they lived in a cocoon, protected on all sides from the chaos and turmoil surrounding the country. Even more than the refugees from Poland that reminded them of the fighting and furor around them, the arrival of the Jewish refugees from Slovakia had truly turned Hedy's entire comprehension of the world inside out.

With the breakup of Czechoslovakia, the Slovaks had set up a homegrown, puppet Nazi regime headed by a Catholic priest named Dr. Josef Tiso. The new Slovak regime was one of the first to implement Hitler's final solution regarding its Jewish population. Many Jews were murdered as soon as they were rounded up, and Slovak Jews were among the first to be sent to Auschwitz-Birkenau. Some ten thousand Slovak Jews escaped to Hungary and those with friends and family in the region had come to Karpatalja. They told unbelievable stories of atrocities.

One of these refugees, a striking young woman named Terez Alexander, found shelter with the Ilkovics family who lived directly across from the Perenyi estate. Living in such close proximity to one another, Terez and Hedy felt an instant affinity and soon became close friends. Their friendship began when they started exchanging books, but soon they were meeting often and Hedy introduced Terez to her other friends. Everyone liked Terez and she was easily accepted by the group. As they walked together about town, they shared stories about mutual friends and flirtations. Terez had brilliant blue eyes and shoulder-length blond hair and when the two stunning young women walked down Verboczy ut together, heads would turn. They were quickly nicknamed the "blond-haired beauties."

Still, months passed before Hedy felt comfortable enough with her new friend to ask why, and under what circumstances, she had left Slovakia. Terez was initially reticent about relating the details of what she had seen but, as they spent more and more time together, Hedy gained her trust and gradually her friend opened up. The story came out in bits and pieces, little by little.

"It's too gruesome," Terez hinted once when they were walking arm in arm. "You won't believe it, just as I couldn't and still can't believe what I saw and heard."

Hedy didn't push her further but, another time, as they sat in the garden of Hedy's house drinking tea, Terez opened up a little more. She was looking around at the tranquility of life in the beautiful garden. "We never saw the hatred in the eyes of our neighbours until it was too late," she said, pausing to take a deep breath. "It began with new laws, with the Jewish Code. Jews were no longer allowed to own land, were excluded from secondary schools and universities, and were not allowed to participate in sport or cultural events." She sipped her tea and unsteadily put her cup down into the saucer in her lap. "Then we had to wear the Star of David."

Hedy sat quietly, afraid to move, afraid that her friend would suddenly stop talking. As horrid as the events were that Terez was talking about, Hedy felt a need to hear them. Her heart pounded so loudly in her chest that she was sure Terez could hear it.

"Then the militias came," Terez continued. "They ordered the Jews in our village out of their homes in the middle of the night." Terez stopped talking. She looked at Hedy, her beautiful blue eyes taking on a cloudy grey hue. "Our homes were set ablaze right in front of our eyes. I'll never forget how the militias kept shouting, 'This is so you will never come back, you filthy Jews.'" Terez's voice broke as she continued. "Over and over again they shouted, 'Slovakia is for Slovaks.' We were sent off with the clothes on our backs. On foot."

Hedy searched her brain for something of comfort to say to her friend, but words failed her. She reached out, took the cup from Terez's hands, and placed it carefully on the little table between them.

Terez blinked back tears and continued with a shrug. "But we were the lucky ones. My family had relatives a few kilometres away. The same thing happened to them but, when they and their neighbours were lined up, they were beaten and shot." Terez put her hands over her face and began to sob. "Our relatives did not survive."

The stories Terez told terrified Hedy. She began having nightmares. One evening, after the little ones were in bed, Hedy had a rare, quiet hour alone with her mother and father. They were sitting around the kitchen table, her mother peeling and coring apples for applesauce. Hedy quietly told them what Terez had described to her. Her mother put the apple and the coring knife down; she went pale as she looked first at her daughter, then at her husband. Hedy saw them exchange knowing glances, as if her parents had already had this conversation. She sat quietly, staring at her hands on the table in front of her, pondering what to say next. Before she could say anything, her father reached across and covered her hands with his.

"Baron Perenyi will never let anything happen to us, my dearest Hedy," Vilmos assured his daughter. "He's a man of influence and prestige. Besides, our family has lived in Hungary for many generations. What is happening in Slovakia won't happen here. Don't worry, my child." He looked across at his wife and smiled. His wife stared back but remained silent. Hedy could tell her mother was not reassured. After a short while, Terez picked up the paring knife and began again peeling and coring the apples in the bowl in front of her.

WITH THE DECLARATION OF war against the Soviet Union at the end of June 1941, there came a series of new edicts, regional and national proclamations, and laws. Karpatalja was directly adjacent to the Soviet Union, the country that Hungary was at war with, and, as such, the region was inundated with new regulations. Newspapers became subject to military censorship. Then came the edict that announced that the spreading of disinformation was equal to treason (*remhirterjesztes hazaarulas*). Radios were confiscated from "unreliable individuals" who were listening to and passing on news disseminated by the enemy.

The army needed areas cleared for operations and announced that agricultural and forestry workers and landowners who lived in the border perimeter would be evacuated and moved to a safer region. Troops began to flood into the region by trains and transport vehicles, and anti-aircraft units were set up just a few dozen kilometres from the border region. The local population, municipal governments, businesses, and civic organizations were asked to volunteer time and resources to assist the work of the national army. The local economy was overwhelmed and soon the rationing of wheat, flour, and sugar began.

The government decided it had to take action to deal with the refugees who had come east from Galicia, Bukovina, and Poland. It was declared that all foreigners who could not prove their Hungarian residency and citizenship were to be taken to Korosmezo, a town near the Polish border, where military trucks would transport all able-

Hedy Weisz (farthest left) with a group of her friends from business school.

bodied persons across the border to work in Kolomea in German-occupied Galicia.

In the middle of July, Hedy's mother quietly told her that she had to go to Beregszasz to obtain documentation to prove that their families had lived in Hungary for several generations.

"Your father says this new law is directed at all the refugees who have been flooding into Hungary recently. The government says they are putting a great strain on the economy." Hedy opened her mouth to speak, to ask the question that hung in the air between them, but her mother continued. "Now everyone has to provide proof of their residency. Even those, like us, who have lived here for generations. It will cause even a family like ours a lot of headaches."

"How are we going to prove our residency?" Hedy asked. She wasn't at all sure she understood what her mother was trying to tell her.

"When your father and I got married," Terez continued, trying to keep the panic from rising to her throat, "we registered our marriage with the county clerk's registrar, even though the ceremony took place in a synagogue. But your grandparents on your father's side were only married in a synagogue; they never bothered to register with the clerk. That means we have to find some other way to prove where they lived and when they were married. Jewish records will not be accepted as proof of residency. We have to find official records in Beregszasz, where I grew up, and in Ronafalva, where your father was born."

Hedy was listening to what her mother was saying, but all of it was a bit much to absorb all at once.

"And it won't be easy," Terez went on. "Your father remembers that one of his great uncles owned land in Ladmoc, in Zemplen County. If we can track down and find that record of land ownership, then our search to find proof of residency will be more or less solved. Landowners have been registered in this country for centuries." Terez smiled bravely at her daughter. "I have to go right away and I need you to take care of Suti and Icuka while I am gone."

"No," Hedy blurted out. "Aliz is older. Can't she look after the younger ones? Let me come with you. Let me help you." She was suddenly pleading with her mother. "After all, I'm in second year of business college. My skills will be useful to you."

Terez looked at her beautiful daughter. How lucky she was to have such a wonderful family. "Fine," she finally agreed. "It would be useful to have you along." She smiled. "And I could sorely use the company."

As THEY SAT ON the train, Hedy watched the yellow fields of rape seed and sunflowers rolling past them. How familiar this land was to her — fields she had seen her whole life. She closed her eyes and let the clickety clack of the train on the tracks soothe her. This journey to prove their identity was bizarre and it frightened her. Suddenly her friend's words reverberated in her head. "It all began with the new laws."

Their trip took longer than they anticipated and was exhausting. With the help of extended family, they had to make several trips to villages and towns where her forefathers and mothers had been born and raised. But Hedy and her mother eventually found the documentation they needed to satisfy the requirements of the new law. They came home successful, but far from reassured.

Hedy realized her family was among the fortunate ones. There were many Jewish families who had lived in Hungary for generations but had not bothered to acquire citizenship. They could not prove residency. In addition, the newly arrived refugee families could not prove any kind of residency and also found themselves in the same precarious situation. By July 1941, these unfortunate people were now being rounded up and driven to Poland to be handed over to authorities in German-occupied Galicia at the rate of around one thousand a day. Their fates were unknown.

In that summer of 1941, when the seemingly safe cocoon she felt they had lived in until then started to slowly unravel, Hedy's carefree teenage years came to an abrupt end. In August, the third anti-Jewish law came into effect, prohibiting marriage between Jews and non-Jews. It also qualified sexual relations between them as a "defamation of race." The new law required documents to prove that there was no such marriage or relationship in order to facilitate promotions, success in careers, and the ability to move forward in society. One's very future seemed to hinge on that single official document.

Suddenly there were endless lines of people in front of the county clerk of Ugocsa — lines that wound their way around the building and snaked down Verboczy ut. Clutching original documents, individuals were desperate to obtain official papers that stated that, extending back to their grandparents, they were "of pure Christian background." It was a pitiful sight to witness some people leaving the county clerk's office clearly ecstatic at having obtained the necessary papers while others walked out in shock, devastated to discover that one of their parents or grandparents had been Jewish.

People watched and waited with trepidation. Then, the entire town was stunned when Lieutenant Jozsef Veress, an amazingly handsome officer stationed in Nagyszollos, committed suicide after learning that his grandmother had been Jewish. He had insisted on being the first at the front of the military lines when the Hungarian army reoccupied Nagyszollos in March of 1939.

One of Hedy's classmates, Eva Sik, was engaged to the handsome young lieutenant. When news of her fiancé's suicide became known, she quit school and left town. No one ever saw or heard of her again.

It seemed to Hedy that a fog had seeped into the very fabric of their little town — a fog that prevented people from seeing things clearly. She decided she had to stay focussed and obtain a higher education so she could pursue employment opportunities. She was grateful that she lived at a time when women were able to do just that.

After graduation, she would seek employment in an office and take her place as a productive member of society. It calmed her just knowing that she had a plan.

chapter 8 | Fall 1941

BELA HAD ALWAYS KNOWN that he would some day follow in his father's family tradition and become a professional soldier. But when, at the age of twelve, his parents told him they were sending him off to cadet school, he felt in his heart that the day had come too soon. To make matters worse, his mother told him that the school — housed in a baroque castle in the town of Nagykaroly — had requested that parents not accompany their children on the five-hour train ride. Somehow, they believed the parting would be less painful if it did not take place in front of the gates of the school.

Bela didn't want to go. He had looked the town up in one of his atlases and found that it was in the part of the country that had been partitioned to Romania following the First World War and had just recently been returned to Hungary. It is so far away, he thought to himself as he ran his finger across the page. He would miss home and his family, particularly his older brother, Tibor.

Knowing that his little brother would be homesick and frightened, Tibor offered to accompany Bela on the train. That made the journey seem a little less daunting to Bela but, still, at the last minute, he secretly tucked a few of his favourite things into his suitcase without Anna neni or Mother finding out.

As he sat on his bed and waited, Bela looked up anxiously when Tibor opened the door. Tibor smiled at Bela and made his way across the room, looking curiously at the suitcase sitting neatly beside his little brother.

"Well, *Beluskam* (my Bela)," he said, "let's take a look at what you've packed."

Bela sat next to the suitcase looking sullen and hoped that his brother wouldn't discover the treasures he had hidden inside.

Tibor sat down on the bed next to the suitcase and ran his hand over the smooth leather. He didn't want Bela to think that he was searching his private things, but he knew his little brother and suspected there would be things in that suitcase that shouldn't be there. Almost as soon as his hand reached into the soft pile of clothing, Tibor felt something hard and pulled out a slingshot. Then, inside an undershirt, he found three perfect little round stones. Tibor pulled them out and looked at Bela.

"Dear brother of mine. You know that one of the things you will learn at military school is how to use far more sophisticated weapons than these."

"But this is my good-luck slingshot. I've had it since I was six," Bela countered.

"It's no good, *Beluskam*," Tibor said shaking his head. "What if another boy finds it and takes it away from you? What if he injures someone with it? Guess who will be blamed if that happens?" Tibor spoke gently but tried to be firm.

Bela knew the answer and stared at his brother sheepishly. His brother did have a point. Then the answer came to him. "But I'll take good care of it. I won't let anyone near my stuff," he shot back.

"The one thing you will learn as soon as you set foot inside that military school is that there is no place to hide 'your stuff,' as you call it," Tibor explained. "Your room captain and commanding officers will come into your room on a regular basis and empty your drawers whether they are perfectly in order or not. Some commanding officers will be fair and decent, but others will simply throw all the clothes in your dressers on the floor because they are having a bad day." Bela sat listening, his eyes becoming rounder as Tibor spoke. "And you will have to get used to that." Tibor waited a moment, watching his brother as he tried to take it all in. "And what if they find something — like a slingshot — that you are not supposed to have? You will be punished and your good luck charm will be taken away from you permanently." Bela choked back his tears and looked pleadingly at Tibor. "But," Tibor continued gently, "if you hide it here in your room, it will always be here when you come home for holidays and in the summertime." Bela looked down at his hands, pondering the alternative. Tibor handed the slingshot back to a pensive Bela.

Bela thought for a moment, then reached into a hidden part of the inner lining at the back of the suitcase and extricated a ten-inch hunting knife sheathed in a fine leather case. He held it lovingly in his hands and looked at the intricately carved handle. Tibor breathed in, trying to camouflage his surprise. He didn't ask his little brother where he had obtained the hunting knife but suspected that one of the many officers who visited their home regularly must have given the prize to Bela.

Bela placed the hunting knife, the slingshot, and the three little round stones in Tibor's hands. "Will you put these in a safe place for me?" he asked.

Tibor hugged his little brother, suddenly overcome by emotion. He knew how much Bela valued these treasures of his and appreciated the confidence the boy had placed in him. "Of course I will," he whispered in his ear.

BELA SAT ON THE train, wearing a crisp, short-sleeved white shirt Anna neni had freshly ironed just before their departure and long cotton pants and polished brown shoes. He was restless and went to look out the window often, watching the rolling hills, towns, and forests pass by. It was a warm summer day and a bit of a breeze offered some relief but Bela was hot and didn't understand why he couldn't wear short pants on such a day. But Mother had insisted. This was a very good school, she had told him sternly. An elite school for children of officers and diplomats. He was going to school in excellent company and he should start his career there by arriving as a well-behaved and properly dressed young gentleman.

Tibor could sense the turmoil in his younger brother and assumed his thoughts were focussed on the conversation they had had earlier in his room. As Tibor watched him, his heart suddenly ached for his young brother. He was still such a child.

Tibor made no secret of the fact that he was a pacifist. He couldn't stand military life. He could barely stomach the basic training he had to complete to obtain the rank of corporal in the reserves for the sake of the family's reputation. After all, they were in the middle of a war, he kept telling himself. Fortunately for him, he was the only male member of the family of draft age who was allowed to remain at home in order to run the family business.

He fingered the picnic basket that sat beside him and motioned to Bela. "Should we see what Mother has sent for lunch?" Bela smiled and Tibor opened the latch. "Bread, cold duck, cheese, and apples." Tibor smiled broadly. "Let's eat!" The two brothers sat alone in their compartment, quietly sharing their lunch until the train screeched to halt.

As they disembarked the train, Tibor looked around. Horse-drawn carriages and drivers, alerted to the increase in passengers arriving by train that day, stood in line, waiting to whisk the cadets to the prestigious military school. Tibor motioned to one of the drivers to take them on the short ride to the institution.

When they arrived at the front gates of the massive castle, Tibor told the driver to wait as he and Bela got down. Tibor took the suitcase out of the carriage and put it down on the ground beside Bela. He stretched out his arms to the boy and hugged him close. "Do well, little brother. Don't let them get you down." He pulled away and looked into Bela's worried eyes. "You can write to me anytime, and I will come visit you if you get lonely, okay?" Bela nodded, not trusting his voice. With that, Tibor turned around and got back into the carriage. He told the driver to take him back to the train station and kept his eyes down as they drove away. He did not want to see Bela's wistful eyes.

When Tibor's carriage finally became a speck in the distance, Bela turned around and looked at his new school. He felt like he was looking at a castle from one of his childhood storybooks. The massive building had four turrets and a moat. The entrance to the castle was about one hundred metres in from the ornate, wrought-iron front gate that surrounded an enormous garden. Bela walked up the long, pebble driveway to the front gate of the castle and went inside to the grand atrium. It looked as if it had just been cleaned and smelled of lemon polish.

As he looked around, he was overwhelmed by the massive entranceway. He felt small and alone and desperately wished Tibor had come with him. The wide, gleaming, marble staircase that led to the second floor had steps that were eight feet wide and a hand-carved, highly polished, cherry-wood banister that was a foot wide. He had never seen such an elaborate staircase and it had at least two landings. At one point, it split into a Y-shape and you could go to the right or to the left. Large paintings of stern, important-looking people hung in elaborate frames on the walls.

The atrium was adorned by three massive marble fireplaces and he noticed what must have been the Karolyi family crest, a coat of arms, engraved into the marble wall above each fireplace. The same four words were written on each wall: *Fide Virtute Famam Querere.*

As Bela stood gawking, trying to decipher the words, a tall, important-looking officer in uniform walked briskly by. He had very short, perfectly combed hair and Bela noticed that, on his collar, he had a blue stripe. He later found out this distinctive rank meant he was a teaching officer. When the officer saw Bela staring at the words over the fireplaces with a puzzled look on his face, he slowed down and stopped beside him.

"That, young man, is the motto of this institution." Bela looked at him quizzically.

"It is written in Latin and the translation means 'To Obtain Glory with Virtue and Loyalty.' Now, come along. Let's get you registered!"

They made their way down a long hallway, down a short flight of stairs, along another hallway and finally arrived at a large, low-ceilinged, well-lit room where tables upon tables were loaded with clothing. There were many other boys already there, all standing in line. At each table, they were handed three each of the different articles of clothing: underwear, shirts, uniform pants, dress shirts, and sleep wear.

Bela watched in awe as each boy received two sets of clothing that had their own special number attached inside each item. There was one

Tibor Schroeder in Budapest, circa 1942.

brown outfit with britches and riding pants that was meant for all outdoor activities, including hiking and military exercises. They also got a blue dress uniform with pants that had a red stripe on each side extending from the hip all the way to the ankle. Each student also received a chrome belt buckle embossed with the coat of arms of the Kingdom of Hungary. Later, each boy would receive a bayonet to wear at his side.

The boy in front of Bela turned to him and introduced himself as Imre Laszlo. Imre had friendly, mischievous eyes and Bela felt an immediate affinity with him. The boys were the same height, although Bela was pudgier. Imre had arrived a bit earlier and already knew a few things about the place. He pointed to a blond boy walking a little ahead of them. "That's Laszlo Haller," he told Bela. "He comes from a famous aristocratic family in Erdely. His father is a baron." He had also found out the nickname of one of the sergeants handing out shoes. "The boys call him *Pacal* (Porker) because he has an enormous head and body," Imre whispered to Bela. The two boys snickered and then saw the boy in front of them handing Pacal back a pair of boots he had received.

"But sir, these aren't a pair," the boy complained.

Pacal looked at the boy and laughed. "That's okay, kid. If they aren't a pair, at least they like each other. Here's another." (*Ha, nem parja, cimboraja.*) When everyone laughed, Pacal put on a grim face. "What is everyone laughing at?" he scowled. "Let's move it. Move it! Move it!"

Once they received their clothing, the boys were assigned sleeping quarters. Bela shared a room with nine other boys. Each student was assigned a bed and a dresser drawer. One of the non-commissioned officers gave a long, boring speech explaining how order was to be kept in the room, how the bed was to be made, how clothing should be folded and stored, how shoes should be shined.

Finally, dinnertime came and they were all led into a dining room with a two-storey high ceiling, wood panelling, and elaborate chandeliers. It could have been the dining room of the Knights of the Round Table, Bela thought. As each student took his place in an orderly manner, white-gloved young men served the students a three-course dinner of cauliflower soup, chicken paprikash with dumplings, and apple strudel. If this is how we are going to eat every day, Bela thought, then military school wasn't going to be as bad as he had feared.

That night, everyone fell into bed exhausted when lights out was called at nine o'clock. The next morning began a whirlwind of activities and, from that day forward, the structure of military school dictated every hour of Bela's day. Wake-up was called at five-thirty and they were immediately ordered to put on their shoes, rush downstairs, and run around the perimeter of the castle four times. When they returned, the boys washed, dressed, made their beds, had breakfast, studied, attended morning classes, and exercised — all before their four-course lunch. In the afternoons, there were more classes in languages (including Latin), history, military history, arts, and sciences. Around four in the afternoon, they practised military formations and marched around the grounds, rain or shine. Six o'clock was dinnertime and, after that, they had a bit of free time. Then, more structured study hours until lights out. They only had unstructured, free time on Sunday afternoons.

For the first two weeks, Bela was miserable and secretly cried himself to sleep every night. He dreaded room inspection and desperately wished he had paid more attention that first day when everything was explained to them about folding and stacking shirts, jackets, underwear, and socks, and about polishing shoes. If the room captain saw a single infraction of the folding rules, no matter how insignificant, every single item of clothing and bedding was thrown out the second floor window. Sometimes, even though only one person folded something wrong, everyone's clothing and bedding were thrown out the window as a collective punishment. Afterward, it took the young cadets hours to collect everything from the ground below, carry it all back upstairs, and put it back in its place. As he folded and refolded his crumpled clothing, Bela remembered Tibor's warnings and finally understood what his brother was trying to tell him.

School work was never-ending. The instructors usually started each class by calling upon the students for oral recitation of their homework. To make matters worse, they always started at the beginning of the alphabet. Since his name was Aykler, Bela was always called upon first.

He was chubby and couldn't keep up with the other students during exercises, so his fellow classmates and teachers teased him. During physical education, one of the exercises the entire class had to do was climb a vertical rope using only their arms. Their physical education instructor carried around a fencing sword and used it as a pointer or to tap the shoulder of a student if he was not paying attention. When he noticed Bela struggling — huffing and puffing as he tried to climb the rope using only his arms — the instructor hit his behind with the fencing blade. When everyone laughed, Bela was acutely and painfully embarrassed. At that moment, Bela became determined that, if he had to attend this school, he would be the best in class.

He began to sneak down to the gym after lights out to practise the rope-climbing exercise. He got hold of a flashlight and studied at night, making sure that he memorized at least the first section of the homework assigned for each class. If his teachers insisted on consistently calling on him first, he would be ready.

By the time he returned home for his first visit two months later, his pudginess had evaporated and the entire family noticed how much leaner and more muscular he had become.

Bela too felt a difference at home and was strangely awkward around his family. In two short months, he had developed a strong sense of camaraderie with his fellow students. They competed with each other and teased each other a lot, but, on that first visit home, he realized he felt more at home at military school with his friends than in Nagyszollos with his family. He missed his friend Imre. Bela and Imre had become best friends. After they saw the incredible movie about the adventures of the Count of Monte Cristo, they even started their own club, the Monte Cristo Club. They were determined to emulate the Count and his fight for justice and the rights of the downtrodden and they had a secret language that no one else understood — a language they decided to call English.

He had also learned many valuable lessons at school — the most important ones being the three rules of survival in military school.

Rule #1: Never tell one parent the other is also sending you money. Bela received money from his mother as well as his father and, so, he always had money when, by the middle of the month, most of the students had already spent all their allowance and couldn't go out on weekends because they were penniless. Bela started to loan students small amounts of cash, but they had to pay interest until they could pay it back, and the interest payments were exorbitant. Bela soon learned that lots of cash meant that you were always popular, not only with your classmates but also with the girls from the town whom you could meet and invite to the local ice cream parlour.

Rule #2: Never miss a business opportunity. Each cadet was required to write home once a week, but writing these mandatory letters was something all the students loathed. Bela realized that a postcard would simplify the obligatory task and hired a photographer to take some exterior shots of their castle school. He asked the photographer if he would take the best photographs to a printer to produce postcards. Bela's classmates lined up to buy the postcards that showed an impressive photo of the school on one side and had a small space to write a short message like "I am fine. Things are going well. Love, your son," on the other. It turned out to be quite a lucrative business for Bela.

Rule #3: Never let anyone know you are scared. Some schoolmates named Bela "The Jew," resenting that he was charging interest on the money he lent them. They decided it was time to teach him a lesson. There was a practice at school known as "blanketing." The victim was lured into an enclosed space, like a classroom or study room, where at least a dozen boys were waiting. Once a blanket was thrown over the intended victim, the other boys would beat him with bayonets and sticks. Bela sensed something insidious was about to happen when a handful of his classmates led him into an empty classroom where several nervous-looking boys were waiting. When he saw the blanket, Bela grabbed the oldest boy by the neck and shoved him with full force toward the window. The window was smashed, the boy's arm was bloodied, and everyone scattered. No one ever tried to "blanket" the kid from Nagyszollos again.

Bela Aykler in his cadet military uniform.

chapter 9 | 1942

THE ADVERTISEMENT IN THE local newspaper leapt out at her:

> Busy office in Nagyszollos looking for full-time office
> stenographer with impeccable experience. Typing, short-
> hand, bookkeeping. References needed.

Hedy felt her heart skip a beat as she read it again. She couldn't help herself as she blurted out, "It's perfect!"

Recently graduated from business school, Hedy was seeking employment close to home. With the war just outside Hungary's borders, she wanted to stay close to her family and knew instinctively that they needed her there as well. There were plenty of talented young people who had graduated with her and she knew the competition within their community was fierce. The courses had been challenging but she loved the feeling of solving problems and completing difficult tasks. She felt she was learning skills that she would use for the rest of her life. In the end, Hedy had finished in the top three — all young women like herself. Women were gaining ground in so many areas of industry and commerce, in large part because so many men had enlisted but also because, Hedy fully believed, the times themselves were changing.

"What's perfect?" Suti asked, looking up from his homework. Icuka was sitting close to him, slowly, carefully drawing each letter he was writing down. Their mother, at the kitchen table kneading bread dough for the weekly baking, looked up, smiled at Hedy, and gave her an inquisitive look.

Hedy smiled back at her and read them the advertisement. "Typing, shorthand, bookkeeping. And the firm is right here in Nagyszollos!" She omitted the sentence about experience. Hedy felt sure she could overcome that small detail somehow.

Without comment, her mother returned to pummelling and folding the bread dough. She was impressed with the idea of Hedy applying for the job, but she wouldn't say so out loud. Terez never lavished Hedy, or any of her children, with praise. Even when she finished at the top of her class, Hedy didn't need to be told it was expected of her to excel in her studies. She realized that her mother's attitude only made her more industrious, more motivated to excel in her studies.

"Whose office is it?" Her mother's voice interrupted her thoughts and she looked up.

"Schroeder and Berliner."

Everyone in town was familiar with the store, which was centrally located on a small street adjacent to the Roman Catholic church. Her mother nodded and went back to the dough. The Schroeder and Berliner families were both well-respected in the community and they operated the only store in town where residents could requisition radios, radio parts, and rubber tires. The store handled salt and yeast requisitions as well — items needed in every household. Since the start of the war these items had been designated "essential" and the government monitored supplies and kept exact records of who requisitioned what. Rubber was also scarce and first priority went to the military. Radios could only be obtained with special permission as they could be used by spies or to listen to the BBC news. The Schroeder and Berliner store handled the paperwork for all of these items. Although she didn't show it or say anything, Terez was proud of her daughter.

Yes, Hedy thought to herself, I will apply for the job. She cocked her head to the side as she studied the name and address listed in the newspaper. The name of the firm had a distinguished resonance to it.

Tibor Schroeder
Electrical and Engineering Enterprise
Telephone: 11
Post Office Box: 32

This wasn't the first time she would have contact with Schroeder and his family. When she was ten, Hedy had been invited to the grand house on the hill by Tibor's sister, Picke. The stately house was situated on a perfect hillside for sledding and, as soon as the first snow fell, the neighbourhood children would all congregate on the hill, their screams and shouts echoing in the distance as they rode their toboggans and sleds down the steep incline. Hedy and Picke had started chattering and laughed all through the afternoon of that snowy day. Picke found Hedy very entertaining and later invited her back to the house for hot chocolate.

As she stepped into the front foyer, Hedy was overwhelmed by the impressive two-storey atrium filled with rows upon rows of books. She had never seen so many books in one collection. Hedy had the urge to stop there and just run her fingers along the neatly organized spines, to just read the titles, but Picke took her hand and led her inside on a tour of the house.

Hedy didn't know where to look first. Mahogany chaise lounges and chairs sat elegantly in the front parlour beside side tables and coffee tables with elaborately carved designs on the sides. Bronze statues of ancient Greek mythological deities and porcelain figurines decorated the tables, bookshelves, and glass-enclosed china cabinets. Flowing landscape paintings and portraits of important-looking ancestors hung on the walls. Rich, ornate Persian carpets covered the main areas of the oak parquet flooring. She ran her hand sensuously over the impressive black Bosendorfer grand piano that stood in one corner.

"Come," sang Picke as she led Hedy into the dining room where the table was being set with Meissen china. Hedy had only seen such china patterns in magazines and watched mesmerized as the maid made her way around the table, polishing the silverware, checking for any spots on the crystal wine goblets as she set three goblets at each place setting. The

Colonel Domokos Aykler as head of the press corps for the Hungarian army in 1942.

maid didn't even notice the two young girls as she went about unfolding each stiffly starched white serviette and folding each again as she laid them on the table beside each dinner plate. Each serviette was big enough to cover a small side table.

"Let me show you my room, and my dolls," Picke said as she marched out of the room, unaware of her guest's awe. They climbed the massive staircase to the second floor, walking past a room whose door was closed. Hedy looked at the only door that wasn't ajar and Picke noticed.

"That's my older brother Tibor's room. He is away at technical college in Kassa and he really doesn't like us rummaging through his room. That's why Mother keeps his door locked. We can only go in there when he's home."

On one side of the house there was a room with a magnificent view of the town. "Look," Picke exclaimed, pointing toward the window. "How many church steeples can you count from here?" As Hedy began adding them up, Picke shouted, "Seventeen!" even before Hedy had a chance to respond. She had never seen Nagyszollos from such a height and Picke seemed thrilled at how enthusiastically Hedy responded to all she showed her. Soon they were exploring all the crawl spaces and crannies of the house. "Okay. Now let me show you my room."

Picke led Hedy to a corner room with a breathtaking view of the vineyards. There were two single beds in the room, each one covered with white lace and decorated, one with teddy bears and the other with dolls. Hedy caught sight of a doll that had an exquisite painted porcelain

A Sunday at home with the family, circa 1943.

face. It was beautiful and its dark blue velvet dress with ecru lace collar matched the fine features of the porcelain visage. She walked tentatively closer and looked at her. There was so much fine detail on the doll; even her socks had a tiny cuff of lace.

"I've named her Maria," volunteered Picke proudly. "My Uncle Laszlo brought it back from Budapest for me. It was hand-painted in China."

Along the walls there were bookcases with row upon row of children's books. There were more books here than even in the local library, Hedy realized.

As they were paging through some of the books, Picke's mother walked into the room. Karola saw the look of wide-eyed wonderment on Hedy's face as she stared at the amazing collection of books. She smiled warmly at the girl and invited Hedy back to the house any time to borrow something to read.

As she sat in the kitchen with the newspaper in her hand and remembered that day, Hedy realized that the warm, engaging woman was Tibor Schroeder's mother as well.

A few years after that snowy day, Hedy had met Tibor Schroeder himself. She was sure Mr. Schroeder wouldn't remember the encounter but she certainly did. The occasion was Hedy's close friend Babci's wedding. The girls studied together at business school and the tall Babci with the perfect hourglass figure couldn't wait to marry her childhood sweetheart who had, by then, finished his degree in law. Babci was a very bright girl but she had married when she was only sixteen. It was at her dear friend's wedding that Hedy first noticed the handsome Tibor Schroeder. Many of the girls in her class were standing around tittering about this tall, broad-shouldered young man with intense brown eyes. At the reception, he entertained and enchanted the women who were continually flocking around him. Hedy watched him from the corner.

Now, years later, she would be seeing him again. She folded the newspaper and laid it on the chair next to her. She wouldn't mention that meeting when she met him. She had been a shy, thin schoolgirl at the time and was convinced that Mr. Schroeder hadn't even noticed her.

Tibor Schroeder could barely contain his excitement as he watched the stunning young woman walk into the office. She was wearing a fitted, light-blue stylish knit suit, her blond hair pinned back in a French twist. He watched through a glass window as his partner, Jaszli Berliner, showed her to a chair in the waiting room. Jaszli asked her a few questions and took the papers she handed him.

A few moments later, Jaszli bought her papers into Tibor's office and said in a barely audible voice, "She has no experience." There was a tone of finality in the statement that Tibor understood, but chose to ignore. He had already decided to hire her. For appearance's sake, however, he told Jaszli that he wanted to ask her a few questions, making it look like he was seriously interviewing a potential candidate. He led her into his office and looked at the pages Jaszli had handed him.

"These are very impressive grades, Miss Weisz. How recently did you graduate from business college?"

Hedy hesitated for a moment; she didn't want to seem impertinent.

"Just now," she stated calmly, with a bit of a smile.

"Of course, of course. It's all here," Tibor replied, studiously examining the transcripts in front of him.

It was springtime, and Tibor wished he could ask this stunning young woman out for a cool drink on a shady terrace somewhere instead of sitting at a desk across from her in this stuffy office. As she sat there, slowly pulling off her white gloves and revealing long fingers and neatly manicured nails, he pretended to continue studying her transcripts. Tibor glanced up at her occasionally. She was a flawless beauty, there was no doubt about it. There was nothing but perfection about her. He couldn't believe she had grown up in Nagyszollos and he had never noticed her before.

Tibor looked up from the transcripts. "Miss Weisz," Tibor said, trying to keep a professional tone of voice, "You have the job. When can you start working?"

Hedy glanced at Jaszli, who was watching Tibor silently.

"Well, anytime, really. Possibly tomorrow morning," she replied, trying to hide her astonishment at being hired so quickly.

"Tomorrow morning it is, then," Tibor repeated as he stood up to escort her to the door.

"Thank you," Hedy said.

"We thank you, Miss Weisz." Tibor's brown eyes glistened with happiness at the thought of seeing her again so soon. "Until tomorrow morning, then."

Hedy turned back at the door and asked tentatively, "What time should I be here?"

"What time?" Tibor looked to his partner for a second and Jaszli promptly replied, "Eight-thirty." She smiled and said goodbye. Once she was out the door, Tibor looked at Jaszli, who just rolled his eyes in exasperation.

As soon as she was out of sight of the office, Hedy practically skipped home with happiness. She could hardly wait to tell her parents and siblings that she had found a job at an important business in town and that her new employer seemed like a very kind man. She'd keep to herself the fact that she thought Tibor was very handsome, too.

Hedy began work at her new job the next day. It didn't take long for Tibor and Jaszli to realize that, in addition to her striking appearance, she was proficient at her work. She typed the extensive lists of the requisition slips without errors and kept the books. The piles of papers that had, until then, been such a nuisance around the office disappeared into newly organized filing cabinets. When townspeople and farmers came from the surrounding villages to requisition the necessary raw materials for their businesses, Hedy processed the applications efficiently. Everyone liked her.

Tibor was twenty-five years old and had quite a bit of experience with women. Although he had been infatuated before, he had been determined not to get entangled with any of the spoiled daughters of well-to-do provincial families in the region. Hedy was different. He had never met anyone as intriguing as her before. She was intelligent and witty and, more importantly, she had something that he was looking for in a woman and rarely found: charisma.

Overnight, Tibor became devoted to his work. Everyone around him noticed how enthusiastic and animated he became when he talked of the business. He made up excuses to spend long hours in the office just to be near Hedy and frequently walked behind her chair to get a whiff of her scent. He was often tempted to touch her hair, her hands, her face, but somehow managed to keep a sense of decorum between them.

Within a week of her employment, he offered to take her to lunch at a nearby café. Hedy looked at him in shock. It was such a small town and there were only two restaurants. But he acted as if it was the most natural thing to do. They both knew they could never go into a café together, but Tibor didn't seem to care. It had been a year now since the law had come into effect making it illegal for a Christian to marry a Jew and qualifying sexual relations between them as a "defamation of race." But Tibor didn't concern himself with laws, especially those that tried to legislate whom he could fall in love with. He simply didn't care what people knew or what they thought. He felt sure that his stepfather's rank and status in the army offered him some protection from this ludicrous state of affairs and continued to mock and openly criticize the changes forced on them by new regimes and wartime situations. She looked at him demurely and graciously declined, but something in her look told Tibor that the ever-deepening feelings of affection he was experiencing might be stirring in her as well.

It started innocently enough. As office manager, Jaszli described her daily tasks in detail, including making coffee in the morning. But Tibor, seeing the amount of work she had to contend with, began to make coffee for her each morning. If clients weren't waiting and the office was quiet, Tibor would bring in a simple lunch from a nearby café.

"You will spoil the professional working relationship we have with Miss Weisz," Jaszli warned him. But Tibor couldn't care less about maintaining the strict rules dictating the relationships between employer and employee. Their conversations went on, sometimes for hours, about their families, their interests, their hobbies, and their surprisingly similar views of the world. Gradually, she began to weave her way into his mind and his heart.

Hedy was impressed with Tibor's impeccable manners. It meant the world to her that he sought out her opinions on all kinds of issues. He often said she brought a fresh pair of eyes to the way they did business at the firm. He convinced Hedy that her work really made a difference. He was so inquisitive yet lighthearted that Hedy didn't mind at all his questioning her.

Soon, he began to actively court her. The flower market was directly adjacent to the office and, at least once a week, he would show up at work with a bouquet of flowers and a simple message card that read, "How did we ever manage before you?" or "To the loveliest young woman in Nagyszollos." Tibor had a zest for life that Hedy had never experienced before in any other young man that courted her. Sometimes, an hour before closing time and much to Jaszli Berliner's chagrin, Tibor would put the CLOSED sign on the door, bring out a bottle of pear brandy, pour it into three separate glasses, and toast the end of the week or the brilliant sunshine or the start of spring or the end of a dreary day.

Tibor was incredibly generous, frequently providing Hedy with tickets to theatrical presentations or movies that came to town. He persuaded Hedy to fill out a form with the ages and shoe sizes of each of her siblings, telling her that the firm needed these for their records. A few months later, each member of the Weisz family received a new pair of leather shoes. In wartime, leather shoes were a rare commodity and Hedy couldn't hide her incredible surprise or sufficiently express her gratitude.

By the fall of 1942, a general curfew had been ordered in the town and power for street lights was curtailed. When darkness fell or they had to work late, Tibor would escort Hedy home, insisting that a young woman wasn't safe on the dimly lit streets of their town. Because they were bundled up in coats and hats, they were rarely recognized. Tibor pulled Hedy as close to him as possible as they walked, stepping in unison.

Sometimes they talked quietly as they walked along the darkened streets; sometimes they didn't say a word and just walked. Often Tibor would lead her on a more circuitous route home, just to extend their time together. During the long walks, Hedy felt a quiver of excitement run all the way down her spine. It was so strong she thought Tibor felt it as well.

A few months after she started working for Tibor, Hedy noticed one evening that Jaszli Berliner left the store early, something he hardly ever did. That left Tibor and Hedy alone in the store. An avid music collector, Tibor had a large record collection with the newest releases of jazz, classical, and big-band music and a Siemens top-of-the-line record player in the store to play them on. That evening, he chose Marlene Dietrich's newest album to put on the turntable. One of the songs was a dreamy tune entitled "Falling in Love Again." Hedy had never heard it before and she was enchanted by the melody and the lyrics.

As she sat listening at her desk, Tibor came over and asked if she would come into his office. She stood up and picked up her pencil and steno pad, thinking he wanted to dictate a letter to her, but he took hold of her hand and guided her deftly to sit beside him on the two-seater couch in his office. When they sat down, he didn't let go and extricated the pad and pencil from her hand. He placed them on the coffee table in front of them where there already sat two brandy glasses, a bottle of sweet Tokay wine, and almond crescent cookies meticulously laid out with lace napkins. It was as if he had been planning this surprise for her. Tibor seemed pensive but then he smiled and began to speak.

"I thought it was time we had a more serious chat, Miss Weisz." He poured them each a small glass of dessert wine and gave one glass to Hedy. "But first, let's have a drink to celebrate our wonderful ...," he paused for a moment, lifted his glass, and then continued, "working relationship." They clinked glasses and he continued. "I feel I must tell you what a great deal of admiration and affection I have developed for you over these past few months. He looked seriously in her eyes. "If this feeling is not mutual or you feel uncomfortable by the subject of this conversation, please tell me now. As for me, I want to talk about ... *us.*"

Hedy felt her neck and cheeks turn crimson with embarrassment as he stared intently at her. His eyes seemed to sear right into her heart. This man was not like any of the boys who had courted her until now. She realized the seriousness of the moment and nodded silently in agreement.

"I have, very simply, fallen deeply in love with you, Hedy," Tibor continued. "I can't imagine my life without you anymore."

Hedy looked at him, her eyes glistening with happiness as she listened to his revelation. Her heart pounded louder than she had ever imagined it could as she whispered in a barely audible voice, "I feel the same about you."

Then Tibor put his arms gently around her and kissed her. No more words were necessary between them. Their kiss revealed just how deeply they felt about each other.

As Tibor walked her home that evening, Hedy felt as if her feet were barely moving. She held on to Tibor's arm tightly, hoping that his sure steps would stabilize her. They walked silently, in unison. Once she got home, Hedy went directly to her room, fearing that if her mother or siblings looked her in the eyes, the secrets of her heart would be revealed. She crawled into bed and pretended to be asleep, her mind racing, her heart pounding as she replayed all that had taken place a few hours earlier. The problem was there was no one in this world she could share her secret with.

The town's chief clerk was a short, wiry, officious-looking man with a nervous pitch to his voice. He wore pince-nez glasses that sat on the end of his nose and he reminded Tibor of a character from the British Punch and Judy cartoons. Tibor would often sit at his desk mimicking the chief clerk, deriding his ludicrous pronouncements. The latest of these idiotic rules had just been announced and, balancing a pencil on his nose, Tibor began with the obligatory "Ahem, ahem" and proceeded to declare that, "In light of this wartime situation, and eggs being such a costly commodity, the painting of Easter eggs should be avoided this spring. In fact, all noisy gatherings of more than five individuals should be cancelled until further notice."

Hedy and Jaszli could barely hold back their laughter once Tibor began his perfect imitation of the chief clerk. But Tibor, once he collected himself, turned serious and a worried look clouded his striking features. "If we can't laugh at it," he said with a shrug, "we would certainly be crying."

As Hedy watched him rail against all the new rules and regulations, she realized he was more affected by them than anyone else she knew. Deep in her heart she understood that what was truly exasperating him was the secrecy they had to maintain about their blossoming love. They couldn't be seen in public walking arm in arm or showing any kind of intimate affection and Tibor was painfully aware that he had to control his feelings in public, even if only for Hedy's sake. They had to be resolute and discreet in their love affair. The consequences could be dire.

As difficult as it was, they continued to address each other in public as "Miss Weisz" and "Mr. Schroeder." Only when they were alone together would they use "Hedy" and "Tibor." Some afternoons, Tibor would simply put the "closed" sign on the front door of the shop, let the blinds down, and they would sit together and listen to the newest album of Edith Piaf or Tommy Dorsey. Sometimes they danced or just held each other. Tibor couldn't get enough of her touch, her scent, the softness of her skin. She fit so perfectly into his arms. Whenever they were in a melancholy mood, songs like "La Vie en Rose" and "Lili Marlene" would lighten the gloominess around them. It was balm to their spirits and reminded them that, throughout history, people in love frequently found themselves in similarly impossible situations.

On warm sunny days, they escaped from the provincial little town altogether. Tibor would get on his motorcycle, provide Hedy with another motorbike, and they would ride away into the rolling foothills of the Carpathian Mountains. As they rode further and further away, the gossip, the rumours, and the war seemed to melt away behind them. The air was full of the scent of mountain bluebells dotting the landscape and edges of the road. The majestic hills offered respite from prying eyes and, for an afternoon, they didn't have to worry about who was watching.

On one glorious afternoon, they sat side by side on a blanket by the banks of the River Tisza. The warmth of the sun caressed their skin as they munched on the cold roast duck, cheese, and bread, sharing sips from a flask of wine Tibor had brought along. Absently, they watched a pair of swallows performing a graceful dance from trees nearby, swooping low just above the water's edge, gently splashing the water as they bobbed and weaved to take a drink.

Suddenly, Tibor sat up and put on his business face. Addressing her as if they were in the office, he said, "Miss Weisz, could you take a letter for me?"

Hedy looked at him with a twinkle in her eye. "Of course, Mr. Schroeder. I will gladly take a letter, but I don't seem to have a pen or paper."

"That doesn't matter, Miss Weisz, you will simply have to commit the letter to memory."

"I will make do my best!" Hedy replied, caught up in his light-hearted, humorous mood.

Tibor cleared his throat and began. "I, Tibor Schroeder, do hereby solemnly declare to the entire world (or at least that part of the world that cares to hear) that I do love Miss Hedy Weisz and will marry her ...," here he paused and looked longingly into her eyes, "... if she will have me. I promise to do so as soon as I am able. Signed this twenty-third day of April in Nagyszollos, Hungary. Tibor Schroeder Esquire, etc. etc."

Tears welled up in Hedy's eyes, "Darling," she whispered as he took her delicate hand in his and kissed it lovingly. He looked into her deep, emotion-filled eyes as if trying to decipher whether the tears were of joy or sadness. Tibor couldn't tell. He looked out at the rushing waters of the Tisza, the swirling currents and undulating waves that seemed to be chasing each other, faster, faster. The sadness of their situation had overwhelmed them both and he avoided Hedy's eyes for a few minutes while he regained his composure.

"Someday, my love, I will build a raft with a little houseboat on it. You and I will get on board and be quietly swept down the Tisza, then into the Danube and out to the Black Sea. We will marry and live freely." He took her hands in his and held them tightly. "I promise you that we will be together forever."

Hedy nodded as tears ran in rivulets down her cheeks. She loved this man, this generous, kind man, but she sensed the world would get in the way. They agreed that, when the time was right, Tibor would speak to Hedy's parents and ask for her hand in marriage. Between them, the matter was settled and the world would just have to go along.

chapter 10 | 1942

HEDY AND TIBOR HAD an unspoken rule between them. When they were together, they talked about anything and everything except the war and the increasingly unbelievable events affecting their neighbours and community. In the American films they occasionally saw at the local cinema, elegantly dressed housewives waved to their well-tailored husbands as they drove off to work in the mornings. The sun was always shining and the housewife, with her tiny waistline and perfectly straight and bright white teeth, was forever smiling. There was always a happy ending. The charade they played, however, of not talking about what they were getting themselves into, of not being able to make any plans, of keeping their secret under wraps, was emotionally difficult.

Although Hedy and Tibor hoped that their lives would turn out like the ones in the movies, Hedy knew that, no matter how hard she tried to envision herself as part of that perfectly sunny, sanitized, happy couple, life in Nagyszollos in the middle of war-torn Europe was far, far removed from that scenario. Still, when she was in Tibor's arms, Hedy felt insulated from it all. She knew in her heart that he would do anything to protect her from harm.

The world outside his arms, though, was harsh and increasingly frightening. Each day brought new laws, new regulations, and war hysteria. Curfews were tightened, rationing of sugar, flour, and coffee became even stricter. Cigarettes became a prized commodity, and "smoke-free" days were held to gather cigarettes for Hungarian soldiers fighting on the front lines. At night, air-raid sirens blared with such regularity that people who had initially been startled awake by them slowly started to get used to them. Newspapers carried more and more horrific stories, some reporting that hundreds of communists and Ukrainian terrorists had been arrested and incarcerated, and some were executed.

Extremist, anti-Semitic groups inspired by the Arrow Cross Party sprung up even in Nagyszollos. Their national leader, Ferenc Szalasi, had been imprisoned in Budapest in the early 1930s for fomenting hatred and violence. One of his followers in Nagyszollos was a captain in the gendarmes named Mezeredi. Tibor realized that the locals had begun to gossip, to inform Mezeredi about his movements and meetings with Hedy. To Mezeredi and his gang, the fact that Tibor Schroeder had hired a Jewish woman was shocking enough; the gossip surrounding a possible romantic liaison between Schroeder and his Jewish secretary was beyond outrage.

The intimidation tactics began with anonymous notes shoved under the front door of the Aykler family home. Finally, Captain Mezeredi's frustration at not being able to do anything about the son of one of the highest ranking military officers in the region boiled over. One day, he boldly telephoned Tibor's mother, Karola. He launched into a tirade against Tibor, calling him arrogant and conceited, a man without virtue. "In light of the fact that the colonel's son is blatantly flouting the law and courting a Jewish woman," Mezeredi said in closing, "the local gendarmes will not take responsibility for what might happen to him."

Tibor always sensed when a threat had taken place but this time was different. Although Karola made her daughter promise to stay tight-lipped about the incident, Tibor knew from the way his mother paced up and down in the parlour, wringing her hands and dabbing her bloodshot eyes with a handkerchief, that this threat had been more serious. On one of his rare visits home, Karola tried to broach the subject of Tibor's love with her husband, Domokos. It was a perfect Sunday and they sat on the veranda enjoying their coffee and an apple tart dessert, Karola noticed how much greyer Domokos's beard had turned since the last visit. As he sipped absently at his brandy, Domi had a distant, vacant look in his eyes and frequently withdrew into himself.

Karola relished this infrequent private time with her husband and although they tried not to talk about the war, she knew Domokos was under tremendous pressure. In the spring of 1942, Colonel Domokos Aykler had been named head of the press corps of the Hungarian army. Those who entered this elite branch of the military had to have already been established newspaper writers, film cameramen, and/or radio reporters. In addition to their skills as journalists, they had to undergo extensive combat training in case the unit came under attack. A small army onto itself, with their own cooks, medics, and ambulances, the corps operated and travelled independently of the rest of the army. The press corps didn't even travel in army jeeps — they drove in large black Tatra sedan cars.

The day Colonel Aykler took command of the regiment was marked by pomp and ceremony and the celebrations were widely covered in newspapers and newsreels. It was the middle of May and the chestnut trees in Budapest parks were bursting with delicate white flowers. A large crowd gathered to watch the impressive gathering and even young boys stopped playing in the park and stood in awe with their parents as some one hundred shiny black Tatra sedans were assembled next to each other in Vermezo Square. Some of the professional press officers stood on the roofs of their cars with tripods and cameras whirring while others stood at attention next to their vehicles as the corps stood for inspection. It was a grand media show of readiness.

The regiment held great fascination for Hungarians, who realized only too well the power of media in the world. They knew that the men in this corps could transmit stories in dozens of languages. Many newspaper reporters had speculated for some time now that Hungary had to become more politically and media savvy in order to gain worldwide sympathy for its cause. Even before they shot a single frame of film, the newspapers in Budapest were already reporting that, "This is the military unit; these are the men who will finally tell the world the story of Hungary's suffering and fight for justice."

These days, when he came home, he was mentally and physically exhausted. Still, even at home, military men continued to knock on the door bringing telegraphs, letters, and correspondence marked "Confidential" for him to read and acknowledge. Karola retrieved a handkerchief from the pocket of her skirt and dabbed her forehead a bit, then she took a sip of coffee and began tentatively to speak.

"Who is that Mezeredi man and does he have power over us?" Karola blurted out.

"Mezeredi?" Domokos asked quizzically. From the look on his face, Karola could see that he genuinely did not know this name.

"You know, of the gendarmes. He's one of the Arrow Cross men."

Suddenly, Domokos was paying attention. "Why? What happened?"

"He threatened Tibor," Karola continued. "He told me on the phone that if Tibor didn't stop courting Hedy Weisz, he would tell his superiors. He said they wouldn't be responsible for the consequences." By the time she finished the last word in her sentence, tears had welled up in her eyes as if a small dam had burst. She started crying, sitting there next to her husband, and it took several minutes before the flood of tears abated.

Domokos looked at her lovingly, with concern. "Dragam, don't worry about Mezeredi. He can't and won't touch Tibor." He wiped at her wet cheek. "I promise you, nothing will happen to Tibor." Simply verbalizing her fears to her husband and hearing his reassurances calmed Karola and they sat together quietly for some time holding each other's hands.

As the sun finally made its way to the horizon, their son, Bela, joined them on the balcony. Karola hugged her son close. He seemed to be growing into a young man at such a fast pace. "Bela is doing so well at military school," she said as much to herself as to Domokos. "He is first in his class."

Domokos eyes glistened with pride as he looked at his son. There was a growing sense of urgency in his voice when he spoke. "I have something on my mind that I want to share with the family." He stood up, stretching a hand out to help Karola up. "Could we go back inside?"

Karola, Tibor, Bela, and Picke gathered around him in the parlour as Domokos lit a cigarette. He asked Picke to make sure the maids were all downstairs in the kitchen and out of earshot and then he began.

"There is a formula," he said slowly, making sure they understood each word. "For every soldier who is fighting at the front, the military needs eleven men to support the infrastructure." He paused, looked at the faces he loved gathered around him, and continued. "These eleven men provide for the needs of each soldier fighting on the front lines. They cook the food and transport water, move the ammunition and gasoline to the front, dig the latrines, provide first aid, and remove the injured and sick. These eleven also include the people manufacturing ammunition and organizing the transport of the ammunition to the front lines." Domokos looked directly at Bela. "Undoubtedly you have learned about this in military school, son." Bela nodded and looked seriously at his father.

"Presently, the number of men supporting the front-line soldiers is continuously diminishing while the territory at the front to be defended is always widening and increasing." He put his cigarette in the ashtray, stared as it burned down a bit, then inhaled again. He wanted to give them all a few minutes to comprehend what he was saying. Then, lowering his voice, he continued even more slowly. "Unless the soldiers at the front are properly supported, the front lines will collapse. It is inevitable." He waved his hand and was suddenly lost in thought. Then he looked up and continued. "Although the men under my command in the press corps continue to provide reports of glorious victories and the politicians continue to say what they will, based on what I have seen at the front, the Germans have already lost this war."

They all sat in stunned silence as the smoke from his idling cigarette curled as it rose from the ashtray. No one spoke; no one responded; no one asked any questions. It was dusk and hard to see but no one reached to turn on the lamps on the side tables. Somewhere, in the distance, a dog was barking.

chapter 11 | 1943

LESS THAN ONE YEAR after Domokos Aykler made his dire prediction, his family came to see that everything he had said was coming true. The winter of 1942–43 was so bitterly cold in Karpatalja that horses, sheep, goats, and cows had to be kept in sheds and barns and cars and tractors wouldn't start. Business and travel ground to a halt as trains became unreliable due to frozen tracks. Schools had to be closed for weeks at a time and local newspapers and radio broadcasts warned people of the risk of frostbite after just a few minutes of exposure outdoors.

As the residents of the region stayed indoors keeping their families and pets close to their wood-burning stoves, they had little knowledge of the tragedy that was unfolding on the Russian front during those same frigidly cold weeks. Some two thousand kilometres to the east, more than 130,000 Hungarian soldiers were being killed, maimed, or taken into captivity, virtually wiping out the Hungarian Second Army in what would later be termed the "Catastrophe of the Don."

Faced with overwhelming odds against Russian forces, the Romanian and Italian armies fled. The Hungarian army, abysmally equipped for the bitterly cold Russian winter and the long impending battle, was ordered to stay and defend the front line. As a result of this completely senseless order, the battle resulted in forty thousand Hungarian soldiers dead, thirty-five thousand wounded, and sixty thousand taken prisoners of war. In February 1943, when the Germans lost their Sixth Army at Stalingrad, it was clear that the tide of the war had turned and Hungarians realized what a horrendous price in lives and human suffering would be exacted by their desire for border revision.

In the fall of 1943, Hedy started noticing that her mother was becoming tired more and more frequently. Normally, their mother was constantly on her feet; always working from the moment she woke up in the morning until she placed her head on her pillow late at night. Lately, however, even when she was performing simple tasks around the house, Terez became short of breath. And she was losing weight as well. Vilmos worried as he watched his wife growing weaker and finally insisted that she go to a doctor. Terez resisted, explaining away her weakness and breathlessness. Lots of women, she told them, went through the same symptoms. Then, one day, she fainted in the garden while hanging laundry on a clothesline.

Within a few weeks after her visit to the doctor, they received the dreaded news: Terez Weisz had cancer, which had already metastasized and spread to several other organs in her body. Vilmos sat down with his older children and explained the gravity of the situation to them. They agreed to shield the younger ones, Suti and Icuka, from the full extent of their mother's illness.

Tibor was desperately worried about the emotional toll her mother's health was taking on Hedy, and offered to help in any way he could. He suggested that she come in later in the mornings so she could help get Suti and Icuka off to school and insisted she leave the office earlier in the afternoons so she could help with dinner and be there when her little brother and sister got home.

Hedy took on more household chores and tried to spend more time with Suti and Icuka, explaining to them as gently as she could that mother was sick and that, until she got stronger, they would all have to look out for one another and help around the house. Suti and Icuka recognized the situation for what it was and quickly adapted, becoming much more sensitive to the needs of the family, hardly ever complaining or quarrelling. Hedy's eyes welled up with tears of emotion as she watched her little brother struggling, without a word of complaint, to drag in large buckets of water from the well or set the table and, with the help of his sisters, wash dishes after dinner.

Before bedtime, they still gathered around their mother for story time but she usually sat, bundled up in blankets and shawls, resting her eyes while Hedy or Aliz read the story. Every once in a while, Terez opened her eyes and smiled faintly, as if acknowledging how pleased she was at how the family was coping.

As her family's need of her grew greater, Hedy turned more and more to Tibor for comfort and advice. It was debilitating to watch her family crumbling around her. Terez became increasingly fragile with each passing week and she had already lost more than twelve kilograms. For Hedy, it became impossible to maintain a brave front. As time passed, words of encouragement became painful to verbalize as the lump lodged in her throat grew larger whenever she tried to speak to her mother, even just to calm her. She couldn't imagine the day they would have to say goodbye to her. She simply couldn't get the words out without feeling like she was going to burst into tears. There was no one else but Tibor she could talk to about her mother's ever-weakening health and the effect this was having on her family.

In December 1943, through their family doctor, they learned of a specialist in Budapest who might be able to offer a cure. But how would they get their mother to Budapest when Jews were not allowed to reserve a place on the train? As always, Hedy turned to Tibor and he offered to make all the arrangements.

A cold mist hung around the hillsides surrounding Nagyszollos on that bleak morning in December as Hedy secured a spot for her mother on one of the few benches on the platform as they waited for the train. She pulled the extra shawl around her mother's frail body and gazed lovingly into her hollow eyes. She smiled and tried to sound cheery as she offered words of encouragement. "Tibor will be here soon, Mother. Don't worry."

The platform was packed with people awaiting the arrival of the train to Budapest. Because of the nighttime bombings, the evening train to the capital had been cancelled a year ago, so this was the only scheduled train route of the day. When the train pulled in, Hedy didn't have any idea how she was going to find Tibor. The crowd was clamouring on board, shoving and jostling each other for a good seat. Hedy couldn't imagine how she would manage the two light bags they had packed and her sick mother who could only walk very slowly and with much assistance. And what if they didn't get a seat? She knew there was no possibility her mother could stand for any amount of time.

Hedy stood on the platform, her eyes welling up with tears, and desperately scanned the crowd looking for Tibor. Suddenly, he appeared from the throng, smiling broadly, and confidently leaned in and spoke directly to Terez. "Are we ready to board, ladies?"

Hedy watched as her mother nodded and closed her eyes in relief and agreement. Without another word Tibor tenderly gathered Terez in his arms, gave Hedy a loving look, then winked as he turned and deftly carried her across the platform and up the narrow metal stairs of the car and onto the train.

It all happened so fast Hedy barely had a chance to realize her worries were over. She grabbed the two light bags and hurried after Tibor as he entered the compartment with her mother. Then she noticed the sign on the compartment door that read: FIRST CLASS. RESERVED — DO NOT DISTURB.

As she clambered in with the bags, she realized that they were the only passengers in the compartment. Tibor must have boarded the train earlier that morning at Kiralyhaza, one stop before Nagyszollos, in order to reserve the first class compartment. She put the bags in the rack above the seats and looked around. There was ample room in the private compartment for her mother to stretch out comfortably and Tibor had already made sure everything was in order. He stood up after tucking the blanket around Terez's legs and told Hedy to lock the door from the inside when he left. Then he asked her if there was anything more they needed. Hedy could hardly speak, she was so moved by what he had done. She simply shook her head and smiled at him, her eyes brimming with tears of love and gratitude. All the way to Budapest, her mother slept peacefully and no one knocked or attempted to enter the private compartment where they sat.

In January 1944, Terez Weisz was sent home from Budapest. The doctors were unable to do much for her because the disease was in such an advanced stage. Within two weeks of her return, she passed away in the hospital in Nagyszollos. Her twelve-year-old daughter, Icuka, whom the rest of the family had tried to shield for as long as possible, sat on the floor near the entrance to her mother's room and cried uncontrollably upon hearing that her mother was gone. No matter what her family tried to do for her, she was inconsolable.

Vilmos Weisz felt as if his life was over. He had lost the love of his life, the woman who meant everything to him, and the pivot around which his family revolved. Even though all the children were in deep shock and mourning, Aliz and Hedy realized they had to forge ahead and organize the funeral.

The news travelled fast and soon relatives from Beregszasz, Munkacs, and Fancsika started arriving for the funeral by train, horse-drawn cart, bicycle, and even on foot. The funeral procession, from the synagogue to the Jewish cemetery, was long and the extensive line of mourners wound its way directly through the centre of town. At the front of the line, directly behind the family, walked two Christian men — the younger Baron Zsigmond Perenyi and Tibor Schroeder — both dressed in black suits and hats, showing their respect for Jewish tradition. According to religious law, all the women were barred from entering the Jewish Orthodox cemetery, but Hedy stood outside the gate, her eyes filled with tears of gratitude as Tibor and Zsigmond stood next to Vilmos, Bandi, and Suti when they placed the coffin of Terez Weisz into her final resting place.

The participation of the two Christian men at this Jewish funeral was a flagrant violation of the anti-Jewish laws. But, despite all the grumblings, the two men were untouchable. It was understandable, and considered a great honour, that the son of the baron, the young, Oxford-educated Zsigmond Perenyi, would demonstrate his family's respect for the Weisz family in their loss. After all, Vilmos Weisz had been an integral part of the Perenyi estate since 1923 when he had taken over management of the distillery.

To anyone who wondered why Tibor Schroeder, the son of a high-ranking military officer, was walking side-by-side with the Weisz family, well-meaning relatives and friends replied, "Well of course. Tibor Schroeder is Hedy's employer. It is a profound sign of respect that he has also come to the funeral."

But for those who suspected that their relationship was more involved, the answer became obvious when they caught a glimpse of Tibor looking at Hedy. The look was undeniably that of someone in love. The secret was out.

After the funeral, young Jewish men vented their anger at Tibor. "How dare this Christian man become romantically involved with one of the most talented, beautiful young women in our community?" Tibor heard about their indignation through Jaszli Berliner and he received written and verbal threats to leave Hedy alone or "he would suffer the consequences." But he remained unperturbed. The funeral was a turning point for Tibor. Despite all the warnings, he no longer made any attempt to conceal his love for Hedy. Considering he was going to marry her, he felt it was only natural that he walk alongside his fiancée and her family as they mourned the loss of their mother.

A few weeks after the funeral, Hedy pleaded with Tibor to let her return to work earlier than they had planned. Home without her mother was an empty dwelling and being there all day every day only made the loss more profound. At least at work she could focus on other things. Tibor agreed, but wouldn't let her work much or stay long hours. When she didn't feel well, or became overwhelmed with grief, Tibor escorted her home. As they walked, Hedy talked at length about the shock of losing her mother, about how life could be cut short cruelly at any time. Tibor told her he regretted not having asked for her hand in marriage before her mother died. He felt in his heart that it would have been the right thing to do and that Hedy would feel comforted in the fact that her mother had known of her plans for the future before she died. He said he felt compelled to speak to her father as soon as possible. Hedy agreed.

In early March, a few months after Hedy's mother passed away, Tibor went to see Vilmos and formally asked for Hedy's hand in marriage.

Suti near the house in April 1944.

"I am deeply in love with your daughter, Mr. Weisz," he began confidently, "and wish to ask for her hand in marriage."

Vilmos looked into his daughter's eyes as Hedy and Tibor sat side by side, and realized it would be useless to object. It didn't take much to see that the two were very much in love and, after what his family had been through, Vilmos didn't have the heart to disappoint his daughter. He consented to their union. Overjoyed, Hedy and Tibor decided they would wed as soon as the war ended. Tibor shook Vilmos's hand and promised his future father-in-law that he would love, honour, and take good care of his daughter.

chapter 12 | march 1944

TIBOR SAT ON THE train as it chugged its way toward Budapest on its slow, tortuous journey. Because of the frequent nightly bombing raids in the countryside, the train engineer and conductors had to slow down, stop, and inspect each spot on the line where possible damage had been reported. Tibor's nerves grated each time the train slowed and came to a screeching halt and he was having trouble focusing his mind on the purpose of this trip: the meetings he had scheduled with a group of engineers at the firm of Weiss-Manfred.

To take his mind off the interminable trip, he concentrated on the dinner he would be having with his family on Sunday. He was looking forward to spending time with his mother, his sister, Picke, and their father, Domokos. He hadn't seen Picke for a while because she had spent the last year in Budapest attending a finishing school for young women. His father also hadn't been home in some time and he had specifically chosen this get-together to announce to his parents that he had asked Hedy Weisz to be his bride and that she had accepted. He very much would have wanted to bring Hedy with him on this trip but he realized that was impossible to do at the moment. But the war would be over soon — he was sure of it — and its end would herald a new beginning for both of them. He smiled as he remembered the meeting he had already had with his older brother, Istvan, and Istvan's wife, Eva. They were both thrilled at his news. Tibor had sworn them to secrecy, at least until he could announce the news to the rest of the family, but he had had to tell someone that he was engaged.

Both Hedy and Tibor were counting on the war being over soon, but the dismal state of affairs all around them just seemed to be getting worse. Once the Americans entered the war, everyone, even the loud-mouthed politicians, realized that Germany and its allies would eventually be defeated. Rumour had it that the Hungarian government had already tried to surrender to the Allies but had been thwarted by the Germans. Tibor closed his eyes and concentrated on Hedy's face. The Russians continue to make gains on the eastern front, he told himself. It is only a matter of time.

Tibor sat on the train daydreaming, his mind obsessed with plans of emigrating to some faraway place with Hedy once the war was over. He shook his head as he remembered his last meeting with their family doctor, Daniel Szabo. In the middle of dinner at a nice little café in town, Dani had announced that he had a brilliant scheme for getting to America at almost no cost. Intrigued, Tibor asked for details.

Daniel Szabo put down his glass and wiped his moustache on the back of his hand. "All right," he said looking around to see if anyone was listening. "Let's volunteer for the western front, surrender to the Americans, and then be transported to the United States for absolutely no charge."

They chuckled and Tibor looked at Dani with affection. "Everyone should be so lucky," Tibor said as he waved Szabo's scheme away. What fond memories he had of the good doctor. Unfortunately, Dr. Szabo was never able to follow his own advice. He had been shipped off to the eastern front as a military physician and had never returned from the catastrophe on the Don.

Finally, the train came to a stop at the station in Budapest and Tibor gathered his things together. He was always amazed at the atmosphere in this city. People continued to flock to restaurants, to shop, to eat and drink well, and to carry on business as usual. It was as if they were completely oblivious to the war thundering all around them. As head of the press corps, Colonel Aykler had been assigned an apartment on Kiralyhago ut, on the Buda side, and Tibor stayed there whenever he went to Budapest. He settled in and got ready for his meetings. He would get them over with and looked forward to an evening out with his friends the next night.

Tibor was out late on Saturday night with his friends and they all had a bit too much to drink. On Sunday morning he was still asleep when he heard knocking at the door. Reaching for his dressing gown he stumbled to open the door and found Picke standing there.

"What are you doing here?" Tibor asked, still in a daze.

"Have you seen what's going on outside?" she asked, glancing at his dishevelled state. "Obviously, you haven't been out yet."

She pushed him aside gently as she walked into the narrow, long hallway of the apartment and Tibor closed the door behind her. "Get dressed and shave. You look terrible. Where were you last night?" She stood with her hands on her hips and frowned at him. "There are German tanks everywhere, they've invaded the city," she continued in an excited tone.

"Calm down, my dear sister," Tibor said, stopping her in mid-sentence. "If you don't slow down and calmly tell me what is going on, my head will explode. What are you talking about, German tanks?"

"They're everywhere. I walked over from school and I saw German tanks on every major street corner. After two blocks, I was so intimidated by them I started taking side streets."

Tibor walked over to the short wave radio and flicked it on. Classical music came wafting through the airwaves into the room. He tried another station. "More Mozart. Great!" he sighed, and he padded off to the kitchen to make coffee. "There are hundreds of hours a week of information about the war but, when something drastic happens right here in the capital, there is nothing about it on the radio." As he took a shower and dressed, he tried to make sense of it.

Nazi Germany invading Hungary? Their ally? It didn't make any sense. It was true that the Horthy regime had tried to surrender to the British, but Hitler's spies had found out about it and quashed the attempt. If it was truly an invasion, then what was the purpose?

As they headed down into the streets, Tibor soon realized that what Picke had witnessed was in fact true. German army tanks lined all the major thoroughfares of the city. They stopped at a newspaper kiosk and Tibor asked for the most recent edition of the *Magyar Hirlap*.

Tibor Schroeder as a reservist in the Hungarian army in 1942.

"It's all yesterday's news," the kiosk manager said in a flat monotone. "We haven't received anything yet this morning."

The fact that no one seemed to know what was going on was frightening.

Tibor and Picke were meeting their parents at noon and the two of them took their time as they made their way through the side streets toward the restaurant. The Zoldfa, well-known in Budapest for its exceptional cuisine and great service, was owned by their mother's uncle and it was full of well-dressed patrons. As soon as Tibor and Picke walked in, the maître d' greeted them warmly and told them their father had already reserved the table. Picke spotted their parents and hurried ahead to kiss her mother and father. Tibor followed and leaned down to kiss his mother. More reservedly, he shook his father's hand then took his place at the table. The waiter handed everyone menus and began stuffily, "I would strongly suggest the goose liver as appetizer, followed by the chicken schnitzel. This is the finest meal on our menu today and, who knows, it might be the last good meal any of us will have in this city for a long time."

Tibor stared at him, aghast by his casual attitude. As the waiter walked away, he turned to his father. "I can't believe the attitude of the people of this city. What is going on?" He was getting angrier by the minute. "There are German tanks everywhere yet there is nothing on the radio or in the newspapers and no one seems to be taking this situation seriously. It seems like everyone is ignoring the facts at hand and talking in some kind of code."

Domokos sat quietly, seemingly studying the menu, and waited for Tibor to finish. His mother pleaded with her eyes for him to stop and, even though he knew that look well, Tibor would not be silenced.

"I find it hard to believe that you," and he looked directly at his father, "as head of the press corps, knew nothing about any of this." He stopped and waited for an answer. When Domokos said nothing, he continued. "Who knew about this? Why weren't there Hungarian troops sent to the border to prevent the German tanks from invading the country?"

Picke looked from Tibor to Domokos and watched for her father's reaction. She was stunned by Tibor's outburst. They sat in an uncomfortable silence as the waiter brought the wine, poured each of them a glass and took their orders.

When he left their table, Domokos took a sip of wine, lit a cigarette, and turned to Tibor.

"Are you finished?" he asked. Tibor nodded, suddenly aware of the spectacle he was making of himself in front of his family. "Son, as we are all sitting here now, I swear to you that no one among the highest military command was informed of the German invasion. We had a report from Lieutenant-General Szilard Bakay, commander of Szombathely, that there had been unusual German troop movements throughout the border region and our general staff officers sent a message to German headquarters asking for the reason. They replied that the troop movements were training exercises."

Domokos glanced around to see if anyone was eavesdropping. When he was satisfied that no one was within earshot he continued. "Our regent was in meetings with Hitler while the invasion was being implemented. You are aware of the fact that our troops are already overextended. In order to prevent the invasion, our commanders would have had to have some prior knowledge of this invasion and our troops would have had to be redeployed from other parts of the country, mainly the east to the western front, which would have taken weeks at best." Domokos stopped, trying to control himself. It was obvious to his family that he was in great distress. "The regent and prime minister are the only individuals capable of ordering such a redeployment." He leaned in and looked into Tibor's eyes. "My information is that Regent Horthy is under house arrest by order of the German High Command." Everyone at the table took a breath and went pale. "I was as shocked as you are to realize what has happened. But I am not a politician, or part of the government for that matter. I am not part of the general staff. I command the press corps. But you cannot blame the press corps for not being informed of the invasion." He sat back heavily and took another sip of wine. He was perspiring, and wiped his forehead with his napkin.

"Let me state, unequivocally, here with my family, that I believe *this is the end*. The invasion by the Germans means we are no longer in charge of our own country or our own destiny." Then he lowered his voice and, with a spark of anger growing noticeably in his eyes, he continued. "Personally, I think the government should resign immediately, en masse. That would signal to the world that independent Hungary as a country exists no more."

Tibor felt suddenly ashamed of his outburst and stunned by his father's admission. He was at a loss for words. "I'm sorry, Father, I never realized ..."

Domokos felt his son's embarrassment and put his hand up to stop him. "None of us realized, Tiborkam. Now, before I get sent back to the eastern front and all of you go back home to Nagyszollos — and you, Tibor, get called into the reserves again — let's try to have a nice, quiet family dinner and hope that somehow the war will end soon and we will all make it out alive."

chapter 13 | spring 1944

Until the spring of 1944, Regent Horthy had resisted Hitler's repeated demands to gather Hungarian Jews and deliver them "to work in armaments factories in Germany." The German High Command was increasing the pressure on Horthy to deport the Hungarian Jews and the invasion of Hungary effectively put an end to any and all resistance. Eichmann was sent to Budapest to personally take charge of the operation, in effect, implementing the "Final Solution" in Hungary. What follows is adapted from Suti's memoirs.

AT THE END OF March, the Jewish children were abruptly sent home from school. They were given instructions to wear a yellow Star of David on their coats. The exact specifications were "a ten-centimetre yellow star to be worn on the left side of the front of the coat, just above the heart."

Suti couldn't believe it when one of the teachers referred to them as "yellows" and said they could go home. Before they went home, the teacher told them they were equal to "war criminals." Suti didn't even know what that meant, but he knew it wasn't good.

Walking home, Suti felt something tighten in his throat. He just wanted to go into the kitchen, lay his head on his mother's lap, and pretend to be eleven years old again. It had all been so much simpler then. But it wasn't to be — his mother was dead and she would never greet him again when he came home from school. He missed her terribly. As he walked, Suti kept his eyes to the ground, fighting back tears.

In early April, instead of going to work, Hedy started to go to the Guttman residence. Suti asked her why she was going there.

"Rezso Kramer instructed me to type a list of all the Jews of Szollos," she replied.

"But you work so hard," Suti said. "Can't you just stay at home with us? What is the list for?"

"I don't know," Hedy said. Then, after a few moments, she added, "Don't worry, Sutikam, this list will be done soon, and then I'll stay at home with you. There are other typists working on it as well and the work is going fast." Glancing sideways at her sister, Aliz, she added under her breath, "There are over five thousand names on the list." No one asked any more questions.

Suti realized there were all kinds of strange, unusual things happening around him. There were occurrences that had no logical explanation, and he had no one to turn to for answers. His father, who hadn't recovered since the death of Suti's mother, had no answers. Hedy and Aliz were always whispering to each other, and little Icuka looked to Suti for answers.

A few days later Suti woke up to eerie silence. He couldn't hear or see his little sister in the house. He rushed out to the yard and called her name loudly several times, knowing that was where they usually played. Hedy came running out of the house, grabbed Suti's hand, and rushed him back inside. Her face was white when she started to speak.

"Suti, promise me you'll never ask about Icuka in front of others again." Hedy was talking in whispers, and she had a sad look in her eyes. "Icuka was taken to the Gyalog family early this morning. Remember her little friend who lives in the mine district?"

Suti nodded. "Marika, she's the same age as Icuka."

"That's right," Hedy said. "They agreed to take care of her for a little while, but under one condition, that no one must know where she is. Remember Peter, the crippled boy who does bicycle deliveries for Tibor Schroeder?"

Suti nodded again and stared at his amazing sister. He was in awe that she had arranged all this.

"We thought it best that Peter take her to the Gyalog family," Hedy said. "Everything's all right. She got there safely."

Suti glanced at her.

"Do you understand, my darling?" Hedy asked. "This is our family secret."

Suti nodded. He loved secrets.

SUTI WASN'T LOOKING FORWARD to the first Passover without his mother. Such family gatherings only reminded him of just how empty their lives were since she passed away. But there was no Passover that year. Hedy woke Suti very early and told him that the entire city was surrounded by the military. The authorities had barricaded four streets near the synagogue and the so-called "Magyar Sor" and were transporting Jews into this section of town. There were Jews being brought in from neighbouring villages and towns. Suti was relieved to hear that for the time being the Weisz family was allowed to remain home.

And there were more strange occurrences. The next day Suti's older brother, Bandi, went to plough the fields. Around noon Bandi received a draft notice calling him up to serve in the Labour Service System and to report to Nagybanya. Running out to the fields, Suti delivered the news to Bandi, who came back to the house. Suti stayed and drove the tractor back on a road parallel to the railway tracks. A train carrying German troops came rumbling by. Through the window Suti saw a soldier raise his fist, then another did the same, then another. Yet another soldier pointed his gun at Suti.

More and more Jews from Nagyszollos were being transported into the ghetto. Suti overheard some say that the situation seemed hopeless and that no one knew when the gendarmerie would come for the rest. Suti's father said that Baron Perenyi was trying to arrange for the family to stay at home, but with little success. Finally, Suti's father received a paper certifying that he was a skilled worker important to the military works and that the family could stay at home until the end of the month. Hedy told Suti that they were all under a strict curfew and could only be out on the streets between ten o'clock in the morning and five o'clock in the afternoon and that he shouldn't go anywhere without telling her. Bandi left for Nagybanya. It was then that Suti realized how much he missed his older brother.

Hedy brought Icuka home! Suti was overjoyed to have her back. How he had missed her. Hedy's eyes were red; she looked as if she had been crying. Suti knew he shouldn't say anything, but later he overheard Hedy talking to Aliz.

"A neighbour threatened to report them," Hedy whispered to Aliz. "The Gyalog family simply couldn't keep Icuka hidden in the cellar anymore. She wanted to play with her friend in the yard. She didn't understand why she had to stay hidden." Hedy shook her head. "Poor child."

ON HIS FATHER'S BIRTHDAY, Suti realized how sad his family had become. One of the young gendarmes came to the house. He was always such a simple fellow who held father in high esteem. But suddenly everything was different.

"Is that you, Vilmos Weisz?" the twenty-five-year-old demanded of Suti's father.

His father looked quite stunned by the man's tone. "Yes, Kovacs!"

"Don't talk to me like that. Do you hear me, Vilmos Weisz? I'm not Kovacs to you. I'm Sergeant Kovacs. Do you understand?"

"Yes," Suti's father replied in a low voice.

"I'll be back in one hour!" Kovacs barked. "You should gather your things and prepare all your gold, silver, cash, and the diamonds you've hidden."

"I have nothing to prepare," Suti's father said quietly. "I had a gold wedding band, which we buried with my wife."

"Be careful what you say," Kovacs said. "We'll be able to check. When you're in the ghetto, we'll dig up your wife's grave. Do you understand?"

"That will be in the hands of the inspector general," Suti's father said firmly but still quietly.

Kovacs didn't reply to that. Instead, he turned and left the house.

With heavy hearts everyone started packing their most essential things. Icuka and Suti collected their favourite toys and books, while Hedy and Aliz grabbed pots and pans, sheets, pillowcases, and towels.

Suti felt that this was the last time he would ever see his childhood home, so he went around and said goodbye to each room, taking a minute more in the one he had been born in.

THE FIRST DAY IN the ghetto Suti's father could still go home but was ordered to return on the thirtieth. The family was assigned a place in the attic of one of the small houses. The house was shared by many families. A window opened from the attic directly onto the entrance to the ghetto. Suti frequently watched what was happening at the gate. He saw the changing of the guard and when the SS were entering. The mood in the ghetto was very bad.

Suti was overjoyed as he watched his father come to the ghetto with a cart full of potatoes sent by Baron Perenyi. Just that morning Hedy had looked so despondent and had told Aliz that the food supplies brought from home were almost gone. It was wonderful to get the potatoes, but they were divided among many people, most of whom already had nothing to eat. Suti took a small basket of potatoes for his family; the rest were distributed.

One day later a large box of yeast arrived in the ghetto. It was sent by the Schroeder-Aykler family, who ran the yeast concession. Everyone could now make bread with the flour. Within a few hours the scent of freshly baked bread wafted through the ghetto. Suti suspected Hedy's employer, Tibor, had arranged all of this!

There was more waiting in the window, more watching the comings and goings at the gate. One day Suti was happy to see his father arrive at the gate for the second time with flour, meat, and potatoes. Suti had been told that this would be it for a while and that there would be no more deliveries of food. His father wanted to stay with the family, but the baron came and, after arguing with the guards, took him out. Hedy said they would get fed up with the young Baron Perenyi, the graduate of Oxford, flaunting the law. After the baron left with Suti's father, Suti saw some officers gathered at the gate and heard them talking angrily. Because they were speaking in German, though, he only understood the occasional "Baron Perenyi" and "Ihr Juden Weisz."

Later in that evening Suti's father was brought into the ghetto by the German officers. From now on he had to stay with them permanently. So much for the wishes of the Oxford-educated baron.

It was May 1, and word travelled fast in the ghetto that sometime during the night persons unknown had tied a red flag onto a tree on top of the hill. This symbol of communism was causing a great stir. The German military began to terrorize the population. All of a sudden the Gestapo was everywhere in black automobiles or on motorcycles and armed with machine guns. Suti learned that the Gestapo had set up an ad hoc torture chamber in the synagogue on Kiraly Street. The first to be taken were the richest members of the Jewish community of Nagyszollos. Everyone was filled with dread and fear.

The next day there were more rumours and whispering. Everyone was thinking the worst. Suti observed a great deal of activity at the gate. The Gestapo and gendarmes appeared here and there to round up the wealthy members of the community, believing that torture would reveal the secret treasure trove of valuables buried underneath a house or property somewhere. It was forbidden to take anything to these poor unfortunates except tea and dried bread. Otto Ilkovics, the prominent landowner and the father of Suti's best friend, was one of the first to be tortured. Because his son was in Budapest, Suti was chosen to take tea into him twice a day.

Suti was truly frightened when he saw the father of his best friend. The torture had taken a toll on the diabetic man — even his scalp was shaved down the middle to further humiliate him. When Suti handed over the Thermos of tea and bit of bread, the elderly man reached out the small window and smiled sadly. After about a minute of conversation, a gendarme grabbed Suti, took him to the gate, kicked him out, and said, "Don't come tomorrow, kid, or I'll shoot you. I won't waste one minute on you, pig!"

Soon there was more disturbing news. Train cars arrived at the station to transport the residents of the ghetto. No one knew where they were going, except possibly Rosenberg, the member of the Judenrat (Jewish Council) and the head of the office of the ghetto.

Everyone was told that each boxcar would hold one family and that the authorities simply wanted to move the Jews out before the Russians invaded. Each minute, it seemed, new rumours surfaced. But one thing was certain: everyone was being transported away from there.

THE DREADFUL NEWS EVERYONE was waiting for only became known in the evening. The order came down that the next morning at four o'clock everyone would be woken up. Everyone was ordered to pack only the most important items to be taken on the trip, such as two shirts, two underpants, one towel, one pair of shoes, two socks, one suit, one winter coat, and two days' worth of food. Whoever packed more than that would have everything taken away from them.

Within a few minutes the entire mood in the ghetto changed. Everyone started rushing in all directions, going home to pack, organizing themselves for the trip. Hedy and Aliz began making backpacks out of tablecloths and sheets.

Two sewing machines were set up near the gate. Men and women lined up at each one to use the machines. There was a limit of ten minutes use per person. Mrs. Grun, who has seven children, tried to cut into the line with her oldest, a twelve-year-old boy. Her neighbour chastised her. "Mrs. Grun, haven't you noticed there are others in this line as well?"

Mrs. Grun, not giving an inch, replied, "What business is it of yours?"

By now it seemed that every woman in the ghetto had some comment or criticism to make, not only about the incident but about one another. Hateful, nasty arguments ensued. Everyone appeared to be arguing, yelling at each other about something or other.

DAWN CAME SLOWLY EACH day now. Suti lay on his straw-filled mattress and couldn't close his eyes all night. He heard voices through the walls. He woke, got dressed, and went to get washed. When Suti returned to the near-empty room, he saw Icuka crying in the corner. He knelt next to her, put his hands on both sides of her face, lifted it, gazed into her tear-stained eyes, and asked, "Why are you crying, Icuka edes?"

"Sanyi, it's so terrible that Mother isn't here with us."

Suti couldn't answer. He simply hung his head, turned, and walked away so that she couldn't see that he, too, was crying.

He went down to the courtyard and noticed an entire row of gendarmes. They wouldn't let him pass. Then he saw a big crowd of people waiting to be told where and when to leave. Two gendarmes were counting the people. Suddenly, Suti heard: "You pig, you'll be exterminated!"

It was Kovacs, the sergeant, the one who had spoken to Suti's father as if he were a dog. Kovacs was one of the counters. He was hitting somebody at the front of the line with his rifle butt.

Suti couldn't watch anymore. He couldn't believe what was going on. He wondered if these men were capable of killing innocent people.

People were leaving. They were already at his neighbour's house.

They were counting: "Twenty more Jews, 3,478, 3,479, 3,480!"

Suti realized that among them were friends and neighbours — the Ilkovics family. He waved weakly to his friends through tears, then went back to his family's room where he saw Terez Alexander, a girl who had escaped from Slovakia.

Suti turned to his father and said, "Father, it will be our turn soon."

"Not today, son," his father said. "Today only 3,500 are going."

chapter 14 | spring 1944

By the spring of 1944, the entire region of Karpatalja was a closed military zone. At night, the residents could hear the Russian troops getting closer and the relentless bombardment was ominous. Fear of the unknown began to creep into people's hearts and minds.

The creation of the ghetto in the heart of Nagyszollos happened over-night, the military operation unfolding with amazing speed. Although the newspapers reported that the "ghettoization" of the Jewish population was being done "for their own protection," there was a sinister feeling about what was happening. An entire neighbourhood, four streets near the synagogue and the so-called Magyar sor (Hungarian way) was walled off and declared to be an area restricted only to Jews. One-third of the population of the town — some five thousand Jewish residents — were ordered to report to the ghetto, where they were joined by another five thousand Jews from other parts of Ugocsa County. In the ghetto, four or five families were crammed into a single family house — one family to a room, if they were fortunate. The air was saturated with lies and propa-ganda, and despite telephones being a rarity in Nagyszollos, rumours spread through the community with lightning speed.

Dire warnings were published in newspapers and broadcast on the radio about contact with the Jews. Anyone guilty of aiding, abetting, and/or hiding Jews would be faced with immediate imprisonment and, most likely, death. Any Jews who did not report to the ghetto or resisted the order would face a firing squad.

Entire neighbourhoods became dark and silent and stores were boarded up. The lifeblood of the town's existence appeared to have been sucked out of the community. Because the community had been so entwined, everyone knew someone in the ghetto: neighbours, friends, business partners. Children asked about their missing playmates but were given ambiguous responses about their whereabouts. Those who believed in the prophesies of the Bible saw this as a sure sign of the arrival of the devil's reign of terror.

Those ten thousand or so non-Jewish residents who remained in the town pulled down the awnings and window coverings of their homes and withdrew to life indoors. No one wanted to speculate about the dreadful events taking place around them. They felt they no longer had control over their own fate, let alone the fate of others. Everyone knew that the war was lost. The Nazis were dictating what was happening in their homeland while the Red Terror's artillery was already pounding at the eastern border. Their hometown would soon be part of the front lines. Yet people pretended to go about their daily business as if everything were normal. Anyone who had a friend or someone they knew or cared about in the ghetto, however, realized that life in the community had been irrevocably altered.

The relatively few local members of the Arrow Cross Party in Nagyszollos became brazen. With the Nazis in control of Hungary, the members of this party felt their time had finally come, and their plans to clean the streets of Jewish "scum" could finally be implemented. Solitary acts of defiance were met with brutality. If anyone dared openly criticize them, they were harassed or beaten.

When the Weisz family was forced into the ghetto, it was a turning point for Tibor. He realized that no one could save his fiancée. He blamed himself for his naïveté. Tibor had, until then, believed that Hedy, her father, and the rest of the Weisz family were in a special category because they were employed by Baron Perenyi and they would certainly fall under his protection. After all, Perenyi was a former governor of Karpatalja. But the protection of the Perenyi name evaporated when the order came. Even Karoly Hokky, the member of Parliament for the district and close personal friend of the family, had written countless letters of guarantee for Jewish citizens of the community. He had personally gone to Budapest to intervene on their behalf. All to no avail. Whether they were decorated veterans of the First World War, deemed essential to the war effort, or had converted to Christianity, they were all, in the end, herded off to the ghetto. Letters, guarantees, past contributions, evidence of loyalty ultimately meant nothing.

Tibor realized that he could trust no one to help find a solution to the problem of how to become reunited with his fiancée. Yet he tried to remain analytical in dealing with what seemed to be an insurmountable obstacle. As much as his heart ached, he vowed to solve the problem.

Tibor first had to find a way to communicate with Hedy, to send her messages, to see her. He knew he could rely on the one person still in his employ: Peter, the delivery boy. Crippled by bone disease as a child, Lame Peter, as he was called, moved with great difficulty because one leg was significantly shorter than the other. Tibor had created a bicycle for Peter with a specially designed pedal system and had given him a job as a delivery and messenger boy. The boy and bike became inseparable. Peter became a whole person on that bicycle. He felt he had no handicap, no hindrance when he rode it. Peter knew it was Tibor who had given him a new life and he was eternally grateful to his employer for this. He was constantly pedalling his way through the main thoroughfares, zipping in and around cars and horse-drawn carts. With time, the lame boy on his strangely engineered bicycle had become part of the flow of traffic in Nagyszollos. Tibor realized no one noticed Peter any longer or thought anything of it when they happened to see him.

Tibor drew Peter aside one day and asked him to do a bit of a scouting assignment. But before Tibor even had a chance to explain what the task was, Peter replied, "Yes, sir!" His loyalty to Tibor was unquestioning.

Tibor asked Peter to ride around the entire perimeter of the ghetto three times a day for one week and note the exact area or areas where there was the least traffic flow. He explained to the boy that this assignment was critically important and top secret. Peter went off to complete the assignment with no questions asked. After five days, Peter reported that there was one section of the outside perimeter where he hardly ever saw any pedestrians, cars, or carriages.

Tibor followed Peter to the exact spot and later, at dusk, returned on his motorcycle with a few tools. He loosened two boards in the fence, just enough for one person to slip through, then attached hooks and latches to the boards so that he could take the boards off any time he wanted to and reattach them. To any casual observer on the outer perimeter, the fence appeared to be perfectly intact.

Tibor stayed at the fence all night and watched until dawn to be absolutely sure that what Peter had reported was in fact true. He had to secure the area and be familiar with the chirping of every cricket if this was to become the place for his clandestine meetings with Hedy. When he felt confident that everything was secure, Tibor had Peter take a message to Hedy. Tibor didn't ask Peter how he got through; he only wanted to make sure that his message had been delivered.

Hedy came to meet Tibor that very evening. Tibor was already at the perimeter of the gate when she approached and Hedy simply melted into his arms. She didn't have to say one word about how dreadful it was in there; he could sense it in her silence, feel it in the tenseness of the muscles of her sinuous arms and back. The only thing Tibor could think of saying to her was how much he loved her, how he missed her. When he whispered it softly in her ear, he could feel her arms tighten around his neck. She nodded and quietly cried.

From that night on, Tibor often went to meet Hedy at their secret meeting place. He was always dressed in full military uniform so that if, by chance, someone would happen by and see a uniformed soldier hugging a woman by a fence, no one would think of reporting or questioning it.

In the third week of May 1944, rumours began circulating daily about the fate of the Jews — where they would be going and when. Each time he met Hedy, she told him about another rumoured destination, another embellishment on what their fate would be. One such rumour was that they were going to the westernmost part of the country to work on the estate of Count Esterhazy and could come back home again once it was safe for them to return.

Tibor also began to ask around and found out that trains had been ordered. But what he couldn't find out, no matter whom he contacted, was where the trains would be heading with their human cargo. Then Tibor's reserve unit was ordered to travel to western Hungary, near Gyor, for military exercises. The reservists were scheduled to leave in three days and Tibor was assigned the task of preparing the train for departure. He realized the timing of the departure of the train to western Hungary was ideal for what he had been secretly planning for weeks.

He ordered twelve train cars for the transport and added two supply cars for equipment, foodstuffs, and ammunition. These two cars would be sealed at embarkation and opened only once they arrived at their final destination, somewhere near Gyor. Each afternoon, after closing the office, he went to work on the inside of one of the supply cars, taking with him tools and pieces of lumber. The station master, Berti Mecseri, heard the hammering and saw the supplies being loaded night after night, but he didn't ask any questions.

Tibor researched the guards' schedule at the front entrance to the ghetto, again making use of the skills of his "invisible" bicycle assistant Peter. He discovered that the SS guards left their posts at 6:00 p.m. each day, handing over the watch to the local members of the Hungarian gendarmes and the new recruits of the Arrow Cross militia. Tibor knew two young men who had recently joined the militia — Dezso Horvath and Tamas Kun. Both their fathers still worked for the winery operated by Tibor's family. Horvath and Kun were typical of the young men recruited by the Arrow Cross in the latter years of the war: they were from simple, hard-working families, had little education, and were lured by the promise of a solid job. Tibor knew they were the types to follow orders exactly. He also knew they were paid very little.

Pretending to be on official business as he walked by their post one evening, Tibor nonchalantly invited them to his office for a coffee and brandy after their shift. When Horvath and Kun came by, their eyes lit up as Tibor pulled out an elegant box filled with Cuban, hand-rolled cigars.

By the time Tibor poured the second glass of brandy, he ginger-ly directed the conversation toward security procedures in the ghetto. Horvath and Kun talked openly about how, and under what condi-tions, passes were obtained for leaving the ghetto. As they talked, Tibor learned about the confidential details of the police bureaucracy guarding the ghetto.

At the same time, he tried to calculate the exact state of their intoxication. Before he proposed anything, he wanted to make sure they were pleasantly inebriated, but not so much so that they wouldn't remember the conversation.

Making a conscious effort to speak slowly so they would hear and understand each word, he began by telling them that he needed their assistance, that he wanted to enter into a business transaction with them. Both looked at him, unaware of the seriousness of what Tibor was about to request. Tibor launched right into the proposal. He bluntly told them that he would offer each of them fifty *pengo* (about one week's wages) to forge a temporary pass and help spirit a woman out of the ghetto. The two sat in stunned silence. Kun pretended to be indignant as he stopped sucking on the cigar in his mouth.

Before he began to speak, though, Tibor reiterated, "Fifty *pengos*, gentlemen. Think of what your wives could do with one week's wages as a bonus. It will be cash. No one will hear or know about it. No one will question why one Jewish woman is being escorted out of the ghetto by a man in a Hungarian military uniform. You'll just hand her over to my custody." He could see that they were on the hook. "Twenty-five now and twenty-five when she is safely out and you provide me with proof of the destroyed paperwork. I need your firm acceptance of this proposal tonight."

"What woman?" Horvath asked.

Tibor knew then, by the tone of his voice, that they would take the bribe.

"Hedy Weisz. She knows this office inside out, did all of the paperwork before she was taken away. And I need her back!" Tibor instantly regretted the explanation, but it was out. They looked at each other and nodded. They agreed to his terms and told Tibor that the next night, when they were on duty, he could come and collect the Jewish woman. Tibor sent a message to Hedy that he would be coming through the front gate to visit her on the evening of May 26, the next day. As

Tibor had instructed, Peter whispered to her, "The boss says to stay calm, Miss Hedy. Everything will be all right."

It was a perfectly still, warm May evening and the full moon shone in the night sky above them. The room where the Weisz family was housed had a direct view of the front entrance of the ghetto. Hedy watched from the window. Compared to the noise level during the day, at ten o'clock at night it was quiet. She could hear Tibor's footsteps on the cobblestone road as he approached. The moon above them lit the night sky; it looked magical. She watched as he approached and saluted the guards, and the guards saluted back. Then he handed over some official-looking papers. Hedy felt as if her legs had turned to jelly.

She heard the guards tell two young boys standing beside them to "Fetch Hedy Weisz." And she thought she would faint. She looked around. Everyone in the room was sleeping. Her entire body trembling, she quickly glanced into her compact mirror, pinched her cheeks for colour, and walked calmly to the front entrance where Tibor was engaged in friendly banter with the two guards and was offering them cigarettes.

Few people noticed the corporal in full dress uniform and his stunning fiancée as they walked purposefully out of the ghetto. Arm in arm they walked, looking to the world like any normal couple. Hedy could feel the strength and fearlessness emanating from Tibor as she clung to him for courage. She kept repeating to herself, "Put one foot forward at a time. Relax. Keep walking." As they walked away from the gate, Hedy expected to hear gunshots. She visualized the two of them, lying on the ground, arms entwined, little rivulets of blood flowing from their upper torsos onto the cobblestone street. Their last moments on this earth, finally, happily together, forever.

They walked at a measured pace and, amazingly, no shots were fired. Hedy really didn't know where they were going but, as the distance grew, each step she took became lighter and lighter. She would have followed him anywhere, she was so giddy with the excitement of leaving that dreadful place.

Tibor led them directly to the train station and to Berti Mecseri's office. He had the key to the station master's office and opened the door.

Tibor guided Hedy over to a chair, motioned for her to sit down, and went to a side table in one corner of the office. He opened the cabinet door, grabbed a bottle of wine and two glasses, and poured each of them a generous serving. As they drank, they let out a sigh of relief, then began talking.

"That wasn't so difficult, was it, my darling?" Tibor asked Hedy as he took another sip of wine. He thought of their boldness and started laughing quietly, more out of a sense of relief than anything else, then he stopped himself.

Hedy was still so shaken by the brazenness of what they had just done, she could barely lift the glass to her lips her hands were shaking so.

She grabbed a handkerchief from the pocket of her dress and wiped her forehead. Her voice shaking, she asked, "How did you arrange that?"

She raised her glass to toast with him, but he held up his hand, as if to caution her.

"You know I'm superstitious, my dear. Let's not clink glasses yet. Our luck could still run out." From the seriousness of the tone, Hedy felt instinctively that Tibor was about to tell her something of great significance. They sat across from each other, each immersed in their own thoughts for a moment. His dark brown eyes, brimming with emotion and love for her, held something more — something serious and troubling. She waited for him to begin.

"I've prepared a place for you on this train," he began. "Come. Take a little walk with me. I must show you something."

They walked out of the main administrative building and headed down to the train tracks, stopping alongside a dark and waiting train at the station. The moon was so bright they could see their shadows. Somewhere a dog was barking — a lonely, plaintive cry. When they reached a railway car elegantly embossed with "*Posta Kocsi*" (mail car) on the side, he helped her up the three steep, iron-forged steps and, once again, extricated a key from his pocket to unlock the door.

Once inside, Hedy's senses were overwhelmed by the delicious smell of freshly baked bread mixed with a slight tinge of ground coffee. Oh, how she loved that smell. How she had missed it. The car was filled with sacks labelled "wheat," "flour," "apples." Hedy looked questioningly at her fiancé. Tibor, still holding her hand, kissed it and led her down the narrow centre aisle of the train car that had boxes and sacks piled up on either side of the central walkway.

At one end of the railway car, small arms ammunition crates were piled on top of each other. Each was made of wood and was 4' x 11' x 14' in size. Tibor removed the lid of the top crate. Hedy peered in and saw that the bottom of the top one had been removed and connected to the one below it, doubling the size of the crate. The sides had been reinforced so that, from the outside, the crates still all looked identical. On one side of the enlarged crate a little doorway had been crafted, also invisible from the outside. Tibor opened it and motioned for Hedy to enter. She squeezed through the door.

Inside, a blanket and pillow were carefully folded. A smaller apple crate was set next to the folded bedding. In it Hedy saw apples, bread, cheese, nuts, and bottles of water. Cloth serviettes were neatly folded over the food. There was even a book to read — a book of verse by her favourite poet, Sandor Petofi. Hedy knew instinctively, from the meticulous way in which the provisions were lined up and from the fresh scent of the sheets, pillow, and blanket, that Tibor meant this to be her hiding place. Her eyes widened. She certainly had not expected this.

"I am the only one who has access to this railway car," Tibor said. He held up the key. "This is the only key. Berti Mecseri is the only other person in the world who knows about this. But we can trust him. He helped me. I couldn't have accomplished all this without him." Tibor turned to Hedy, placed his hands gently on her shoulders, and looked into her eyes. "Come away with me, my darling. We will go together on this train to a place where no one knows us. This war will be over soon. Let's start anew in a brand new place. After all the destruction things will have to be rebuilt; there will always be work for an engineer." He pulled her close and she buried her face in his uniform shirt.

Hedy said nothing. Her mind was a blur trying to absorb all that he was saying and she was trying to imagine how the plan might work. Her heart was ready to go away with him. The idea of never going back to that dirty, overcrowded, lice-infested place was very enticing. She had only been out for an hour or so and already felt so much calmer, so much more like a human. But the thought of what would happen to her father, her brother, and her sisters was nagging at another part of her brain.

As if reading her mind, Tibor whispered, "There's nothing you can do for them by staying here. I've heard rumours that the Jews are going to be transported to a place called Waldsee. Once this nightmare war is over, we'll find them together, you and I. I promise you that you will be reunited with your family. Come with me, my darling."

Hedy realized she couldn't possibly give him an answer right away. He would have to give her a few hours to decide. They sat down side by side on two apple crates and talked in whispers, laughing quietly and shedding a few tears. They talked about their lives together in this new place, a city where they would start life all over again as newlyweds. They talked about the mundane details that would make up their daily routine. As the hours passed, it became cool and Tibor pulled out a blanket and wrapped it around them. They grew silent, both of them finally feeling the emotional toll of this exhausting day. Tibor kissed the moistness left by the tears on her cheeks, then his kisses became more passionate. "Life is but a day, our lives are but a single kiss."

It was two in the morning when Tibor departed. Hedy promised to spend the rest of the night in the hidden train compartment. In the morning, after a few hours rest, he would come back and they would finalize the details.

Tibor left with a heavy heart. He knew he had to go through the motions of life as usual and couldn't let anyone in the house know that this might be his final night at home, that he was planning to disappear forever the next day. He pushed away thoughts of what his disappearance would mean to his mother, who had come to rely on her son more and more. He shut his mind to his family. He couldn't bear to think of anyone but Hedy.

He hardly slept that night and no one was up yet when Tibor left the house the next morning. As fast as his feet could carry him, he went directly to the train car. It was empty. He dashed over to the station master's office but, before Tibor could ask anything, Berti Mecseri picked up a note from his desk and said, "She left this for you."

"What?" Tibor stammered. "When?"

"Around six in the morning. I had just arrived for my shift," Berti said.

Tibor looked at his watch. It was just after seven. "Did she say anything? What direction did she go?"

"She really didn't have to say anything. Her eyes were red from crying. She looked wracked with sorrow."

Tibor mumbled something under his breath as he walked out of the station master's office in a daze, ripping open the letter.

My dearest Tibor,

Forgive me for writing you these lines. I do so because I could not bear to see the sadness in your eyes when I told you of my decision. I don't know if going back will make any difference to my family's future or, for that matter, our fate. All I know is that I have to go back and face that fate together with them. I cannot abandon my brother, my sisters, and my father now, in their hour of greatest need.

Forgive me, my darling.

Love,

Hedy

Tibor stood staring at the note, trying to let the message sink in. When it did, he came to the realization that he had been selfish in trying to save her. Since her mother's death, Hedy had become mother to her brother and younger sister — she was all they had. How could he not have seen the obvious?

As Tibor headed back to his office, he thought about how he had worked to secure Hedy's safety. He had planned everything, right down to the smallest detail, but the only scenario he had imagined was the one where they would leave together. He had never thought she would decide to go back into the ghetto.

chapter 15 | may 1944

HEDY FELT CONFIDENT THEY wouldn't lay a hand on her. She had returned to the ghetto through the secret entrance and was on her way to her family when a guard recognized and stopped her. Dezso Horvath, the same guard Tibor had paid off to get her out of the ghetto, had a devilish look in his eyes.

"Where do you think you are going?" he insinuated. But before Hedy could think of a possible answer, he continued. "We'll have to teach you not to sneak out again. There can be no waltzing in and out of here whenever you choose. Who do you think you are to assume you can break the rules?"

Hedy was so exhausted she found these questions almost comical. Horvath had taken Tibor's money and now he was making a show of his loyalty to the cause for the small group watching them. She was tempted to say something, here in front of witnesses, but she bit her lip. Horvath's beady brown eyes sat in a head that was narrow, but top-heavy like a turnip. He looked at her with a mixture of disdain and lust and pursed his thin lips. "You'll be sorry you tried to escape," he hissed, coming very near her face.

The kosher butcher shop was cold and humid. The refrigerated shelves were turned off and stripped bare of any produce. What goods there were had long been taken to feed the ghetto or pilfered by the gendarmes. Hedy guessed there were twenty other people there already, watched over by four guards. They ordered everyone to sit down on the cool tile floor. Then, for no apparent reason, two guards grabbed a reluctant man off the floor and dragged him out the door. The man's protests and screams pierced the air as the guards started to beat him. Hedy put her head down and tried to muffle the horrible sounds by putting her arms up against her ears.

Possibly to camouflage the noise, the two guards in the shop started berating those left inside. "You are all here because you are guilty of not following orders. No one will leave here until they learn that rules are made to be followed exactly. No one is exempt from these rules. Now, repeat after me: Lipit-Lopat."

The recitation went on for at least twenty minutes and was followed immediately by another series of nonsensical tongue-twisters. What is the point of this stupid exercise? Hedy wondered. Already exhausted from being up most of the night, she tried to follow the instructions of these guards who had probably never finished grade school. Her mind wandered back to the events of the previous night. She saw before her the intense look in Tibor's eyes, felt his loving caresses on her cheek and arms and felt a pang of love as she went back over in her mind the planning and thought he had put into creating that hidden compartment for her. She realized for the first time the tremendous risk he was taking in doing all this for her.

The repetition went on for another hour. Then they sat in silence for hours more. Suddenly, more of the stupidity of repetition. Hedy glanced at the clock on the wall. It was almost evening; she had been there since 8:00 a.m. How could I have possibly thought that I could help my family? Hedy thought. They must be sick with worry right about now. She tried not to think about what Tibor must have felt when he found out she had returned to the ghetto. She looked down at her beautiful calfskin shoes and second-guessed her decision to leave the train car.

During the night, the beatings outside stopped and the guard who had ordered them to repeat the nonsense phrases also became silent. Hedy curled herself into a little ball, trying to retain the little warmth left in her body. Her fatigue and the damp, cool surroundings left her shivering all night. Toward dawn, everyone inside and out became silent. Then they heard the muffled footsteps. At first, it sounded to Hedy like there were just a few, then what sounded like hundreds of people walking past the butcher shop. Eerily funereal, it seemed like hundreds of people were shuffling by on the street outside, with hardly any other sound than the occasional baby crying or child talking. Panic set in as Hedy realized that another group from the ghetto was being taken to the train station. One thought kept running through her mind: They can't take my family without me.

SUTI PROMISED HIS FATHER that he would look after Icuka, who wanted to play a counting game as they walked. He didn't feel like playing — he felt hot and irritable. Who wears a coat on a warm day at the end of May? he thought. Yet Aliz, his older sister, had told him he must wear the coat or carry it. It was easier to wear it. He was already wearing a knapsack on his back, even though his wasn't as big as the one Aliz and father were wearing on their backs. He still couldn't understand any of this. Where were they going? When were they going to be allowed back home?

"Let's play a silent game," Suti said to his sister. "When you see something and you want me to find out what it is, squeeze my hand and I will try to guess what you are thinking of."

Icuka smiled, pleased that, finally, someone had agreed to play with her. Within a minute she squeezed Suti's hand. He guessed a bluebird on a tree. Icuka was amazed at his quick guess. He had secretly been admiring it, wishing he could be that bird and just fly away. The game continued. Suti was soon tired of the game. He told Icuka to count a hundred cobblestones in between guesses. The cobblestones were close to one another, in an arched, half-circle repeating pattern. It would take her time to count them. She looked at him sadly but reluctantly obeyed and began counting in groups of tens.

As the long row of people slowly made its way down Vasut utca (Railroad Street), Suti noticed that nearly every one of the houses they passed had their shutters pulled completely down. The street was devoid of people. No cars or horse-drawn carts were moving. The sun's rays beat down on the row of neat, whitewashed houses and the sun-bleached cobblestones of the old street and seemed to melt both together, transforming everything into a scene of translucent white.

The family seemed to be just around the corner from the train station when the long line came to a halt, inching forward only every once in a while. They were in front of the Liga, an old medieval-looking school structure that had been an orphanage for as long as anyone could remember. Suti could see that a table had been set up in the street.

Behind it were three chairs where two men and one woman were busy writing. As they inched closer, Suti could see his teacher, Ortutay bacsi, sitting at one of the chairs. As the line snaked over to the table, each family was assigned one of the three stenographers. Suti was pleased when they were assigned to Ortutay bacsi. He really liked his teacher.

His father, Vilmos, gave him the information: the family's last name, their address, the names of the members of the family in line and dates of their births. Suti stood next to his father as his name and date of birth were being given. He looked for some sign of recognition from this teacher he loved, but Ortutay bacsi kept his head down as he wrote and seemed to be totally concentrated on what he was writing.

After he wrote Suti's name and address down, Ortutay stopped, put down his pen, then, methodically, took off his glasses, rubbed his eyes with his hands, and wiped his eyes with his handkerchief. He did not greet Suti or look at him. Suti tried to imagine how hot it must be just sitting there at the table writing all day. He felt sympathy for Ortutay bacsi.

The line continued to crawl at a snail's pace. Icuka was quiet now, trying to catch the eye of a child near them. Suddenly, there was a bit of commotion behind them and a small group of people, some of whom Suti recognized from the ghetto, walked by. Icuka recognized Hedy in the group and ran to her.

"Hedy, Hedy, thank God you're here!" cried Icuka, grabbing her sister by the waist and hugging her. Not waiting for an answer, she grabbed her older sister's hand. "Where were you? I missed you!"

No one else asked Hedy anything.

Aliz glanced at her with a worried expression. Hedy looked relieved, but her eyes were red, as if she had been crying. Suti was so happy his sister was back with them. He saw Tibor, dressed in uniform, following right behind Hedy. Tibor greeted everyone and smiled.

He was pushing a bicycle and there was a very official-looking black leather bag in it that looked like the kind of bag a doctor carried. Suti noticed it had "T.S." engraved in fancy lettering on the top, next to the lock.

The line was moving a bit better now and they were heading toward the only train standing at the station. The long line of open cattle cars standing on the railway tracks couldn't be waiting for them, Suti thought — they were for transporting animals. But he could see that those people in the front of the line were already being herded into the cars.

Tibor stayed with them as they were loaded onto one of the cars. "Sixty. Seventy. Eighty." Suti heard the guard counting every tenth person as he ordered them into one of the boxcars.

Inside, it felt very cramped. The air was still and there was hardly any room to stand, let alone sit or lie down. Suti was incredibly thirsty. When their car was full, the guard began rolling the heavy, steel, windowless door down in order to slam it shut. But before he could, Tibor spoke to him quietly, discretely, pulling a bottle of vodka out of his briefcase and handed it to him. The guard looked at the bottle then, without glancing at Tibor or saying a single word, he put the vodka into his pants pocket and moved on. Their door stayed open. Another set of guards came by and handed them two buckets: one was empty and the other was full of water. When they saw Tibor standing at the door, they didn't question why the door was still open. They just handed in the buckets and walked on.

Tibor pulled more surprises and treats out of the leather-bound case: a bottle of wine, glasses for Hedy, father, Aliz, and himself, bread and cheese, candy and apples for Icuka and himself. Where could he have stored all these goodies? Hedy sat with her legs dangling over the edge of the doorway and Tibor stood by her side. They leaned in close together and talked and talked. Suti could hardly hear a word — no one could, they were talking in such low tones. What could they be talking about for so long? he wondered.

For the next six hours, the train just stood and waited in the blazing, late-May sunshine. As the hot afternoon wore on, Suti heard cries from the other boxcars.

"Water, water. Please, we're dying of thirst." The guards watched, unmoved.

"We can't breathe. Please, open the boxcar. My wife is suffocating." But all the other cattle cars remained closed.

The tar on the train tracks seemed to melt from the heat. No other trains came and went. Late in the afternoon, the train whistle blew. Tibor leaned in close to Hedy. He seemed to be saying something very serious to her now. Finally, he took a small white book out of his briefcase and handed it to her. She took the book in one hand, put her other arm around his neck, and hugged him. Suti saw tears rolling down her face. The guard came over and motioned for Tibor to step away. The door had to be closed. Tibor took Hedy's hand in his and gently kissed it, then, reluctantly, he stepped away from the train. There were tears in his eyes.

Hedy stood up and the door rolled shut and was sealed from the outside. Slowly, it rumbled out of the train station.

Tibor stood and watched as the billows of white smoke from the steam engine became smaller and smaller. Even long after the train disappeared, he remained there, staring into the distance, as tears of disbelief and grief rolled down his cheeks.

THE TRAIN OF CATTLE cars pulled into its final destination of Auschwitz-Birkenau. From the moment it came to a final stop, Suti was in shock, stunned by the series of unbelievable events taking place around him.

For almost three days, Suti, his sisters, and his father, along with some seventy others, had sat scrunched back to back, side to side in the dark cattle car. As the train had pulled out of Nagyszollos, tears were rolling down Hedy's face but, once she stopped crying, she showed Suti the little, white, leather-bound book Tibor had given her. Through the thin stream of light coming in the opening at the top of the boxcar, he could see the book was full of beautiful pictures. Hedy explained to him that this was Tibor's prayer book. As she tenderly stroked the soft leather cover, she told Suti that she and Tibor were in love. They were secretly engaged. Once the war was over, she confided, they would be married. It took Suti a while to absorb everything she told him, but he was happy for his sister.

THE NEXT THREE DAYS were like a nightmare. The cattle car had a small opening at the top (ten to twelve inches maximum) that ran along the uppermost sides of the car; it was the only place light and fresh air could come in. No one was tall enough to see out of the opening so, each time the cattle car slowed down for a station, some of the men lifted Suti up on their shoulders so he could read the station sign and tell them what he saw. People were anxious to find out where they were and what direction they were going. At one point Suti realized that the language on the signposts had changed. The place names were now written in what was Slovak or Polish — Suti wasn't sure which. But he read the names out dutifully, hoping that one of their fellow passengers would recognize where they were.

Suti and Hedy tried to keep up appearances for the sake of twelve-year-old Icuka. They told her stories during the dark and terrifying journey, reassured her that they were going to a place called Waldsee and that there would be a playground there and a beautiful lake where they would go swimming. In the dark, Hedy and Suti took turns comforting her, quietly talking and singing songs.

It smelled dreadful inside the cattle car. The bucket that was provided for waste had filled up by the second day and people started relieving themselves wherever they could. As the train slowed down and lurched forward on the journey, the contents of the bucket splattered and spilled out. Their fresh water was gone and so was the little food they had packed. There were whispers that an elderly man had died on the second day but they couldn't see because it was too crowded to stand and walk around. Suti lost track of time. As the train pulled into a station on the third day, he hoped this would be their final stop on what seemed like a never-ending journey.

The cattle cars were sealed from the outside with heavy iron latches. Everyone inside sat in silence, listening to the terrifying sounds coming closer to them. It sounded like a series of shotguns going off right outside their door. Suti soon realized the noise was the smashing of a sledge-hammer against the latches, unsealing the doors from the outside. When their door rolled back, the sudden burst of sunlight was blinding and felt like a lid being lifted from a coffin. Suti had to cover his eyes. Almost immediately, uniformed SS guards began barking at them, shouting in a language Suti couldn't understand. "*Raus! Raus! Schnell! Schnell! Raus, schnell!*" ("Get Out! Get Out! Fast! Fast! Out fast!") Many of the adults in the cattle car could hardly move, their legs and backs stiff from days of sitting in the same cramped position. Suti saw many of them struggling to stand up, trying to collect themselves and their belongings. Everyone seemed to be shouting at them.

Suti looked at his sister, Hedy, who had become the most important woman in his life since their mother died. He watched her stand up, run her hands over her wrinkled blouse, and straighten out her pretty pleated skirt. She looked beautiful, even after the long, harrowing journey. The lack of sleep and stress of the frightening journey hardly showed on her face.

But Suti didn't want to look at his little sister Icuka's face — not now, with dogs barking and uniformed SS officers shouting. He didn't want to see the betrayed look in her eyes as she realized everything they had told her about the beautiful lake was untrue. He was glad when Hedy grabbed her hand. Stunned by the sudden blast of air and sunlight that burned into his brain, Suti felt his senses were in shock, allowing him to move only in slow motion.

More yelling. Men with shaved heads in striped pyjama-like clothing jumping onto the cattle cars as the new arrivals tried to get off. To Suti they looked like convicts or escapees from an insane asylum. He didn't know what they wanted but they seemed to be devilishly determined in their task. They started grabbing bags, searching, looking for something, picking up bags, emptying them of their contents. As they worked, some of them spoke to the new arrivals, giving advice under their breath. They were speaking Yiddish, a language Suti didn't understand, but a neighbour who stood close by translated. "Give us any jewellery you have. They'll take any and all valuables away from you anyway."

One of them stared at Suti and said something directly to him. "Say you are seventeen and able to work," the neighbour translated. "Say you are a skilled worker." A frightening-looking man pointed to a building where flames were shooting out and said something. The translator turned white and became silent. Suti tugged at his sleeve for the translation. "See those chimneys over there?" he said. "That's where they gas and burn people to death." Suti was shocked by their rudeness. How can they tell such monstrous, unbelievable lies? he thought. Why, they were nothing more than a gang of thieves. One of the prisoners grabbed a baby from the arms of its screaming mother and handed the newborn to an elderly woman next to her. He pointed to the old woman and yelled at the young mother, "She takes the baby. Now go!"

A one-metre jump separated them from the ground. His sisters and father were being helped down by others and, when Suti jumped, he felt relieved to be on solid ground again. There was dry dust everywhere. Then Suti noticed another kind of putrid smell. It seemed to permeate this place. There must be a slaughterhouse nearby, he thought.

By the time they emptied the cattle cars, Suti, his family, and the other Hungarian Jews from Karpatalja were already being herded into a long lineup that seemed endless. Everyone was trying to see what was happening in front of them but there were too many people for Suti to see anything, even though the line was moving quickly.

As they neared the front of the line, Suti saw that they were being sorted into three separate groups: women and teenage girls were being ushered to the left, men and older boys to the right, and there was a third line for just older women and men and very young children.

Two uniformed officers stood behind a table examining long lists; a third stood in front of the table. They looked very stern. The one in front, a senior officer who wore wire-rimmed glasses, seemed to be directing the operation. When the family got to the front of the line, the senior officer didn't ask them anything or address them in any way. He barely glanced at them, simply pointing in the direction they were to go. A flick of a finger, like a conductor, Suti thought. Deciding their direction in a split second. Suti and his father were sent to the right. Hedy and Aliz were sent with the women's group. He was relieved to stay with his father, relieved that his sisters were also together. But, while all this was going on, Suti looked back to see Icuka being sent to the third line made up of children and older men and women. As he helplessly watched her being herded away, he saw an elderly neighbour from back home, Mrs. Rosenberg, take Icuka's hand. "Come with me, Icuka," he heard her say. "We'll stay together." Suti was relieved that Icuka would not be alone, that someone they knew was with her. The image of shoulder-length braids and the back of her favourite light blue sweater was the last glimpse he, or any of them, ever had of her.

HEDY HELD ON TO her sister, Aliz, feeling that as long as they walked arms linked, nothing could happen to them. No one could separate them. Herded and rushed as they were, they barely had a chance to think or react to everything that was happening around them. To cope, Hedy let her thoughts float away to memories of Tibor. Like a drug, his image and scent, his last words, stayed with her, shielding her a bit from all the frightening things happening around her. She stroked the white prayer book concealed in the pocket of her skirt — the last thing he had given her. There had been a deep sadness in his face as he said goodbye and whispered, "Let this talisman protect you from harm until we're together again."

As they were being led past a fenced-off area, they saw more people with shaved heads in grey garb. "Look, just look at those women," Aliz whispered to Hedy.

"Maybe they're more inmates from an insane asylum," Hedy replied softly.

The inmates were yelling at them as they passed. It was too dreadful to watch them and Hedy kept her eyes ahead of her, on the women guards guiding them through this maze. They looked decent enough, with well-kept hair and clothes.

"They're like us," Aliz whispered to Hedy, motioning toward the guards. "I heard some of them speaking Slovak, but others speak Hungarian. They've been here longer, though. I heard they were brought here some years ago."

Maybe it was possible to survive this place after all, Hedy thought.

"Surely they will give us water soon," Aliz continued. "My throat's like sandpaper."

Hedy was going to reply, but one of the Slovak women yelled back, "No talking!"

They were herded into a large, cavernous building where one of the Slovak women, the one with a round face and black-framed glasses, stood in front of them and yelled out a series of orders. "In the first room," she explained, "they will shave you." Hedy and Aliz looked at each other in shock, as did most of the other newly arrived women. "Next, you will have a shower. And then, you will be assigned to barracks. Everything that's done here is done for the sake of cleanliness."

The shavers were quick and efficient in their task. Hedy couldn't bear to open her eyes and see her blond curls falling to the floor. She thought back to her last haircut and tears welled up in her eyes. But she wouldn't give them the satisfaction of seeing her cry. Then the Slovak guard with the black-framed glasses was back, barking more orders.

"Hang up your clothes along the wall. Each hook has a number. Remember the number. When you are finished with the shower, you will get your clothes back. Keep only your shoes with you and prescription eyeglasses. Leave everything else on the hooks." She waited a moment to see if they were following orders and then screamed, "Move it!"

The women undressed obediently, quietly. Hedy undressed slowly, her mind still trying to comprehend her body's feeling of nakedness. She didn't want to touch her bare scalp or look at her bald sister. She stared at the hook, trying to engrave the number 31 into her brain. The number kept going out of focus as tears kept building up in her eyes. She bit her lip hard and once again told herself not to cry. She hung up her blouse, bra, socks, panties, and, finally, the skirt that held Tibor's prayer book in the pocket. She lovingly ran her fingers over it as she left it, hoping that stroking it would bring her good luck. As she made her way to the next room, she grabbed her beautiful burgundy calf's-leather walking shoes. They were all she had left now that linked her with everything she cherished.

The female guard in the next room was big-boned and taller than any of the others. She had a hardness about her that was accentuated by her piercing blue eyes. Her job was to check their mouths and shoes as they entered the showers. While the big one went about her task, the one with the black glasses, who stood nearby, continued her shouting.

"If you're hiding anything, we will find it, and the punishment will be severe."

Hedy tightened her grip on her shoes as she and Aliz neared the guard. She was naked but, somehow, tried to cover herself with the shoes and her hands and arms. Aliz went through the humiliating examination within seconds. Then the tall Slovak guard indicated for Hedy to open her mouth. She grabbed the shoes, turned them upside down, looking inside, and, without saying a word, put them on a shelf behind her. Without skipping a beat, she looked toward the next person. Hedy couldn't believe what had happened. Something broke in her as she looked the big-boned guard straight in the eyes and said, "Excuse me, those are my shoes!"

"Get moving, if you know what's good for you," the guard snarled back at Hedy.

"I want my shoes back!" Hedy demanded through her anger. She wouldn't move, she told herself, sweat rolling down her naked body, her heart pounding.

The guard, who had already turned to face the next person, turned back to Hedy. Without moving a muscle on her cold facial expression, she raised her palm and slapped Hedy across the face. "Do you want more?' Then just stay here," she shouted. The room became very quiet as Hedy felt all eyes staring at her.

For the first time in her relatively short life, Hedy felt she could kill someone with her bare hands. Aliz grabbed her arm and pulled her toward the next room where the showers were. As the women around her opened their mouths to wet their parched throats, they noticed it had a strange taste. Hedy didn't notice. The shower didn't last long but, while the water hit her face, she could finally release the torrent of tears.

Her thought's raced back to what Aliz had told her about the guards. They were inmates, too. Unbelievable. They knew what it felt like to be stripped of everything. She couldn't believe that someone who had gone through what she was going through now would be capable of such cruelty.

There was no soap in the shower, no towels afterward. As they stood dripping, they were handed clean, used dresses, most of them threadbare from repeated washings in strong detergents. As she slowly put on the light cotton dress that fell to her ankles, Hedy thought back to her clothes hanging on hook number 31 in the other room. She realized now that the hook and the number were just part of a series of lies. They would never get their clothes back. She would never get Tibor's prayer book back again. Stripped of her clothes, her hair, her shoes, and her precious talisman, she had been deprived of all that she had ever been and hoped to be. Hedy glanced at her bald-headed sister and saw a mirror image of herself.

"I won't cry if you don't cry," Aliz said to Hedy. "Let's not give them the satisfaction."

chapter 16 | june 1945

SUTI AND HIS FATHER hardly spoke. Initially, Suti whispered questions: "Where was Icuka?" "Where are Hedy and Aliz?" "What is this place?"

But when no reply came, Suti could no longer bear to see the vacant, helpless look in his father's eyes. This was not the father he knew — the confident, knowledgeable man Suti could turn to with any question. His father seemed to be like the other adults around him: frozen with fear, unable to comprehend why they were here or any of what was going on around them.

Their heads were shaved, but not completely. It was as if the barbers wanted to make them all look ridiculous with their mocking design. They shaved a strip of hair down the centre of the head, with the two sides trimmed very short, just three millimetres above the scalp. The men and teenagers were given hats.

Orthodox Jews wept as their heads and beards were shaved — they simply couldn't cope with this violation of their religious beliefs. They huddled in small groups in shock, some burying their heads in their knees, rocking themselves back and forth in disbelief, murmuring prayers of mourning. Using makeshift scarves, they attempted to cover the areas where their beards would have covered their faces.

Following the humiliation of the shaving, the new arrivals were led to the men's barracks. As they walked in, the smell of human sweat combined with a disinfectant-type cleaning fluid overwhelmed Suti.

Three rows of wooden storage shelves were stacked on top of each other, with a few feet in between each where heads peered out. The rows were narrow in front — long enough to lie down, but not high enough to sit up. Six to eight skinny men were crammed into one section, like spoons in a drawer. Suti was mesmerized by the rows of eyes staring back at him with blank, empty stares as he and the others were led down the centre aisle.

Suti had, until then, never had to share a bed with any of his siblings, let alone strangers. He and his father settled into one of the shelf-like boxes to try to sleep. If someone wanted to turn over, they all had to do so at the same time. He tried to quiet the growling of his stomach, but it was still the thirst that was consistently clawing at his throat.

The next day began in the dark before dawn at four o'clock, with loud whistling and shouting going on outside their barracks.

"*Raus, raus, schnell, schnell.*"

Suti could hardly move he was so tired. His entire body ached. His father nudged him and helped him get up. Everyone seemed to scramble out of their bunks, as if they dreaded what would happen if they didn't jump when ordered. The group fell silently into exact rows at the front of the barracks. Suti, his father, and the other newcomers didn't know where to stand, but were pushed and shoved into their places by the others.

Jewish women of Karpatalja in Auschwitz at the end of May 1944. Reproduced from Az Auschwitz Album *by permission of Yad Vashem/Auschwitz-Birkenau Állami Múzeum.*

The *zehl appel* (roll call) lasted one hour. The older inmates told the new arrivals they were fortunate: the *zehl appel* had been relatively brief that morning. Suti learned as the days wore on that the roll call sometimes lasted one to three hours, sometimes a half day.

After a few days, Suti's father was taken away on a work brigade, leaving Suti completely alone. His daily life became a fusion of loneliness, boredom, and fear.

Outside, nothing grew: no grass, no trees, not a single flower. Suti noticed there were no birds. The stench of death hung over the place like a pall, there was no place to escape from it. This smell of death, mixed with human excrement, urine, and disinfectant were the primary smells of the camp.

Even the food they received didn't provide any relief, however temporary, from the smell of death. The so-called bread came in the shape of a brick — it was hard and tasteless. Sawdust was used by the bakers to keep the brick-shaped bread from sticking to the pan — the tiny bits of wood were baked right into the loaf. The soup was suspiciously devoid of colour: it was consistently a tinge of dull grey and brown with a few bits of vegetables floating on top — primarily beets and turnips. Occasionally, there were bones cooked into the soup. Suti later learned the bones were leftovers from meals prepared for the SS.

With a mixture of defiance and desperation, Suti began to scrape an atom of beauty from the desolation. He noticed little red fragments of bricks randomly crushed into the dirt here and there on the ground. He started collecting the bits of brick and, out of these, he constructed geometric designs in the dirt. In scouring the ground, Suti found a small, discarded, single length of string. He considered it a great treasure — something he could use to create uniform lengths for his flowers. Hunched over his outdoor artwork for hours, he created perfectly shaped flowers out of the little bits of red-brick debris where no real flowers grew. The creation of the artwork required precision and concentration, and it filled the hours between meagre meals and consumed moments that would have been lost in memory and fear. Finally, Suti thought, this was a tiny part of his universe where he was in control.

The block altester noticed his meticulous work and took an immediate liking to the decorative motifs. The recognition was brief — the first time since their arrival that anyone had spoken to him directly or acknowledged him as an individual. Suti's symbolic flower garden decorated the entrances to their barracks, and distinguished their barracks from the rest. For his efforts, Suti occasionally received a little more soup, and an additional morsel of bread.

Housed in barracks full of Hungarian Jews from his home district, Suti nevertheless felt completely alone, isolated, and lonely. He turned inward for solace and comfort and decided he couldn't relate to any of the people around him. He already lost everyone in his family — he couldn't bear to lose any more people he cared about. He decided not to make any attachments.

There was one inmate, however, who went out of his way to engage Suti and consistently had a kind word for him. Everyone simply called him Dr. Braun. He spoke to Suti often, reassuring him that this would all be over soon, trying to instill a glimmer of hope in the boy. In the midst of all the hardships around them, Dr. Braun injected humour in their everyday lives and shared stories that made Suti smile.

On one occasion, a shipment or horribly pungent cheese was delivered to the lager. The cheese was packaged elegantly in wooden crates, each small portion wrapped in fine wax parchment paper. By the way it was packaged and prepared, one could see that this cheese had been intended for an upscale market. The cheese was repugnant to smell, however, and it was crawling with live worms.

Suti was part of a group of young boys repelled by the idea of looking at it, let alone eating it. But they were all hungry. Dr. Braun realized that what these young boys needed to survive was protein — something almost entirely devoid from their diet. He decided to make them believe that the cheese was an amazing delicacy.

Dr. Braun gathered the boys around him and, as if he was letting them in on a secret, leaned in close to them and began, "This is so delicious — an expensive gourmet treat. It is destined for very exclusive restaurants in Paris and London. The worms in it are specially bred in this cheese to make it more appealing to the taste buds: they make it crunchy, like eating almonds. You have no idea what you are missing if you don't taste it."

Dr. Braun unwrapped one of the elegantly wrapped portions from the wax paper, and as he held the cheese in the air, the worms were so plentiful they were falling, writhing as they landed on the ground.

"Mmmmmmm, this is soooo good. Delicious!" Dr. Braun said as he popped the entire chunk into his mouth at once. The expression on his face demonstrated sheer enjoyment as he continued to masticate the mouthful. Suti and the other boys were aghast. Then their growling stomachs sent encouraging signals to their brains: maybe it didn't taste as disgusting as it looked.

Although he pretended to be aloof and withdrawn, Suti couldn't prevent hearing the constant mutterings and discussions going on around him. While most adults were pessimistic about what was to come, others tried to convince themselves that there was reason to believe the war and their incarceration would be over soon. The arguments, sometimes in whispered tones, sometimes louder, went back and forth.

"We're never getting out of here. The simplest thing to do is to hang ourselves, commit suicide. They're going to kill us anyway."

"Listen to me; the Allies have landed in France. This is the end for the Nazis. The Americans are coming from the west, the Russians from the east. We will be liberated soon."

"Liberated? Soon? Are you crazy? With the smoke from those chimneys billowing out smoke and soot, operating around the clock, we will all be exterminated before the Americans arrive. They don't even know about us."

Sometimes Suti desperately wished he could block his ears to stop his hearing. But he was a curious boy, and found that, as a skinny young kid, he could easily go to the front of the crowd to find out what they were gathering to see.

Sometimes he regretted being so curious, such as the day he saw his first "jumper." By the time he fought his way through the crowd to see what the focus of their attention was, the unfortunate man was still clinging, with both hands firmly clutching the electrified fence. His hands were smoking and red-hot, partially turning black from the electrification. Those watching had to cover their noses with their hands as the putrid smell of burning flesh filled the air. The torso and head of the man were thrown back from the force of the electrical charge. The unfortunate man's eyes were wide open, the eyeballs nearly popping out of the sockets, his tongue hanging out of his mouth. He was obviously dead from the force of electrical blast, but his head, torso, eyes, and tongue kept moving with the powerful current still coursing through his body.

The camp guards were irritated by such "jumpers" as they had the task of cleaning up the mess. They ordered the gathered crowd to disperse immediately, swearing at them under their breath. But even as the onlookers stepped back just a few feet, they were mesmerized by the gruesome sight. They continued to watch as the camp guards turned off the electricity and removed the burnt corpse from the fence by hitting the lifeless hands with the butt of a rifle to dislodge the charred limbs from the fence, then dumping the dead man unceremoniously into a sack. Bits of burnt flesh were simply left on the fence. Some around him had already started praying for the dead man, some were praising him, muttering about his courage, about what a glorious, simple way it was to end this miserable existence.

Within a few weeks of landing in Auschwitz-Birkenau, Suti began to have serious doubts about the existence of God. It was all a story. No God would allow so many horrible things to happen to so many innocent people. How could God tolerate a place like this? Nothing made sense.

Suti went out of the barracks on a particularly melancholic evening, turned his face to the cloudless night sky, and, like a wolf howling at the moon, screamed obscenities at the heavens and challenged God to prove his power by striking him dead, right there, right then. The wind took his words away quickly.

Nothing happened. He yelled again. No answer except for the distant sounds of dogs barking, guards yelling orders, a train whistle blowing far away.

Suti listened again. His yelling at the heavens became more muted. Still no response. He had no more fear of anything: punishment for such blasphemy, the wrath of God, were concepts that were completely meaningless to him.

AFTER SIX WEEKS IN Auschwitz–Birkenau, Hedy had become obsessed with finding her brother. Hedy and her sister, Aliz, were inseparable: looking out, protecting, soothing, comforting one another. They shared their meagre portions, thoughts, small joys, and sorrows. But both were sick with worry about Suti and their father, and still held out hope, despite the horrible things that they heard around them, that Icuka was alive.

In a place where inmates would kill each other for a soup spoon, they learned to cope. Finding Suti, however, was one of their triumphs. It wasn't easy because they were moved from lager B2C to B2B, when the latter was emptied of a group of Czech Jews. Suti, they later found out, was also moved from the kinder lager to a men's lager (B2D), adjacent to the main entrance. Hedy cautiously approached anyone she thought could help in her search for him.

There was a young, serious-looking doctor in the camp. He was Jewish — an inmate as the rest of them — but could move between the women's and men's barracks. He came in one day and approached Hedy.

"A new group of women just arrived from Lizmanstadt. Could you please assist in finding my fiancée? I've heard she's with the newly arrived group. I'm desperate for news about her. They can't move around the camp yet, and I can't get in to see them. Please help me get word to her."

"If you describe her for me, I'll see what I can do," replied Hedy. The doctor provided a good description so that even without the colour, length, or type of her hair, Hedy found his fiancée and delivered the message.

After a few days, Hedy reported back.

"I've found your fiancée. She's fine and sends her love."

The young doctor was overcome with emotion upon hearing the news.

"How can I thank you?" he asked sincerely.

Hedy paused for a second, then replied, "My younger brother is in your lager. He's very young — he's called Suti. Could you bring him in as a worker the next time you come?"

The young doctor's face turned gloomy. "My movements are restricted, unfortunately, but I know the kapo who is in charge of the disinfection commando. I'm sure he could do something. I'll bring him over to meet you."

The doctor kept his promise and arranged a meeting with the kapo, who was very different from Hedy's expectations. He was a red, freckle-faced, pert Polish Jew called Dzeidjic. Of average height and stocky, Dzeidjic seemed quite arrogant. His thick auburn hair was combed straight back. Hedy could tell by the way Kapo Dzeidjic stared at her that he was impressed with her looks. He stopped when she approached, and his mouth opened just a bit, as if he wanted to say something, but no words came out. He simply stood in one spot, tapping one foot on the ground, curling the end of his little red moustache with his fingers, looking uncomfortable. But he didn't leave.

"What do you want?" he snapped at her in a gruff manner.

"My brother is in the same lager where you are," Hedy replied, unfazed by the tone. "The next time you come in, could you bring him as a worker? I simply want to see him for a short visit."

"How old is your brother?" the kapo asked. He seemed to be impressed with the courage of this young woman.

"Fourteen," Hedy replied cautiously.

Softening his tone a bit, the kapo then asked with a half-smile, "Is he as pretty as you are?"

"He's much better looking," Hedy said as she returned the smile.

"Does he know any languages?" Dzeidjic asked.

"Yes, he does."

"Okay, here's my word: tomorrow you will see your brother."

While Hedy realized that, even without any hair, in a torn old burlap dress, she had managed to make an impression on the kapo, she was skeptical about whether this arrogant man would actually make an effort to carry through with his promise. Hedy went back to the doctor, thanked him for his help, and asked him to personally find Suti and take him to the kapo.

The next day, in the middle of the morning, Hedy and Aliz heard their names being called from a distance. They looked at each other quizzically. The yelling came from the direction of the railway line, beyond the electrified fences. The voices were male and sounded strong, confident. The rail line ran parallel to one side of their barracks, and they stared in the direction of the voices. There, on an open rail car, side by side, stood Suti and Kapo Dzeidjic. Suti had his arms stretched up toward the sky, as he yelled for the attention of Hedy and Aliz. Suti looked so pleased! Hedy and Aliz shot their hands up as well — tears of joy were streaming down their faces as they yelled Suti's name.

A few hours later, the kapo brought Suti in to them and they had a chance to talk. Hedy and Aliz both hugged Suti for minutes before they would let him go. Suti was breathless in his excitement, anxious to tell his sisters about all the things that had happened to him in the past twenty-four hours.

"The kapo said he will take me to the *kleidungskammer* (place to get new clothes). I have a job cleaning his shoes, and I already got more food."

Hedy was so pleased. She fought back tears of joy as she saw her younger brother's beaming face and new-found happiness. The excitement poured out of Suti as he explained how Dzeidjic had found him and given him a job: he would be cleaning Dzeidjic's boots. Suddenly, Suti stopped, as if he had remembered something. He moved in close to Hedy and whispered in her ear, "The kapo wants to marry you."

"Really?" Hedy replied, feigning a look of surprise.

Suti nodded, his brown eyes becoming rounder, more animated.

Hedy didn't realize it then, but later learned that Kapo Dzeidjic was an individual who wielded tremendous power and influence in the camp, one of the kapos connected to Commando Kanada.

Commando Kanada consisted of several groups. The name itself was associated with wealth within the concentration camp, because this group collected and sorted through all the packages, foodstuffs, and other objects the new arrivals brought with them. The inmates who worked within Commando Kanada could get things because they had a seemingly never-ending supply of food, clothing, carpets, silver, jewellery, and other valuable objects to barter, trade, and sell. The early Polish prisoners gave the group this name because it evoked the land of legendary wealth to which many of their relatives had emigrated before the war.

One of the brigades of Commando Kanada climbed through the boxcars like hyenas, poring over left bags — lifting and recognizing within seconds what was salvageable and disposing of everything else.

After the boxcars were emptied of their human cargo and left luggage, Kapo Dzeidjic and his group took charge. Their job was to disinfect the boxcars of the stench of human feces, urine, and vomit, and to remove dead bodies.

The men in the Dzeidjic brigade lugged a large barrel full of two hundred litres of disinfectant with them. The barrel was pulled on wheels. Two men pumped the barrel while the third sprayed the boxcar using a directional hose. As the disinfectant was pumped out, there was more and more room in the barrel for found treasures. As they worked, they lifted the lid and dropped the valuables into the barrel.

When Dzeidjic marched into the barracks, everyone became silent, watching him with rapt attention. He was the commander of the prestigious unit. The kapo could be furious when provoked, but most of the time, his crew followed his instructions to the letter.

Suti polished the kapo's boots. The storage area had all kinds of brushes, shoeshine creams, and leather polishes. He spent hours scraping and brushing away every centimetre of dirt and coaxing a brilliant shine out of the dull leather. When Dzeidjic witnessed the thoroughness of his work, he named Suti his personal boot cleaner. From that point on, Suti realized he had a critically important task to do and no longer had to spend hours of solitary time in making geometric patterns in the dirt.

Another bond eventually developed between the two. Dzeidjic let Suti discover one of his most guarded secrets: Dzeidjic couldn't read. Once or twice, Dzeidjic simply handed Suti a note and ordered, "read this out loud to me." By the third or fourth time this happened, it dawned on Suti that the kapo was incapable of reading and that this was another way Suti could make himself indispensable.

To deflect attention away from his inability to read, Dzeidjic gave Suti notes in Polish, a language he knew the young boy didn't know how to decipher.

When Suti was ordered to read the notes in Polish out loud, Dzeidjic laughed heartily and ridiculed the young boy's pronunciation. But Suti didn't mind. Dzeidjic couldn't read and Suti couldn't pronounce Polish words. In Dzeidjic's mind, they both had a handicap.

Day by day, a bit of hope crept into Suti's heart and mind. He considered himself fortunate. He felt that as long as he was under the protection of Dzeidjic, he was impervious to the monotony and hunger of the camp. And, even more importantly, the kapo provided Suti a purpose, a patron, a light through the despair.

chapter 17 | fall 1944

HEDY AND ALIZ SOMEHOW adapted to the heat and stench, to the hunger and the desolation, but still their long. hot days in Auschwitz-Birkenau seemed interminable. News and rumours flew through the camp, at times bringing optimism to their miserable existence, at other times pushing them deeper into despair that their suffering was never going to end. They were overjoyed to hear that the Americans had landed on the shores of France and would come to liberate them, but the anticipation of their arrival slowly diminished as the days wore into weeks, and then months.

The sisters developed ways of coping with daily life inside the concentration camp. The two became inseparable — they shared everything. At night they snuggled close to each other, comforting each other merely by their physical presence.

Aliz had one leg that was shorter than the other: this disability caused her to limp. Physically, it was much more exhausting for her to keep up with the rest. Hedy balanced out her sister's physical ailment with her zest and energy. If at four-thirty in the morning Aliz was too exhausted to get out of bed for *zehl appel*; it was Hedy who willed her strength into her sister and pulled her to her feet.

The lager they were in contained thirty-two barracks, with one latrine in the middle. The toilets consisted of a cement hole, and there was no paper, no soap, no privacy wall. The length of the first dress Hedy received extended all the way down to her ankles. She tore strips off of her long cotton dress and used these bits as toilet paper. As the days passed, the hemline of the dress got shorter and shorter.

Within a few months, their menstruation stopped. Hedy thought it must have been something — a drug — they added to their food that suppressed their monthly cycle. Hedy didn't know how they would have coped with that.

Once a month, they were taken for an *entlausung* (delousing bath). Ordered to strip and throw all their shoes, dresses, and underwear into a pile, they were assigned new clothing from piles of over-washed, over-bleached, and threadbare clothing. They stood in single file and were handed a bundle of clothing — whatever they were doled out is what they had to wear for the next month. On one such occasion, Hedy was handed a dress that did not cover her left breast — the fabric was completely ripped away. Realizing she had to wear this dress for the foreseeable future, Hedy managed to find a discarded piece of cloth to cover the gap, and somehow tied it to the rest of the dress so it wouldn't come apart.

If Hedy was handed a better pair of shoes, she passed them on to her sister. A shoe without proper support only made Aliz's limp more pronounced. Sometimes Hedy was assigned a pair of shoes that were mismatched. These things didn't seem to matter. In Hedy's mind, these were all challenges, all obstacles to be overcome by ingenuity and determination.

Hedy and Aliz were frequently selected to work in the Essen-Commando, a group that helped distribute the daily rations. If either got one more carrot or bit of soup, they shared it. As there were no utensils or dishes to eat with, four or five women shared a bowl of soup, counting the spoonfuls for each, making sure each spoonful was distributed equally. A discarded soup can was considered a great treasure, as it was immediately transformed into a highly prized eating utensil. If Aliz got a piece of a radish or potato in her soup, she wedged it between her teeth until Hedy bit the other half off. Hedy always reciprocated her sister's generosity. The bread was the size of a brick: at first they divided it among six, then eight, then ten. By the end of this game of division, each was left with a quarter of a slice each.

Between the mind-numbing activities of their daily routine, *zehl appel*, and talking about how famished they were, some women organized impromptu gatherings when and where they could, to tell stories they recalled from books and recite poetry. Often Hedy took the initiative. She remembered that as a young girl she couldn't comprehend why they had to memorize so many poems by rote. Now she was grateful for the many hours she spent learning poetry as the poetry recitations and the songs they sang at home with their parents all came flooding back, providing the only escape from the present environment of dread and boredom.

Among all the poetry, storytelling, and singing they all shared, Hedy's favourite piece was Sandor Petofi's "*A Rab*" ("The Captive").

> I battle for you, freedom
> My arms and legs in chains.
> Light, I crave after you
> As a mole, existing underground.
>
> When will freedom's hour strike?
> When will the happy hour be
> When I breathe from freedom's air again
> And you will shine on me, oh bright sunshine?
>
> And hope sustains him that he will someday be free
> Despite the time that marks half his life
> Hope that the other half of his life
> Will be spent in sweet freedom.

But each time she recited it, anyone who heard it was in tears — the poem reminded them so much of their own situation and how they had to somehow gather the strength to survive. At the end of the poem, after so many years of hoping, craving after freedom, just as they remove the shackles and unlock the prison cell, the captive dies of a broken heart.

Despite the tragic end of the poem, everyone kept begging that Hedy recite it, over and over again. She became convinced that reciting a brilliant piece of poetry or discussing a classic work of fiction brought their intelligence to the forefront and reminded them that they were still thinking, feeling human beings. The storytelling sessions kept their humanity intact.

The singing and poetry also seemed to transport her back to Nagyszollos and her mind became full of memories of Tibor. She still saw his face clearly in her mind's eye, his deep, emotion-filled, brown eyes, so full of love the last time she saw him. But the memories evaporated once she looked down at her dress, felt her hairless head, or smelled the putrid air around her.

Blokkova was the title of the prisoner in charge in the female barracks. In their barracks it was mainly Jewish women from Slovakia who were in these positions of power — they supervised the newly arrived Hungarian Jewish women. Hedy and Aliz quickly learned to avoid the cruel ones, those who meted out harsh punishments for no reason and were consistently looking for new ways to taunt them, verbally and physically. Although they knew exactly what it felt like to arrive to this place and be stripped, shaved, and humiliated, they seemed to have nothing but disdain for the newly arrived group. They spewed an endless litany of cruel, disparaging remarks.

"Why are you crying? Do you want your mama? Well she's not here and no one else is going to help you get out of here." The Slovak women arrived almost two years before the Hungarians, which seemed to be another reason for their deep resentment and hatred.

"You were still dancing and sleeping in comfortable beds at home when we were already dying in here!"

One Slovak Jewish blokkova named Judit was an exception; she treated them with kindness. Of average height and weight, with an oval face and deep brown eyes, Judit looked plain, but she had a lovely cream complexion and a kind demeanour that intimated a background of education and civility. She didn't yell or scream like the others, but when she spoke, she did so with an authoritative voice and commanded respect. Judit was one of the few who protected and cared for the women in her barracks. It was only later that Hedy and Aliz realized how her invaluable instructions saved their lives on more than one occasion, especially in times of the selections.

The word *selections* itself evoked dread, and was mentioned only in whispered tones; it was synonymous with annihilation. These selections were usually quite arbitrary, and no one knew when they were coming, or who was targeted, or on what basis they would be selected. Everyone understood that those selected or sorted out were automatically sent to the gas chamber.

On one occasion, when the inmates from every other block were outside of their barracks, Judit imposed *blokk sperre*, or lockdown, for no apparent reason, forcing all the women to stay incarcerated in their barracks for many hours. It was only later, when they were released, that they learned that, while they were confined to their barracks, SS officers had implemented such a dreaded sorting.

When no advanced warning came of the sorting, and Judit was unable to lock them inside the barracks for their own protection, she coached them on how to avoid getting selected.

"Hold your skirts above your knees and show them a bit of thigh — that way it won't be as obvious that you've lost a lot of weight. They will be too busy looking at your legs. Act like young, energetic women," she cautioned them. "Run, don't walk. Run so fast that Mengele won't have a chance to pick you. Pinch your cheeks. Smile!"

Judit coached them on how to run like a pack of gazelles, protecting each other from being selected. She organized the group so that the youngest, most agile would sprint on the outside, thereby protecting the weaker, thinner, older on the inside.

When camp commanders asked for volunteers for work brigades, the inmates frequently had no idea whether it was to go to work, or be sent to the gas chamber. It was a life and death lottery. Sometimes members of the work brigade received a bit more food, sometimes they didn't.

By the fall Hedy and Aliz were assigned to a work brigade that went to construct a drainage ditch to the Vistula River. It was back-breaking, exhausting work and their daily rations were not increased, but by working Hedy and Aliz hoped that their chances of survival would probably be better than if they stayed in the barracks. Each morning, as they walked down the Lagerstrasse to be led out of the camp, Suti and Kapo Dzeidjic walked along the inside the fence, saying goodbye, in effect escorting them as they headed off to work. Dzeidjic and Suti stayed at the fence as long as they were within sight of Hedy and Aliz. No matter how exhausted they were in the morning, the two sisters acted energetic, and smiled and waved at the two of them, comforted by the fact that Suti also had someone looking out for him.

BUT THE FEELING OF being protected melted away for Suti one day in September when a sudden selection was implemented, targeting the younger teenaged boys. Those who were under the designated height were selected out. Dr. Mengele was there, personally supervising this selection. It was a quick movement of his finger that was the final arbiter of life and death.

Before Suti could fully comprehend what was happening around him, he had been selected, along with many hundreds of others. Suti and the others were taken to empty barracks, where they were locked up. Emptying barracks for a specific reason took a matter of minutes: the guards simply entered and ordered everyone out.

The young boys and teenagers knew instinctively that this meant the end. The next step was inevitably the gas chamber.

Suti was shocked and dazed. Everything had taken place with such incredible speed. His protector, Dzeidjic, wasn't around when the selection took place. No one from the Dzeidjic group saw Suti being taken away. It would be hours before his sisters would return from their day labour on the Vistula River.

The barracks were packed with hundreds of boys. Suti looked around and estimated there were at least 699 boys — he being the seven hundredth.

It was the eve of Yom Kippur 1944, the Day of Atonement, the holiest of all Jewish religious holidays. Some of the boys began to recite the *Kol Nidre* — the prayer of contrition and consolation that is the climax of the holy service. The prayer spread through the group. Within minutes, they were all praying together. All except one.

Susan M. Papp

Suti couldn't and wouldn't pray to a God who he believed had abandoned all of them. God did not exist. Ever since the day when he howled at the heavens, soon after entering Auschwitz, he relinquished his faith in God.

The others saw Suti's atheism as the cause of their own condemnation. Two boys from Nagyszollos — Sanyi Lebovics and Chayim Teitelbaum — challenged Suti. "Why won't you pray with us?" they demanded. "Your arrogance will cost us our lives. It's the Day of Atonement. If you don't pray with us we'll all be condemned!"

"*Szégyeld magad Weisz Sanyi!*" (Shame on you Sandor Weisz!)

Suti was unmoved, simply staring at the door.

No living boy could convince Suti of the existence of an immortal God.

This was the scene on that eve of Yom Kippur — minutes turning to hours, hundreds of wailing, crying, praying children and teenagers crowded into the cramped corridors of the death barracks, muttering, chanting, whispering psalms and prayers for deliverance. All except one.

Suti fought his way through the dense crowd, trying to find a place to stand at the nearest point to the entrance so he could see anyone entering or exiting the barracks.

Trying to fight back the overwhelming feeling of panic that was creeping into his body, Suti saw Janek, one of the men who worked in the brigade run by Kapo Dzeidjic, enter the barracks. Janek headed in the direction of the block altester's room for dinner. He was alone.

In a panic, Suti yelled to Janek — from about a metre and a half — as loud as he could. "It's me, tell Dzeidjic I'm here! Please tell Kapo Dzeidjic I'm here!"

Janek looked, recognized Suti, mumbled under his breath that he would tell Dzeidjic, and proceeded into the block altester's room, closing the door behind him. Suti had little choice but to wait patiently while Janek and the other workers ate their dinner. After what seemed like an interminable length of time, the door opened again and Janek came out. Suti whispered (as loudly as he could), "Please don't forget to tell the kapo about me." His heart pounded loudly as the words came out of his mouth. No matter how hard he tried to control it, his voice was quavering.

172

When Janek left, Suti hardly noticed the desperate teenagers around him anymore. A numbness descended upon him. There was nothing he could do but wait.

An hour later, just as Suti convinced himself that all hope was gone, Janek returned with another man. Dzeidjic's assistant never even glanced at Suti as he went directly to the block altester's room once again and closed the door. After a short time, the visitors opened the door and came back out. Janek walked directly toward Suti, pointed to him, and yelled in an angry tone, "You are coming with us, now!"

The room fell silent and everyone seemed to hold their breath in shock as Suti was grabbed and taken out of the barracks.

The men took Suti directly to an empty barracks where Dzeidjic was standing in the middle of his small working group. Everyone around him was sitting. Suti looked at Dzeidjic, hardly able to speak. Dzeidjic gave him a steely look, put his finger to his lips as a signal to be quiet, and pointed to the upper bunk at the farthest end of the barracks.

Suti could barely find the strength to pull himself up the stairs — his legs had been drained of all energy — but he somehow scrambled to safety. There, to his surprise, was a Greek Jew who comforted him by putting his arms around him until he stopped shaking. He began talking to Suti, first by telling the boy his name — Chaim Raphael — then telling him stories in a soothing, comforting tone.

He sensed by the trembling of the young boy that he had just survived a devastating experience, the seriousness of which the Greek man could only guess at by the length of time it took to calm him.

To take Suti's mind off the trauma, Chaim Raphael quietly sang Italian folk songs and encouraged him to sing along. After more than an hour of quiet singing, the boy finally stopped trembling.

Suti later learned the price Dzeidjic had to pay to extricate him from the death barracks: five cans of sardines and twenty U.S. dollars. Such was the appraisal of a single human life at Auschwitz-Birkenau in the autumn of 1944.

Before dawn, the other children and teenagers were exterminated. All except one.

chapter 18 | fall 1944

TIBOR HARDLY SLEPT ANYMORE. His days melted into nights as he tried to get through the seemingly senseless existence he had been living since he last saw Hedy. He lay awake at night wondering where she was, what might have happened to her since they parted. His thoughts were filled with a steady series of self-recriminations. What more could he have done to save his beloved? How could he have enticed her to stay? Why didn't he think of spiriting away the entire family? Tibor knew deep in his heart there was little he could have done other than to get on board that train and go with his fiancée, but the recriminations continued. Each time he replayed the events on the train the night before they were taken away, he felt an additional thrust to his wounded soul.

The nightly aerial bombardments that could be heard for hundreds of miles did not help. Each member of the household lay in their bed at night, listening for air raid sirens. The steady, rumbling noise of exploding shells from tank turrets and the long guns reverberated through the earth itself. The fighting on the eastern front seemed to grow louder and louder and closer and more deafening with each passing day. It was an ominous, never-ceasing roar that invaded every moment of their lives.

Each window of their expansive home was covered from the inside with thick, dark-blue paper that completely blocked out the light. The entire town had to be pitch black at night to evade the bombers. The inside of their home, dark both day and night, reflected the mood of its inhabitants. Tibor's mother, Karola, who had until then emanated so much strength in the family, was a broken and utterly depressed woman. She hardly ever came down before noon and sat listlessly in the darkened parlour, seemingly listening to the radio, in the afternoons. Ironically, the grape crop was bountiful that fall but, no matter how often the estate manager came to her with positive news, he was unable to engage Karola in the details of the harvest and the many tasks that lay ahead.

When he could no longer wait for Karola to make the decisions, the estate manager came to Tibor. Tibor and his younger sister, Picke, helped out as much as they could. Picke volunteered at the local hospital, taking crates of grapes to the sick and injured. Tibor assisted Hunzelizer with the hiring of hundreds of local Rusyn workers. Although Tibor felt the entire charade was ludicrous, "The harvest," as his mother explained in her more coherent moments, "was something that had to be done, especially this year, for appearance's sake. People look to us for leadership in this community," she would insist.

One day, while Tibor was walking in the fields, he overheard two women who were harvesting grapes talking.

"You know, when the Russians arrive, this will all be ours," one said.

"Why would you think that?" the other woman said in an incredulous tone.

"Because I heard that under communism we will all be equal and the land will be divided equally. Just think how many of us will become landowners if the Ayklers are thrown out!"

Tibor tried not to listen, tried not to see the dissolution of everything around him. But he knew all was lost. He remembered that, before his little brother, Bela, had gone back to military school in the fall, the boy had saddled a horse and rode around Nagyszollos, through the centre of the town, the estate of the Baron Perenyi, up and down the outlying hills. When Bela returned, his mother and Tibor were waiting for him.

"Where did you go?" Karola had asked her son. "You were gone for so long, I was worried."

"This is the last time I will ever see this place," Bela had replied. "I just wanted to take one last good look around."

How pragmatic Bela was, Tibor thought. How realistic. Bela had left for military school in September already knowing the end was near. Yet here was the rest of the family, incapacitated by fear and depression, keeping up shallow appearances, not quite knowing how to prepare for what everyone knew was inevitable.

Colonel Domokos Aykler came home with increasing frequency now that the front was just beyond the nearest mountain range. Rumours swirled about an impending ceasefire and armistice with the Allies. Romania had switched sides and negotiated an armistice with the Allies in 1944. Hungarians hoped that, like Romania, Hungary would also be able to switch sides and reach an agreement.

On October 14, Domokos Aykler returned home and, as always, Karola came to life. The first thing she wanted to do when he returned was to retire to the parlour with her husband and talk to him privately about how he was and how things were progressing. But this time, he arrived with a few other officers and Karola could see in his eyes a sort of sad pleading. Domokos has such expressive eyes, Karola thought. She knew what it meant. He was telling her he couldn't talk openly in front of these military men and to just be patient a little while longer. She got the message right away. During the simple meal that followed his arrival, Domokos asked his wife to tell the officers how the harvest was progressing. Karola repeated the cheery news of the bountiful harvest and all the details of the work like an automaton. She didn't have to think much about what she was saying — the details of the tasks that needed to be done seemed second nature to her. But when her husband calmly turned to her during the meal and said that tomorrow she should order the slaughter of two pigs, something in his tone of voice made her afraid. Get ready to leave, he was telling her in code.

After supper, the officers went on their way but Domokos stayed. That night, they lay together in bed, clinging to each other and whispering. This was such a rare moment, when Karola had her husband to herself, but Domokos was completely worn out. He asked her to trust him. He told her that soon, all would be known. Soon. He fell asleep and slept well for the first time in a long time.

Karola lay beside him and looked at his face. She knew that, ever since he had become head of the press corps, her husband had a stash of pills that he ingested regularly. "They keep me going when the demands of the military require it," was what he said when she asked him what they were for. But the years of popping uppers had started to take a toll on her husband. There were deep crow's feet around his eyes and he smoked incessantly. His beard had turned stark white.

On October 15, Regent Horthy himself made an important announcement on the radio. The regent declared that Hungary had signed an armistice with the Allies and the Hungarian army would lay down their weapons. The news that everyone had been hoping for had finally come. The family was elated but a bit numb at hearing the good news. After so many years of war, they could hardly believe it. Karola asked Tibor to pour everyone a glass of red wine. But Domokos sat in silence. The nearby crashes of exploding shells and the sounds of the long guns reverberating in the earth continued through the night.

When Tibor awoke the next morning, the house was silent. It was Sunday and he came down to find his mother and father sitting silently across from one another, drinking coffee in the dining room. They looked anxious. His mother was still in her dressing gown, a bit of lace from her slip peeked out from the fold of her robe. Domokos was in full uniform. Tibor was afraid to ask what was wrong.

Before he had a chance to say anything, his mother said, "There's going to be another broadcast from the regent today. I'm sure its just more details of the ceasefire." The look on his father's face made Tibor realize that there would be more to it. Something momentous was happening.

At the time of the radio broadcast, the entire family congregated in the parlour and sat in rapt silence. The minutes seemed to tick by ever so slowly as they waited for the regent's address to begin. Tibor looked at his father and noticed, for the first time, how white his beard and hair had become these past few months. And he had deep, dark circles under his eyes. Domokos's hand lay quietly on the coffee table next to him as he smoked. When he inhaled, Tibor noticed that his hand shook noticeably.

Suddenly, the telephone in the parlour rang. Domokos held up his hand as if to let everyone know that he would answer the telephone himself. He got up slowly and walked toward the phone. The family listened, but could only hear him occasionally say, "Yes," and then "I understand." He returned the telephone to the receiver without saying goodbye and returned to his chair. They all looked at him but no one dared to ask any questions.

The news broadcast began shortly after the telephone call. This time, the regent sounded terribly sombre. Horthy rescinded the announcement of the day before and declared that Ferenc Szalasi, the head of the extremist Arrow Cross Party, was now in charge.

Karola Aykler covered her face with her hands as she broke down in tears. Her daughter, Picke, sat by her mother's side on the carpet and hugged her knees, silently rocking back and forth. After giving his wife several minutes to express her sorrow, Domokos leaned over and gently stroked her arm.

It wouldn't be until much later, when all the details were known, that it would be discovered what had actually happened on October 15, 1944. After concluding an armistice with the Allies through a delegation in Moscow, Regent Horthy announced on the radio that Hungary was defecting to the side of the Allies. The Germans knew about the agreement beforehand and, because the announcement had been made without appropriate military and political preparations, they were able to kidnap the regent's son Miklos on the day of the attempted capitulation. In order to achieve his son's release, Horthy was forced to withdraw his proclamation and legalize the government takeover by Szalasi, the leader of the Arrow Cross, who would now organize a Nazi puppet regime.

"Let's pack up what we can," Domokos said. "We leave tonight for Ungvar." Karola looked at her husband and understood. She knew her family was counting on her. They made their plans and tried to go about the packing and departure hastily and quietly, without alerting all of their neighbours to what was going on. The maid and cook were sent home. Only Anna, their devoted household helper, remained.

One of the horse-drawn carts normally used for shipping grapes was packed with what little they could fit on it: four crates of clothing, some family albums, tablecloths, and the silver. The valuable Meissen china, their paintings, porcelain, Persian carpets, books, and all the furniture would have to stay.

Tibor took charge of organizing the food: one sack of flour, one sack of wheat, a tub of lard, freshly baked bread, and the smoked meat of the two pigs that had been killed a few days before. As he watched the cart being loaded, Tibor realized that his mother concentrated on collecting and packing family treasures like the silver, photo albums, and tablecloths. She had hardly packed any practical, useful things they would need for such a journey. At the last minute, he went back into the house and fetched six horsehair mattresses, six comforters, and a pillow for each of them and tossed them into the back of the cart. He also wrapped his most prized possessions — the Siemens radio/record player and a few records — in a blanket and put them onto the cart as well.

Domokos decided that their chauffeur, Marton Pek, would drive the family in the black Tatra sedan car. Another dependable employee, Endre Szege, drove the horse- drawn cart with all their belongings. Now they were ready to depart.

"Just one more thing," Picke begged her parents as she jumped off the cart and ran up the stairs of the house to her bedroom. She gently picked up her Chinese doll with the porcelain face, the one her Uncle Laszlo had bought for her so many years ago. She felt silly going back for it, after all she was over sixteen years old, but she wanted to take something, an object that would link her to her happy childhood here. She kissed the doll, wrapped it in a pillowcase, and raced back down the stairs and out the house to the car.

The family dog, Buksi, kept jumping onto the cart as Picke and Tibor took turns comforting him and whispering that they would be back and that the overseer, Mihaly bacsi, would take care of him.

Picke gave the dog one last hug and got into the back seat of the car. Mihaly bacsi held Buksi so that he wouldn't run after the vehicles. The dog had a puzzled, hurt look on his face as the black sedan and the cart made their way down the driveway and turned left, disappearing into the dark night.

The family travelled toward Ungvar, a few hours drive away. Later that night, Tibor returned with the empty black sedan to pick up their close friends Senator Karoly Hokky and his family. Margit Hokky took a long time coming out of the house and, when she did, her eyes and face were red from crying. She was accompanied by her daughter, Kato, whose face was also tear-drenched.

"Mother doesn't want to come with us," Margit neni said, wanting to somehow explain to Tibor why they had taken so long. "She can't face being a refugee again. I told her it wouldn't be for long, that we would be back, but she doesn't believe me." They travelled all the way to Ungvar in silence.

Five days later, the Fourth Ukrainian Division of the Soviet army, led by Commander Ivan Petrov, entered Nagyszollos. Not a single shot of resistance was fired; the army was gone. Petrov instructed his deputies to pick the highest point in the region and set up their command post. In very short order, Sergeant Gouzov told his superior officer that they had found the perfect spot with a great view of the surrounding region. As Petrov was driven up to the massive house on the hill, he saw that some of his soldiers were already going through the rooms, pilfering the contents. Two soldiers walked out carrying rolled-up Persian carpets on their shoulders, others were stuffing silver bowls into their knapsacks. Many of them were gleefully showing off bottles of wine. When they saw Commander Petrov arrive in the jeep, the men scattered.

Sergeant Gouzov met Petrov in the yard and reported that the house was empty of inhabitants. He said that, in the basement, they had found over two hundred bottles of jams and pickled vegetables, crates of dried fruits, and over four hundred litres of bottled wine. There was still meat in the smokehouse. Gouzov also reported that the overseer, Mihaly Hunzelizer, a Rusyn, was living in the basement. Hunzelizer told them that the owners, a high-ranking colonel in the Hungarian army and his family, had left the country and were not coming back.

As he walked up the front steps, Commander Petrov saw a dog lying motionless on its side with a full bowl of food next to him. "What happened to the dog?" he asked.

"We don't know for sure, sir," replied his sergeant. "The dog was like that when we got here."

"You might as well bury him," ordered Petrov.

Commander Petrov was pleased to have such pleasant surroundings for his command centre. He knew they would be stationed here for a while. As he went inside the house and looked up at the two-storey entranceway, he thought, "Yes, this will do quite nicely."

Petrov and only a few of his deputy commanding officers knew that this part of Hungary would soon become annexed to the Soviet Union. He had been sent here with specific instructions to quash any resistance to the Russian occupation and make sure the consolidation of the region into the Soviet empire went smoothly. One of the first things that had to be done was to change the name of the town to Vinogradiv.

Within a few days, a group of able-bodied men and women volunteered to help rebuild the destroyed bridge over the Tisza. Petrov wrote in his official report that the population of the region was "docile and compliant, totally exhausted by the war."

chapter 19 | january 1945

BY JANUARY 1945, GERMAN military troops were being pushed back by unrelenting pressure from American forces from the west and Russian forces driving them from the east. The pounding of Russian artillery could already be heard from Auschwitz-Birkenau. The SS was ordered to empty the concentration camps and to destroy evidence of the atrocities committed there. The plan was to march prisoners to territories and areas still firmly under German control.

The SS ordered a mass evacuation of Auschwitz-Birkenau on January 18, 1945 in the middle of the night. The walls of the last crematorium still standing, crematorium #5, were dynamited. The barracks containing the loot of Commando Kanada were set ablaze, but the mountains of clothing, housewares, and carpets were so heavily packed that it would take weeks for them to completely burn — time the SS didn't have.

The "death marches," as they came to be known, were haphazard and chaotic. No one knew where they were going or how to organize such a mass evacuation. Those remaining, Suti among them, could sense the panic in the voices and actions of their captors. When they heard they were being ordered to march out, those who could tried to grab what few blankets were left, wrapping them around themselves as flimsy protection against the cold. Others tore strips out of pieces of blankets to bind their hands and feet.

The first group were marched out in columns of five. Suti was near the head of the five- to six-kilometre-long line of barely clad, emaciated survivors who trudged along in the snow-covered countryside. Most had no protection from the cold, and they were given nothing to eat or drink.

Rumours swirled around the camp like small brush fires.

"We are being sent to a place called Gross-Rosen."

"The camp guards had orders to shoot everyone who couldn't march."

"The Americans are coming to bomb Auschwitz."

Hedy, in a desperate panic to find her younger brother, searched for Dzeidjic. She found him with two of his men, their noses buried in a list of typed names. They were counting, verifying, and counter-checking names on a long list.

As Hedy approached and called Dzeidjic's name, he looked up anxiously, but when he saw it was Hedy, a look of relief crossed his face.

"I can't talk now," he mumbled, "but I sent the kid ahead earlier with the first group. Bad things are going to happen here. I wanted him to get out of here quickly."

"What have you heard?" Hedy pleaded.

Dzeidjic looked uncertain, insecure somehow.

"Go back to your barracks. I'll come to find you later."

With that, he abruptly turned and returned to working on the lists.

Kapos and guards counted then recounted everyone in their barracks. Hedy and Aliz stood in line for what seemed like hours. One of the guards, who they nicknamed "Burly" because of his thickset, stocky build, came toward them, counting the women in each row as he proceeded. Hedy focused on his chunky hands and fat fingers as she started hearing the numbers he called out:

"Nine hundred ninety. Nine hundred ninety-one. Nine hundred ninety-two."

Hedy quickly did a head count of the inmates between Burly and themselves.

"Nine hundred ninety-five."

They had to stay together, no matter what, Hedy thought.

Hedy pushed Aliz ahead of her; Burly pointed to Aliz, counted "one thousand," and yelled, "That's another one thousand that can head out."

Hedy grabbed Burly's arm and pleaded, "Please, sir, that's my sister. Please don't separate us."

Burly barely looked at her, completely oblivious, yelling to someone up at the front, "Move them out, it's a full group."

"Please let me go with them — I'm begging you," Hedy pleaded in tears.

But Burly had already turned and gone to organize the count somewhere else. A guard was placed at the end of the line, preventing Hedy from simply joining Aliz and the departing group.

Hedy's world collapsed. How was she going to survive now without her sister? How was she to go on?

She was overcome with sheer and utter desolation.

AFTER ABOUT FIFTEEN TO twenty kilometres of walking, Suti realized he didn't have the strength to go on. He was starving, and with the temperature ten degrees below zero, the cold was biting at his extremities. Although he, along with the other prisoners, had begun to eat the snow from along the roadside, he was still desperately thirsty. He felt he couldn't take another step.

Suti collapsed by the side of the road. When he did, he felt his legs become paralyzed; they would never allow him to stand up again. He curled his legs underneath him and lay on his side, gently placing his head on the snow. Closing his eyes, he envisioned his mother's tender face before him. It became eerily silent around him, except for the soft crunching of the snow of those who were still walking past.

Suddenly he heard boots crunching on the icy snow toward him. Suti opened his eyes.

A rifle-toting SS guard was stomping in his direction. Although Suti realized he was coming to shoot him, he felt he couldn't and didn't want to move. The SS guard came up to within a few inches of Suti, looked directly down at him, and kicked him.

"March! You are too young to die!" the guard shouted.

Suti didn't know where the strength came from or why the SS guard didn't shoot him, but he jumped up and started running.

HEDY REALIZED SHE HAD to be at the front of the next group of women leaving the camp —the one that was directly after her sister's group. They began their march an hour later in the bitter, January cold.

Please God, she prayed, let me find Aliz. I can't survive without her. She repeated these few lines of her prayer over and over again until her senses became inured to the cold and the pain.

After about a dozen kilometres, the winter light diminished and they were ordered into an enormous barn for the night. There, Hedy's heart jumped as she saw some women from the previous group. Aliz must be here, Hedy decided. Determined as ever, she made her way through the groups of women as they lay on top of straw bundles, numb from the day of walking and the freezing cold. On the upper level of the barn, on one of the furthest straw piles, Hedy was overwhelmed to find her sleeping sister. She crawled in next to her, wrapped her arms around her, and cried herself to sleep, grateful to have found her sibling, and feeling like a whole person once again.

AFTER WHAT SEEMED LIKE an endless two to three days of marching, stopping at barns to rest a few hours, they ended up at a railway station where they were unexpectedly ordered into boxcars. No one knew where they were heading. Occasionally, the doors were opened and they were handed some containers of water or a watered-down version of soup. The train stood for hours without movement. Then it moved for an hour or so, then was halted again. This went on for days. Suti was sure that even the commanders of this death march didn't have any idea where they were going anymore. The fighting was moving closer, and they frequently heard bomber aircraft flying overhead.

At one point during the journey while the train was standing for hours at a station in the town of Tichau, Russian planes flew overhead and riddled the train with machine-gun fire.

Crammed in as they were for hours on end, Suti was standing next to and occasionally talking with a Jewish boy named Walter from Prague when the shooting began. His friend fell silent. Suti spoke to him, but he didn't answer. Walter had been hit by a single gunshot to the head. No blood came out from his head — the pumping of his heart stopped immediately. Shortly afterward, the authorities simply opened up the boxcars and the dead bodies were thrown out.

When the transport arrived to the train station closest to Mauthausen in Austria, they were taken by trucks up a hill to the concentration camp. The relatively short (three-hundred-kilometre) journey by foot and by train took thirteen days (from the eighteenth to the thirtieth of January).

Emaciated, with practically nothing to eat during the two-week journey, Suti felt frozen right down to the marrow of his bones. As soon as they arrived, they were sent to the showers. Suti was certain he knew what this meant. The only time groups of prisoners were sent to the showers at Auschwitz-Birkenau was to be gassed. But, by this time, he didn't have the strength to even think about death. Resigned to his fate, he followed along as they were herded into the showers.

To their disbelief and surprise, though, it wasn't gas that came out of the shower heads, but water. Warm refreshing water! After the nightmare of their journey, the warmth of the water revived their chilled bodies and they started to feel somewhat human again. Awestruck, they could hardly believe this strange and unexpected twist of fate as they received clean, disinfected clothing and were assigned to their barracks.

In Mauthausen, the blocks were built differently from Auschwitz-Birkenau. Wing A and Wing B were in the same building — the same block but on different ends — the block altester and block schreiber were in the centre of the block.

The block altester assembled everyone twice daily for *zehl appel*. On the A side, the block altester wanted a certain round number. If it happened to be two hundred, and there were 195 already assembled, he would yell over to the B side and get the missing number of inmates to come over. The numbers had to be consistent, at least on the A side.

On this particular day, five men were called over — and ran over from B to A. Among them, Suti, stunned, recognized his father, Vilmos. He was much thinner and seemed much older than the last time he had seen him. Overcome by the emotion of seeing his father again, Suti yelled. Vilmos froze, reaching out his arms, before even seeing where the familiar voice was coming from.

"My son, my son, I've found my son!" Vilmos cried out.

Just then an SS guard wandered by and noticed the silence of the assembled group. He looked at Vilmos, who explained again, without any hesitation, that he had found his son.

The astonishing reply of the SS guard: "Well, go and hug your son."

Vilmos and Suti embraced in a tearful reunion that touched all the assembled. As Suti put his arms around his father, he realized he could feel his ribs. Still, it was amazing to be reunited with him again.

Vilmos and Suti remained in Mauthausen together, spending their days completely occupied with the constant gnawing feeling of hunger in their stomachs. The other activity was the never-ending task of removing lice from their bodies and clothes.

On March 12, 1945, less than two months before the collapse of the Third Reich, the last constructed concentration camp, Gunskirchen, was opened. That same day was Suti's fifteenth birthday. Gunskirchen was built from the logs cleared right out of the forest. Built because of the overcrowding at Mauthausen, Gunskirchen consisted of six or seven huge hangar-type structures assembled out of the freshly cut tree trunks. Long and wide, each hangar had a few doors but no windows. The floors were hardened mud. Suti and Vilmos, both suffering from typhus, were herded into one of these hangars. There were two or three thousand men in each hangar with barely room to sit or lie down.

On the last day before they were liberated in early May, an SS guard came into their hangar and tried to get their attention. By this time the inmates sensed that changes were imminent — there was a lot of noise in the hangar and they barely paid attention to the guard. The SS guard took out his revolver, pointed it at the inmate sitting directly next to Suti, and shot him in the forehead, killing him instantly. Bits of blood and brain spattered onto everyone around him, including Suti. The killing silenced everyone. Then the guard yelled something unintelligible and left. The next day all the guards simply vanished.

Susan M. Papp

Gunskirchen was the last concentration camp to be built by the Germans and the last liberated by the Allies.

chapter 20 | spring 1945

WHEN GUNSKIRCHEN WAS LIBERATED in the first days of May 1945 by the 71st Infantry of the United States Army, most of those still alive there reacted with shock, disbelief, and gratitude. The guards had fled four days before. The liberators found nearly ten thousand bodies in a huge communal grave. But what really shocked them was the indescribably awful smell of the place.

The liberators were greeted with cheers, shrieks, and groans. They stopped in their tracks from complete disbelief of what they were witnessing: the skeletal shells of human beings.

The well-dressed and fed American soldiers, desperate to do something immediately for these poor unfortunate souls, started handing out boxes of food and cigarette rations. Some survivors simply fell upon the food rations and devoured them, including the tobacco rations. After so many months of starvation rations, their digestive tracts could not absorb the rich caloric foods, such as cold corned beef, and they died shortly after consuming the army rations.

Suti and Vilmos simply stared at the soldiers, and at the box of food rations handed to them, which they didn't have the strength to open. The army commanders asked a Hungarian-speaking survivor to translate for them. "Don't leave this place. The commanders are pleading with us not to go — they will look after us here. They will have water and food and medics for everyone in a matter of hours. Don't go, there is nowhere to go to."

But a type of mass hysteria took hold of the survivors, who simply wanted to leave this hellhole. The emaciated father and son, Suti and

Vilmos, both sick with typhus, their bodies covered in lice, trudged out of Gunskirchen.

The road leading out was clogged with hundreds of survivors walking slowly but determinedly, many hanging on to relatives or friends, trying to place as much distance between themselves and this place of horrors as possible. Joining the parade of fleeing skeletons, not knowing how they were mustering the strength, Suti and Vilmos walked and kept going until they found themselves in front of a house in the nearby town of Wels. They stopped and knocked on the door of a stranger. After what seemed like many minutes, an elderly Austrian woman tentatively opened the door and peered out. The old woman couldn't hide the look of shock on her face. Neither she nor her visitors said anything as the two pushed past her and walked into the house. She closed the door and followed them inside.

They walked to the back to the kitchen and sat down on handcrafted wooden chairs that surrounded a small wooden table. The kitchen was sparsely decorated. They simply stared at her.

"I have no food, nothing to eat," she began, wringing her hands and looking very nervous. "My husband and son are gone — lost on the front. There's no one here but me — I have nothing to give you. I have lost everything during this war. I've lost my entire family."

The silence in the room was deafening. Minutes passed. Then, she noticed Suti and Vilmos scratching themselves and realized that she had to act quickly to prevent the lice from spreading. She collected herself, put some water on the stove, and lit the fire underneath. She made tea and introduced herself as Frau Hans Asen. Pouring hot water in a pan, she led them into the garden and motioned for them to wash themselves. Finding some clean clothing from her husband and son, she suggested they change and directed them to throw their lice-infested clothing into the fireplace in the garden. She then lit a fire under the filthy clothes.

Within a day or so, trucks with loudspeakers roamed around the district announcing that a place had been prepared for camp survivors. The American army gathered the survivors into a German military facility, which had been the last active airbase of the Luftwaffe at Horsching.

The airbase was transformed into a place where survivors would be able to gather their strength and obtain meals.

Suti and Vilmos were transported to the base. They lived in a room originally intended for five or six soldiers, but now housed twenty or more concentration camp survivors. They slept on straw mattresses and blankets strewn about on the floor, most still comatose and dazed from their experiences, some dying, some recovering. The daily death rate of the survivors was sizeable: some seventy to one hundred dead bodies were removed from the facility to be buried in a mass grave designated as such in front of the building.

The American army was not prepared to deal with this legacy of the war — there were no kitchens set up to prepare hot food. They were provided with bread, tea, and some other food supplies, but survivors frequently helped themselves to U.S. rations in the storage areas.

Suti realized that his father was gravely ill, but didn't want to face the reality of the situation. He continued to bring his father tea and coaxed him to eat a bit of bread, but most of the time Vilmos didn't even open his eyes. When he did, Suti noticed he had a distant, dazed look in his eyes. Suti needed his father, however, now more than ever.

An American Jewish doctor who was a major in the U.S. Army created a clinic to rehabilitate those concentration camp survivors who were, in his assessment, capable of regaining their strength. Suti was chosen to go to this ad hoc clinic nearby in Horsching. Choking back tears, trying to put on a brave face, Suti said goodbye to his dying father, who was by then in a comatose state. But Suti's anxiousness was turning into anger by this point: anger toward the remoteness of his father. Why wouldn't he snap out of his haze? They were free now, he was getting medication and nutrition, and more than ever Suti needed his guidance and help. Why was he shutting himself off from his son?

Suti spoke straight to him, saying his final farewells. No response came. No motion, no sound was made as Suti left, feeling his father had already abandoned him.

At the clinic, Suti fell into a deep sleep that lasted ten days. He was fed intravenously. When he came to, no one could explain to him whether he had fallen into a coma, or had slept so long and so deeply from sheer exhaustion.

Suti awoke one morning to overhear the attending doctor telling the nurse that he was being sent to a sanatorium in Switzerland for long-term treatment and recovery. Suti knew that under no circumstances did he want to be sent west. He grabbed some clothes out of a closet and made his way surreptitiously out of the clinic and back to the base where he left his father. On arrival, he was told that Vilmos Weisz had passed away on May 22, 1945. To the great chagrin of Suti, he learned his father had been buried in the mass grave at Horsching Air Force Base, directly in front of the building where they had been housed.

In May 1945, the fifteen-year-old concentration camp survivor found himself completely alone in the world. At that point in his life, he felt the tremendous pull of home. There was only one direction he wanted to go: east, back home to Nagyszollos.

chapter 21 | spring 1945

THE SPRING OF 1945 was particularly cold and rainy in Europe. It was as if nature were trying to cleanse itself of the immense amount of blood, death, and hatred that had spilled onto the continent during the war.

Tibor and Bela learned of the end of the war in Europe while sleeping in a barn, near Altenfelden in Austria, along with thousands of former combatants, Hungarians and Germans, under the watchful eye of American soldiers. The German soldiers threw their caps in the air, yelled, and became hysterical with joy. The war was over — nothing mattered anymore. They had had enough. They were going home. Some cried from happiness.

The reaction of the Hungarians was more muted. No one knew what the future held. Bela had a feeling of more hardship ahead. Tibor's only thought was to find Hedy.

The previous day they had been registered and ordered to head out on a march.

Not having any idea where they were going, they were allowed to bring their belongings — anything they could carry in their backpacks.

They marched in platoon formation, and stayed mainly on country roads. The march led through the Austrian countryside, traversing hills and valleys, through oddly quiet villages. Intermittently, along the roadside, in ditches and ravines the bodies of dead soldiers remained from recent local skirmishes. By mid-morning, as the rays of the sun grew hotter and hotter, the marching men began throwing away heavy gear, raincoats, extra jackets, and boots.

As they marched, Bela tried to retrace how they had ended up here and all that had happened to him in the last half year. The military school Bela attended was transferred to Sopron, the westernmost city in Hungary, then disbanded completely. As one of the school's oldest cadets, Bela was ordered to gather up the youngest class, fifteen eleven-year-olds, and spirit them out of harm's way to Austria. The group of frightened cadets joined the hundreds of thousands of fleeing civilian refugees. They were desperately trying to maintain a distance from German and Russian lines, but roads were bombed and became impassable; they came under frequent fire. Despite it all, walking most of the way under deplorable conditions, Bela, incredibly, delivered the young boys to safety.

Once in Austria, Bela found his older brother, Tibor, whose unit had been pushed westward and disbanded near a small town called Altenfelden. The men were assigned to live with farm communities, along with other military personnel and their families. The brothers pitched in with the chores at a dairy farm — they milked cows and delivered the milk to the surrounding farms.

As they approached, the American forces destroyed much of the old town of Altenfelden with tank bombardments. Two American soldiers arrived at the farm where the brothers lived and demanded that all ex-military report for inspection in the yard. The American soldiers were inebriated and repeatedly shot rounds of ammunition into the air — one narrowly missed Bela's ear. They shouted questions that no one understood and seemed to become increasingly incensed that no one was able to provide answers. The Hungarian solders and some non-commissioned officers were frozen with fear. The intimidation continued for hours. Eventually the Americans grew tired of this and left.

Within two days, more American soldiers in jeeps arrived. Tibor and Bela watched from an upstairs window of the farmhouse as the vehicles screeched to a halt below. Tibor looked at his brother and whispered, "I bet they didn't count us the first time."

"They were too drunk," Bela added.

Without saying another word to each other, the brothers slipped quietly behind a wardrobe upstairs, listening to what was going on outside from their hideout.

The yelling continued as before, and once again gunshots were fired. This time, however, the Americans not only lined up the men, but to their families' great consternation, marched them away. Everyone assumed they were being taken to some kind of registration and holding facility.

When Tibor and Bela came out of hiding, they saw that only the women and children were left. Some of the women were happy to see that there were still two able-bodied men remaining to perform the daily back-breaking labour that needed to be completed around the farm. But one woman, Ilona Nagy, the wife of a sergeant major, accosted them when she found out they had stayed behind.

Jabbing her finger at Tibor's face, she yelled in a shrill voice, "Don't think for a moment you'll get out of this. If you don't go after the rest and report to the Americans, I'll report you myself!"

Tibor could see that Ilona Nagy had once been a stunning woman. She still had a voluptuous figure, even after nine children, but her long brown hair was unkempt, with streaks of grey running through it. She tied it up in a bun, loosely, but some strands fell out into her eyes and face. It was obvious the years, the children, and the war had taken their toll on her, she had become slovenly about her appearance.

When Tibor and Bela didn't react, her angry tirades continued and became more frenzied. Bitterness and exhaustion became evident in her eyes and face. Her lips were moving and words were pouring out, but the real meaning behind her rant soon became evident.

"Why should my husband suffer in some holding facility run by the Americans while you two, who have enjoyed a privileged upbringing as the sons of a colonel, enjoy freedom?"

Tibor and Bela realized there was no way this woman would stop her tirade against them until they left. Bela couldn't understand any of it: if they left, there would be no one left to do the heavy tasks. Ilona Nagy relied on the two brothers for practically every task, from bringing in water from the well early in the morning to milking the cows and transporting the milk for sale to the neighbouring communities. They were of invaluable help to her in looking after her children and making sure they were provided for.

Resigned to their fate, Tibor and Bela packed a few things in preparation: dried smoked meat, canned sardines, extra socks, underwear, a shaving kit, and as much clothing they could take for what they suspected would probably be difficult times ahead. Tibor hammered together a little cart using the wheels of a discarded baby carriage so they could pull their few worldly possessions behind them in a wooden crate.

Currency was worthless by the end of the war in Europe. Jewellery and gold were the only items that were worth anything, as they were always good for barter and trade. The brothers acquired a range of watches. They placed the cheapest ones closest to their wrists, the more expensive ones were placed higher up, closer to the elbow. Under long sleeves, all the watches were hidden, but if they were stopped by robbers on the road, the brothers always had an inexpensive watch to reluctantly hand over.

They knew they had to find an imaginative hiding place for the few pieces of gold jewellery and U.S. dollars they had between the two of them. It had to be in a place no one would even think to look. Tibor spliced the end of a tube of toothpaste open, extricated some of the toothpaste, then gingerly pushed the jewellery and cash into the flat end and rolled it up.

As they walked along the country roads, Bela felt full of foreboding, but reassured himself that all this had to be over soon and they would be going home.

When they arrived at a rocky hillside with small springs running down from it, they were allowed to pause for a cool drink of water. Bela removed his shoes and socks and washed his aching feet. It was a method he had learned in military school — a way to increase circulation and renew your strength while hiking. Soon the entire platoon was following his example. As a result, their group picked up the pace.

Not having any idea of where they were going, they sang as they marched. Some of the American soldiers guarding them were impressed — their enthusiasm was rewarded with the occasional cigarette, chocolate bar, and stick of chewing gum. By comparison, the other platoons were dragging their feet.

It was late in the afternoon on the second day when they arrived at a farmer's freshly ploughed potato field just beyond the village of Tittling in Austria. Tibor stopped, taken aback by the sight before them: as far as they could see thousands of men were crowded onto the muddy field. Many were dressed in military khakis, some were in civilian clothing.

The entire area sloped down to the bottom of the hill, where a small creek flowed, with just a trickle of water running through it. On the other side of the creek stood thousands of German soldiers, jammed in, encircled on all sides with barbed-wire fences.

The platoon Tibor and Bela were part of was directed to the bottom of the hill, to the first row, directly adjacent to the small creek.

Once they were assigned their spot, Tibor looked around more carefully, squinting his eyes to see that there were many young boys and teenagers in the crowd as well. Not quite believing what he was witnessing, he made sure his eyes weren't playing tricks on him, but upon closer examination became convinced that there were twelve-, thirteen-, and fourteen-year-olds here with them, swept up in the net of postwar sortings.

As Tibor looked around, he guessed that, similar to his younger brother, every tenth person was simply too young to have taken part in any combat. He surmised they were probably members of a compulsory youth military league, the Leventes. Or, he wondered, could there have been that many cadets still remaining at military schools?

Tibor noticed Bela staring at him. Not meeting his brother's eyes, staring directly in front of him, Tibor whispered to his brother in disbelief, "This has to be temporary, just a holding area. These are the Americans, after all."

During the next few hours, hundreds more new arrivals descended onto the sloping field, taking their places in rows of military precision.

They didn't have to wait long before the order came to lie down, on their backs, shoulder-to-shoulder, feet to head on the ground. Tibor looked up at the late afternoon sky, tinged blue puffs of clouds forming here and there. He felt like calling out to God loudly, publicly, but instead decided to say a prayer in the silence of his heart: "Dear Lord, let the suffering of this war end. Enough already, God!" He closed his eyes, comforted in the knowledge that his brother was with him.

His prayers were interrupted by the rumbling of jeep motors. Tibor couldn't tell if it was one jeep or more, but could hear that one of the engines was screeching on and off from exertion. It was then that Tibor turned his head to see three jeeps very near to them. A drill had been attached to the back of the first jeep. With it, the driver was digging a deep hole in the ground every five metres or so. The second jeep, following closely behind, placed a heavy duty thick wooden pole into the freshly dug hole and secured it.

The men on the third jeep were unwinding a barbed-wire mesh fence and nailing it to the inside of the posts. Tibor closed his eyes once again as he lay on the ground, too terrified to accept what was going on around them.

By the time they finished, and the men were allowed to stand up, they saw that the Americans had encircled the men on each side of the hillside, and the fence separated them from the creek running on the bottom and up the other side. Darkness had descended on the hillside by the time the fence was finished and a steady cold drizzle of rain had begun pelting down on them.

A few men were given shovels and ordered to dig a latrine at the bottom of the hill, inside the fence, parallel to the creek. The ditch was ordered to be narrow but deep, just enough to straddle your feet on two sides and defecate or urinate. There was no cover to the ditch, nothing to hold onto and nothing to wipe yourself off with when you were done.

The brothers settled in the small space they had on the ground, covering themselves with the sweaters and the raincoats they brought with them. They and the thousands of other prisoners slept under the open sky.

During the night, they heard the terrifying screams of a man being beaten and tortured. The screams pierced the night and seemed to go on for hours. The dreadful sounds came from the other side, where the German prisoners were held. Tibor shut his eyes as he tried to sleep, covered his ears with his palms.

At dawn, they were woken and ordered to stand in line for food. Each section was instructed to receive their food at a specific time of day. Tibor and Bela's platoon was assigned four in the morning and four in the afternoon.

Food consisted of a bowlful of pinkish water the Americans referred to as "tomato soup." It looked as if a few cans of tomato soup had been tossed into hundreds of litres of water. The soup had a stench of gasoline — the water to make the soup was transported to the camp in tanks that formerly held gasoline.

The available drinking water was also permeated with the same stench of gasoline. Tibor and Bela consumed some of the soup, but avoided drinking the water for as long as they could. They still had some food (smoked meat), and ate small amounts of it in the dark, making sure no one else saw or heard them. But, after the first few days of their incarceration, the food they brought with them was gone and they were famished like everyone else.

After one week, as they stood in line for the soup, Tibor was elated to see that the men in front of them in the line were being handed entire loaves of bread.

"See?" Tibor said to Bela. "I told you the Americans would start feeding us. They simply weren't prepared for all these people. Now they're getting organized."

Three American soldiers were in charge of the distribution. One soldier translated and kept repeating, "Every thirty-eighth gets one."

It was when Tibor reached the front of the line that he saw that they meant every thirty-eighth man was handed one loaf of bread.

Bela was the thirty-eighth in their group. The private who was counting and distributing looked at Bela smugly and handed him the loaf of bread.

Great, Bela thought, as the famished men gathered around him. Now the rest are going to slit my throat for a piece of bread.

He realized he had to find a way to make sure the loaf was equally distributed. He spread out his raincoat and began by breaking the bread into chunks, then further working the bread into smaller and smaller piles of crumbs with his hands. He could feel the eyes of the thirty-seven men on his hands, watching his every move, making sure each pile was equal, while practically salivating like dogs.

It took at least twenty minutes to prepare the anthill-like piles of bread crumbs, and only seconds for each man to swallow his tiny ration — about a teaspoonful each. Bela was surprised there wasn't an outcry, but everyone could see that not a crumb was wasted or distributed unevenly.

The next time they divided the bread in this way, it was mutually agreed to let a different prisoner have first choice each time — this way the person dividing up the loaf could not be accused of favouritism. Bela was chosen to be the one to divvy the loaf up each time.

The brothers spent their entire waking day and night trying to make their day-to-day lives more bearable. Then, as if the heavens were mocking their cruel fate, cold dark clouds brought spring rains, saturating the ground beneath them. Tibor and Bela were grateful to have a couple of raincoats to crawl under.

But it rained for days on end and they realized they had to find a centre pole for their makeshift tent, as the raincoats had to be propped up away from them. By the third day, they were soaked by the seemingly unending downpour, despite their raincoats.

The only possibility of escape might have been underneath the barbed-wire fence on either side of the creek, where the ground was soft because of the latrines and groundwater. Their captors, however, had a strategy to thwart any plan of escape. Each night, American soldiers drove two new Volkswagen cars to either end of the creek, parked each parallel to the water on opposite sides, then turned the motor off with the lights burning. It was like an amazingly well-lit soccer field during the night. By the time the batteries on the cars went dead, daylight broke.

The vehicles with the burned-out batteries were left there night after night. A few prisoners were allowed out the next day to take apart the useable parts for shelter. They ripped out the seats and upholstery with their bare hands.

After a week, the ground near the creek was covered with automobile carcasses, picked clean of any useable parts.

Those who weren't fortunate enough to find a bit of material for shelter or fend for themselves died of exposure. They lived and slept under the open sky. Unprotected from the driving unrelenting cold rains and blistering winds of early May, many caught colds that turned into pneumonia. Those who survived until the warmer weather arrived at the end of May sometimes collapsed from dehydration.

The gasoline-tainted pinkish soup and drinking water made many sick with dysentery. The first sign was body-wrenching diarrhea, eventually leading to dehydration and ultimately death. The brothers were camped on the first row, on the bottom of the hill, closest to the latrine. As the days turned into two weeks, the stench of human feces and vomit became unbearable, yet there was nowhere to move to — the rows higher up were covered with prisoners. Worst still was seeing the lineup of the sickest and weakest, distinguished by the yellowish sallow skin, and the hollowness of the eyes. Those most affected by dysentery barely had the strength to move away from the area of the ditch-latrine. Weakened from disease and hunger, often they would simply fall into the latrine and die where they fell.

The young boys were the first to go. Tibor couldn't imagine how these young kids ever ended up here. Their mothers were probably still waiting for their safe return home. Every once a while, Bela reminded his brother of his earlier comments that the Americans were just getting organized, that they weren't counting on this many people, that they wouldn't allow so many people to starve. Tibor was fascinated by the United States and its history — to him the country represented higher ideals. He remained adamant, stating he still couldn't believe that this was being done purposefully.

While in military school, however, Bela had studied the international treaties governing the treatment of prisoners of war. Countries, including the United States, had to abide by these international rules. After two weeks of living out under the open sky and being given starvation rations and tainted water, Bela suspected something more sinister.

A local Catholic priest was allowed into the prisoner-of-war camp to say daily mass for the prisoners. He brought with him the wafers of unleavened bread used as hosts. The brothers went to mass every day.

Bela stood in line to receive communion three or four times during the mass. Tibor admonished his brother and told him what he was doing was sacrilegious, but Bela replied he didn't care. He didn't have the energy to pray anymore — he just wanted to have the feeling of something in his stomach.

After two weeks, Tibor was already starting to show the first signs of dysentery — he had developed a severe case of diarrhea. He didn't want to alarm his younger brother. Tibor felt the energy drain from his body, and when he stood up to drag himself to the latrine, he felt dizzy. He simply wanted to lie down and be left alone. Bela noticed with dread Tibor's increasingly gaunt face and the dark circles under his older brother's eyes.

Each night the screams of men being tortured and beaten on the other side went on unabated.

chapter 22 | may 1945

As HE WATCHED TIBOR's strength slowly hemorrhage out of his body, Bela knew he had to do something and quickly, although he didn't have an inkling of how he could get his brother something solid to eat. He wracked his brain for some solution.

While part of him still clung to his past, everything he had been trained to believe in was slowly crumbling. Military discipline and honour, respect for fellow enlisted men, lending a helping hand for those in need ... Bela had witnessed these noble ideals trampled in the mud and muck of Tittling. He felt like an empty shell, drained of his youth and any hope the future held, robbed of the lofty ideals he had been taught at military academy. He thought of the motto of his military school with disdain. *"Fide Virtute Famam Querere"* — "To obtain Glory with Virtue and Loyalty." Indeed. It turned his guts inside out to think about how much he used to believe in all of it.

There was nothing ennobling about the behaviour of the military men he had encountered on either side. No military honour or regulations were observed here. It was survival of the fittest, rule by the most powerful. For the second time in his life, he realized that he didn't care whether he lived or died. If he died, however, he would choose the route, and he knew he wouldn't expire like the others around him: weakened by hunger, felled by dysentery, thrown onto the back of a jeep and dumped into a communal grave with hundreds of others. He wondered how long it took to die of hunger. How many more days of this would he be able to endure? How would he ever be able to face his mother if Tibor died and he survived? He would never be able to come home again.

He scoured his knapsack and found the last dress uniform jacket he had. It was relatively clean, all the buttons in place. The jacket was the last symbol of his attachment to the past: it was decorated with two stripes and two decorative gold buttons — indicating he was the best in his class. Silently, he pulled on a pair of safari pants that were about the same beige colour as the uniform jacket — each of the pants legs had several big pockets.

Without having a clear idea of what he was going to do, Bela decided to head toward the administration building. He surveyed the distance. He would have to walk two hundred metres past an American guard with a Tommy gun slung over his shoulder.

Bela had seen enough of American soldiers to be able to imitate their air of self-confidence. He simply had to imagine being part of the victorious side. No matter how hard he tried to build confidence, however, his knees were turning to pudding at the thought of the distance he had to cross.

Fortunately, he still had one last piece of chewing gum, saved from the pack the Americans had given them during the march. Bela knew the gum was a critical part of the "American look." As he put it in his mouth and started to chew, he realized the gum also helped calm the queasiness of his knees and his stomach.

If he was going to do anything at all, he had to do it now. He felt his courage already dissipating.

Bela garnered his last bit of strength, put on the best swagger he could muster, and walked toward and past the American guard with the Tommy gun. The young private was also chewing gum, checking him out with a look of disdain. Bela walked calmly. The guard didn't seem to be suspicious, probably thinking that if Bela was trying to escape, he would have been walking away from the administration building, not toward it.

Bela forced his feet to take slow, measured steps. If he was going to be shot, it would happen any second now. He braced himself and realized taking a bullet in the back would be a quick, easy, relatively painless way to go. The shot never came, however, and Bela didn't look back, only ahead.

As he reached the door of the administration building, he froze. What will I do now?

As he stood there in a frozen stupor, he saw through the glass pane that a uniformed officer was heading out of the building. Bela grabbed the doorknob, opened it, saluted the soldier, and closed the door behind him. With his heart pounding so loudly he was convinced the entire camp could hear it, he cautiously looked around. All was calm. The private with the Tommy gun wasn't even looking at him.

Another soldier came in, another officer went out. Bela opened the doors for both.

Until noon that day, Bela dutifully opened and closed the door and saluted everyone entering and exiting. No one asked what he was doing there. There were two doors — an inner and outer door. By noon Bela was opening and closing both doors from inside the building. At lunch time one of the staff approached him and said, "Come on kid, help pass out the lunches."

Bela understood, nodded, and said, "Yes, yes," trying not to seem overanxious.

Bela was directed to the basement where there were boxes of food piled to the ceiling. He was shown where the prepackaged boxes of lunch rations were, and instructed to bring up a dozen — one for each of the clerks upstairs.

Bela dutifully passed out all the lunch rations, ate a lunch portion as well, then went down to the basement again and helped himself to more food, grabbing packages at random from cartons full of chocolate bars, crackers, cookies. He even found a hen laying eggs in the basement. He grabbed two eggs, cracked them carefully, then poured the insides straight into his mouth, swallowing the raw whites and yolks whole.

After lunch, Bela returned to his post at the door and continued working until the staff in the administration building finished their day. Around four o'clock, when he completed his task, he casually went down to the basement again and filled his pants pockets: cans of spam, sardines, condensed milk, crackers, chocolate bars, and cheese —everything he could grab. Walking very carefully, with each pant leg looking like an overstuffed sausage, Bela sauntered past the guard again. Trying to look nonchalant, Bela even gave him a little wave. The guard was smoking and busy reading a paperback book. A scantily clad woman with voluptuous, half-exposed breasts decorated the cover. Bela thought the soldier must have been reading the sexy parts, as the guard barely looked up to acknowledge the greeting.

"Where were you?" Tibor asked when he returned. "I was worried about you!"

Bela motioned to his brother to come under cover of their tarp and, looking around to make sure no one was watching them, slowly unpacked the packages of meat, fish, crackers, cookies, and chocolate bars hidden in his pockets. Tibor grabbed a chocolate bar ravenously, ripped it open, and practically swallowed it whole. Then another. He smiled at his brother. "You're amazing."

Bela told him about his stint as doorman.

Then Tibor's expression changed to a look of concern.

"You stole all this food? They're going to come after you. What were you thinking?"

"What was I thinking? We're starving! Are we just supposed to lie here and die of starvation? Anyway, if they want to come after me, let them. Sooner or later we're all gonna die with what they're giving us to eat."

That night they went to sleep, without feeling hungry, for the first time since they arrived.

The next day everyone woke to the sound of sirens blaring: six military policemen in two jeeps were driving through the camp. There were no roads — the jeeps simply drove wherever they wanted to, the prisoners jumping up and out of the way like pigeons scattering before a speeding car. The sound of those sirens confirmed Bela's worst fear.

"This is it," he said to Tibor. "I'm finished. The Americans found out I stole their food." It was probably the two missing eggs that gave him away. There was only one chicken, after all.

As the jeeps sped through the camp, almost running over several prisoners, flattening tents and sleeping areas, one of the military police ordered a stop and began to study the faces of the prisoners.

Then, one of the MPs recognized Bela and shouted to the others, "That's him!"

Two MPs grabbed Bela and got him into the jeep. The jeeps turned around and drove back to the administration building.

When they arrived the MP who identified Bela pointed to the front steps and motioned to Bela.

"Get back to your post!"

Still incapacitated with fear, Bela was incredulous. He simply couldn't believe what he was hearing.

The MP thought maybe Bela didn't understand and yelled again, louder and slower this time, emphasizing each word.

"We need you o-o-o-pen and clo-o-o-o-ose the door." With that, he stretched out his arm and pointed to the door.

Bela's fear dissipated into an unbelievable sense of relief. No one had noticed all the food he had taken — they just wanted him to get back on the porch and be a doorman!

Each morning from then on, he left the fenced in prison encampment, walked past the private guarding the main entrance, made his way over to the administration building, and saluted everyone going in and out until noon. Then, he dutifully went down to the basement and brought up the lunch rations and distributed them to everyone in the offices. He was courteous, friendly, and helpful.

His English was improving rapidly, as was his ability to deftly gather and hide foodstuffs in his pants. He learned to walk effortlessly as he smuggled cans and packages of condensed milk, spam, corned beef, cookies, and chocolates in his pants pockets. He took a lot less than on that first day, and learned how to pilfer it — one can here, one package there — without anyone noticing a large stash missing from any one box.

Other inmates were also given the chance to work. The camp commanders asked for volunteers to work outside the camp. Everyone who was still healthy volunteered for such a chance. Tibor was chosen to work in such a brigade, and he and his group were taken to a lumber mill to sort wood. The volunteers were not paid, but were given real food. Tibor brought back pieces of wood for a tent frame.

Food became the currency of the camp, and Bela and Tibor were able to trade for a better spot, further up and away from the first row, directly beside the latrine and the horrible smells. As the days became warmer, the smell became worse.

With the wood Tibor bought from the lumberyard, they had a new centre pole and created a makeshift frame. In camp terms, they started to become relatively well-off.

Bela and Tibor were hounded by others to share their tent and food. It was an impossible situation — they couldn't share their food with thousands of others, no matter how much Bela took from the American food-storage facility. They did, however, take in two others who they knew from their hometown.

Hungarian army officers who ended up in this camp received the same treatment as the rest. They were still in a position of authority vis-a-vis their own men, but could do little except share in the hunger and humiliation of their prisoner-of-war status.

A few commanding officers pretended nothing had changed, such as Major John J. Varga, who was constantly barking orders at everyone. Varga surrounded himself with yes-men to reinforce his own delusion that he was still in charge. The major was a tall man with big bones, somewhat overweight, with thinning hair. He wore black-framed glasses, sported a goatee, and always had a stern look on his face. Everyone was convinced he was crazy as, on hot days, he stripped off all his clothes and walked around naked.

Once a week each company received flour rations. While there were several military cooks in each company, they didn't have anything to cook with. Without any ingredients or utensils, they tried in various ways to make something with the flour.

Major Varga surreptitiously stole some of the company's communal rations, gave it to his camp cook, and ordered him to make *langos* (fried bread) for himself and his entourage. Tibor became aware of this thievery and threatened to expose the major if he didn't stop stealing the company's flour rations, especially when everyone else was always hungry.

Bela's job as doorman gave them the kind of independence and security others simply didn't have. But while Tibor's stomach was full, his heart still ached from witnessing the miserable conditions of the others around them. Tibor couldn't tolerate that an officer, someone whose rank still commanded respect, was stealing from those entrusted to his care.

The major found out about Tibor's accusations through an assistant. He was incensed.

"What is this little nobody, a reservist, accusing me of?" he screamed at one of his assistant's. "You tell this nobody to report to me for a hearing tomorrow at 8:00 a.m. promptly."

Tibor was informed of the "obligatory" hearing and told Bela where he was going. Bela was furious.

"Why are you going? Major Varga has no power over us!"

"I'm just gonna have a chat with him."

"He has no right to order you to such a hearing," Bela snapped. "Who does he think he is, and where does he think we are?"

"The whole thing is ridiculous," Tibor replied. "If I don't go, he'll just call me a liar. Plus, who knows what stupid things he'll say about us."

Bela insisted on going with his brother.

Major Varga sat like a king holding court, stark naked, but fortunately for everyone around him, the overhang of his belly covered most of his genitalia. Tibor and Bela stood before Major Varga, who looked at them sternly and shouted, "How dare you come before me like this, undressed. Your buttons aren't done up all the way!"

The brothers shot a side glance at one another, not quite believing what the major had said. They didn't know whether to laugh or cry.

"Sir, this war is over. You are just as much a prisoner of war as we are," Tibor replied in a quieter tone.

Major Varga's face became crimson, and contorted with anger. He started shouting even louder.

"I will report you to the authorities!"

"What authorities?" Bela shouted back.

By this time everyone within hearing distance started to pay attention.

Major Varga seemed startled that someone had yelled back. He started to say something, but Bela cut him off.

"If you don't stop stealing the company's rations, we'll tell everyone what you've been doing. You know men here have killed each other for a piece of bread. As an officer, you should be ashamed of yourself!"

Major Varga took a hard swallow, collected himself, and yelled in a steady dictatorial tone, "I will have you both court martialled —"

But before he could finish, Bela once again cut him off.

"I look forward to that, Major Varga, but before we get there you will be dead, torn from limb to limb and decapitated by our fellow prisoners once we tell them what you've been doing."

The beady eyes of Major Varga glazed over. Something registered. The message slowly sank in. His massive chest seemed to collapse under the weight of comprehension. The argument was over. The half-crazed major felt the pain of defeat at last.

In the middle of June 1945, after roughly forty days in captivity, an unexpected announcement was made at Tittling:

"The Hungarians can gather their gear — get whatever belongs to you. You are being transferred."

Nothing was said about where they were going, and no one asked anything.

Tibor was elated — they were finally leaving — but Bela looked disappointed.

"Now, when we have shelter, work, and a whole system of survival worked out — now we are probably going to be sent to a new place where we have to start all over again," Bela said with a long face.

"Don't be so pessimistic, little brother. You'll see we're going to a better place."

The Hungarian prisoners of war were assembled, put on open trucks, and, within a day, transferred to a refugee camp called Pocking, inside Germany near the border with Austria.

chapter 23 | june 1945

KAROLA AYKLER SAT INSIDE the little chapel in Micheldorf, immersed in prayer. Her favourite spot was the pew directly in front of the statue of the Virgin Mary holding a plump, but serious-looking baby Jesus. The statue was of carved wood, but Karola marvelled at how the painted cloak on the statue seemed to flow, as if it were real blue cloth. She stared at the face of the Virgin as she prayed. Possibly it was the candlelight falling onto the statue from below, flickering and dancing, that lent a soft, mysterious glow to the face of the Madonna, but Karola was convinced that the countenance of that wooden statue softened and occasionally looked right at her. Local residents claimed that this chapel was a holy place and there were numerous reports that, at certain times of the year, the eyes of the statue came to life. During the war, worshippers provided sworn testimony that wet droplets appeared on its face of the statue.

Karola felt calm, safe, and serene inside this place. Gazing at the statue brought back the warm memories of when her children were young. In her mind she was transported back to the place and time when she held them in her arms and cuddled them, played with them, kissed their tender, dewy skin. She realized that giving birth and raising her children was the happiest, most fulfilling part of her life.

Here, in the chapel, Karola felt she could bare her soul to the Virgin Mother. Mary alone understood her heartache at this juncture in her life — as a devoted wife and mother. Each day she prayed for her sons Tibor and Bela. No one seemed to know where they were. It was June 1945, the war had officially been over two months now, and still there was no sign of them. Karola felt at peace here, praying for them, but as soon as she left the chapel, the feeling of restlessness and panic about their fate swept over her like a bitter windstorm from the nearby mountains.

Since leaving their home in the fall of 1944, Karola and her family had endured six months as refugees, scattering from one temporary shelter to another — sometimes not knowing where their next meal would come from or where they would rest their weary heads at night. For a while they lived in a tiny apartment in Sopron, the westernmost city closest to the Austrian border, yet still inside Hungary.

Karola prayed for her husband as well — prayed that all of them would have the strength to accept their present situation and bear all their adversity with dignity. After months of uncertainty, when the war finally ended, they were herded into a displaced-persons camp near Micheldorf in Austria in the American Zone. It was fortunate for them that Domokos spoke English reasonably well. He went to pay an official visit to Colonel Arthur Harris, the local American commander of the district, in order to offer his services as a translator. Domokos knew they needed someone who could oversee the repatriation of the Hungarian enlisted men and their families. The rules of military conduct dictated that when a war ends and peace treaties are in force, the displaced enemy combatants are sent home, including prisoners of war. Colonel Harris accepted the offer.

A few days later, Harris took a tour of the displaced-persons camp where they were living. It was housed in a cavernous school where the refugees slept in large classrooms on floors, tables, benches — wherever they found space. Colonel Harris hardly had a few square metres left to walk through the enormous rooms. One communal bathroom was used by about three hundred people. When he asked where Colonel Aykler and his family were housed he was shown to a niche at the end of one of the rooms. The entrance to their small living area was blocked by a blanket hung on a rope drawn across two dresser drawers, providing the only bit of privacy. As her husband drew the blanket aside to welcome Colonel Harris into their tiny abode, Karola could see on the look of embarrassment on the face of the sympathetic American officer. Inside, four cots and a few trunks shoved together offered the only place to sit or lie down. They offered to make tea, but Colonel Harris kindly refused, seeing how impossible it was to make and serve tea or anything in the cramped quarters.

After the tour, Colonel Harris was overheard saying to one of his deputies, "Shame on the Hungarians for subjecting their commanding officer and his family to such appalling conditions. I hope if we are ever in such a situation, my men will treat me and my family with more decency."

Colonel Harris gave Aykler Domokos the mandate to make lists of all the Hungarian ex-enlisted men under his command. A mutual respect and friendship developed between the two men, both of the same rank but one on the victorious side, the other on the side of the vanquished. It would take time and resources to organize the repatriation and Harris looked upon Colonel Aykler as someone he could rely on to get the formidable task accomplished.

Massive prisoner-of-war camps run by the Americans for ex-enemy combatants were rumoured be operating in several places in the American zone. Domokos Aykler was informed that such places were merely clearing centres where the military sorted out war criminals among the ex-enemy. Domokos heard that his sons might be in such a place near Tittling. When he informed his wife of this possible lead, Karola felt her heart was being crushed by the news. After the initial shock, she peppered her husband with questions.

"How could they possibly be considered enemy combatants? Tibor was a reservist — he didn't take part in any fighting during the war. Bela was in military school — he had no rank. Can't they see he's still a boy?"

Domokos replied with silence.

Domokos went to Tittling, with a letter from Colonel Harris, asking the commanding officer of the camp "to extend all courtesy to the bearer of this letter in finding Bela Aykler, sixteen years old, and Tibor Schroeder, twenty-seven years old, both Hungarian nationals."

Domokos returned with the news that Tibor and Bela had been transferred out of Tittling just two days earlier. No one could tell him where they had been transferred to or why. Karola was dazed and shocked by the news. For a few days, she stayed in her cot, feeling like an empty shell. But seeing the helpless, stunned look on her daughter's face, Karola realized she had to collect her strength again — her family needed her. It was from that point forward that Karola decided to put her trust in Mother Mary. No one else could possibly understand her complete and utter devastation upon hearing this news.

chapter 24 | june 1945

TIBOR AND BELA WERE part of a mass movement of millions of displaced refugees on the move across Europe, all trying to get back to someplace called "home." Tibor in particular felt the pull of home and Hedy and their life together. After surviving Tittling as prisoners of war, they were discharged to a refugee camp called Pocking. Following ten days there, a surprising announcement was made: everyone born in Karpatalja was now a Soviet citizen and would be provided papers to go home. Bela and Tibor reported along with a group of about thirty men and teenagers who assembled for the journey.

Railway lines were bombed out — only partial lines were running sporadically here and there. No one had tickets, currency had no value, yet everyone was trying to get somewhere. The trains were crammed, at each stop more and more people jumped on. There were even people lying on top of the railway cars, everyone covered in black soot — like chimney sweepers — from the smoke belching out from the front of the coal-fired locomotive.

SUTI STARTED HIS JOURNEY home by hitching a ride on a U.S. Army truck leaving Linz and going east. Let off at Melk (still in Austria), he crossed the Danube on a river ship, as all the bridges were either bombed out or blown up. He entered the Russian-occupied part of Europe.

Here he joined with other refugee teenagers and became a group of almost twenty. They "borrowed" a cart with a horse from a farm for the next leg of their journey — stopping by farmhouses along the way to ask for, and if refused, take food. They went from Wiener Neustadt to Bratislava — a distance of thirty kilometres. After days of travelling by foot, by cart, and whatever means, they arrived in Bratislava, from where they knew there were some trains running.

This is where Suti met Kornelia Weisz, an older girl and neighbour from Nagyszollos. Although they had the same last name, they were not related.

From Bratislava they took the train.

THE TRAIN TIBOR AND Bela travelled on, headed east through Czechoslovakia. When it reached the Slovak-inhabited eastern part of the country, they were told that most of the bridges had been destroyed and that each time they reached a crossing the train would stop and disgorge all of its passengers. They would have to walk through the town or village and find the other end of the destroyed section of track where the railway continued. The first couple of times they had to do this they didn't notice anything unusual about the townsfolk, but the third time, it was as if the locals had been forewarned of their arrival.

"Filthy Hungarians — you started all this!" yelled one man at the side of the road as he watched the group walk by. Tibor couldn't help but notice the man's ugly wife and children, who were all screaming at them, taunting them.

"We hope you die, you pigs. We should kill you ourselves, with our bare hands," a nearby neighbour yelled.

"War criminals!" screamed a woman who was carrying a pitchfork.

To Tibor, it all seemed surreal. He remembered how the Slovaks became rabid Nazis early on in the war. They set up a special, homegrown Nazi regime run by a de-frocked Catholic priest. Slovakia had the dubious distinction of being one of the first countries to deport their Jewish population to Auschwitz-Birkenau and to willingly fight on the side of Hitler. When the Slovaks terrorized and finally ousted their Jewish population, many fled to Hungary.

War criminals indeed, thought Tibor as the group became more belligerent.

Their steps quickened as the local mob started ripping the knapsacks off their backs, throwing stones, and kicking dirt.

"Don't ever come back here, rotten Hungarian scum!"

By the time they reached the next railway station they were exhausted and filthy. Tibor, still breathless, looked behind him and noticed his brother had fallen back a bit. Tibor waited for him and saw that Bela was short of breath and fighting back tears.

"I don't have the strength to go on. They stole my knapsack and boots, and my last clean shirt is gone." Tibor looked at his brother and noticed for the first time how thin he had become. His prominent nose had become even more pronounced, as had his high cheekbones. A fine coating of dirt covered his face, interrupted only by little streams of tears. The look on his face was like a child who had been beaten up by a bully. Tibor wanted to just put his arms around Bela and comfort him, but he didn't know how he would react. While they were prisoners, Bela had stayed tough — it was as if every obstacle became a challenge. Bela provided for both of them. Now he had reverted to childhood again, not knowing what to do about all the cruel things that happened around them. He looked to Tibor for every decision.

It was almost dusk and they found an abandoned farmhouse and took a drink of water from a well. Tibor washed the spit off of Bela's back — the saliva was mixed with dirt and stuck to the back of his shirt. The washing left a sizeable mud stain on his back. Tibor didn't want to tell him how he looked now — Bela was always so meticulous about his appearance.

Tibor pulled Bela aside, and extricated a can of sardines from one of his deep pants pockets. He opened it deftly and tried to encourage his brother.

"We'll eat like kings tonight. Don't worry about your knapsack, little brother."

They travelled after dark from then on, finding hiding places and resting during the day.

SUTI, KORNELIA, AND ANOTHER boy kept hopping onto and switching trains. They had to jump on a train going through Debrecen in eastern Hungary in order to catch a train that went further northeast of their destination to Kiralyhaza, where they finally switched to an overcrowded train going west to Nagyszollos. Trains that were running seemed to be going east-west and not north-south. Finally, they reached Nagyszollos — or, as the Russians had renamed it, Vinogradov.

It was almost midnight when the train pulled into the train station. Suti and Kornelia were warned that the train would not stop, only slow down. It was the last train of the day carrying Russian soldiers west, and the station master, Palyuch bacsi, was ordered to stay and salute as it went by. There was one dim twenty-watt light bulb still burning in the office of the station master. Otherwise, a thick blanket of darkness enveloped the train station. Suti and Kornelia jumped skillfully off the train in time, without injuring themselves, and saw Palyuch bacsi just as he was collecting his things and locking up to go home.

Palyuch bacsi was a short, pudgy, bald man with glasses. He was an ethnic Rusyn and spoke Hungarian with a local accent. Suti and Kornelia knew him. When Palyuch bacsi saw them coming toward him in the dim light he knelt down and made the sign of the cross. He recognized them, but didn't quite trust his own judgement — he had already imbibed a couple of shots of homemade brandy by then. Waiting for the last train was tedious and time-consuming. As the two small figures drew near, he whispered in disbelief, "Is it really you?"

As they assured him they were truly Sanyi and Kornelia Weisz, tears began rolling down his face. The two teenagers helped the station master to his feet. After touching their hands, feeling their faces, Palyuch bacsi collected himself and declared,

"You are coming home with me tonight." Suti and Kornelia were surprised by the generous offer and accepted, and the three of them walked the two-kilometre distance to his home.

After gently inquiring whether or not they had any lice, Palyuch bacsi and his wife gave Kornelia and Suti each their own bed to sleep in. That night, for the first time in over a year, Suti slept in a bed with clean sheets,

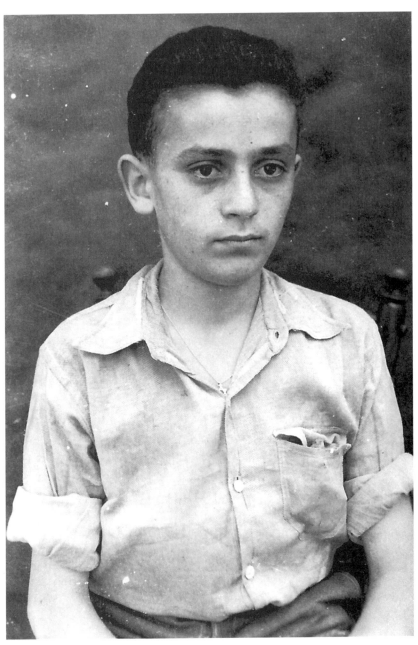

Suti in August 1945 in Budapest.

a pillow, and a comforter. As he settled in, he savoured the softness and thickness of the down comforter.

TIBOR AND BELA ARRIVED at the border station of Csap at dawn. The train they were on was scheduled to go further east to Nagyszollos. Bela remarked that it was practically empty of passengers.

Bela mentioned this again, but Tibor didn't take note. Nagyszollos was close — they were practically home. Home to Hedy, Tibor thought.

They entered a compartment with a man already inside, and took the seats across from him. Tibor looked out the window, watching the events taking place on the platform, ignoring the fellow passenger. When he sat down again, he noticed that the man was staring at them, not in threatening manner, but in a way that made Tibor nervous. The man had an unusual handlebar moustache, with dark hair and eyes, and round, wire-rimmed glasses. Tibor guessed he was about forty-three. There was something about him that was familiar, yet Tibor didn't know where to place him.

"Aren't you the sons of Colonel Domokos Aykler?" the man asked.

Tibor nodded tentatively.

"And are you Tibor Schroeder?"

"Yes," Tibor stammered, taken aback by the recognition.

"What are you doing? May I ask where you are going?" the man asked.

Tibor just stared at this stranger. Bela, snoozing a bit, opened his eyes and also stared. They both sat in silence.

"I'm sorry, how rude of me, I should have introduced myself. My name is Endre Kaposi. I used to have a business in Nagyszollos. I am now shutting down my business there and moving back to Budapest."

"Of course." Tibor finally recognized the man and remembered they had once met. "I remember you."

"Where are you going?" Kaposi asked again.

"We're going home to Nagyszollos. Our home is still there and my business is waiting for me," Tibor stated in a matter-of-fact tone, and then adding with a bit of a smile on his face, "and if my fiancée will still have me, we will be married soon."

Kaposi stared at both of them for what seemed like minutes. He went to the door of the compartment of the train, looked up and down the hallway of the car, then closed the door. Making sure it was securely locked, he returned to his seat, took a deep breath, and began talking in a low voice.

"I'm not sure where to begin. Do you have any idea what has happened in Nagyszollos? Your estate has been ransacked and plundered. A gang of Russian soldiers broke most of the furniture in the house into pieces and used it for firewood." Without waiting for a reaction, he continued. "The property is now in the hands of the Soviet state. Your business is no longer yours. All signs that it was even once yours are gone. The authorities searched for your father for weeks. They questioned everyone who used to work for your family. Your brother-in-law returned; he's since lost his mind. His new occupation is digging out the weeds between the cobblestones on the streets. They've pinned a sign to his back that reads, 'This is what happens to kulaks, the enemies of the state.'"

Bela's eyes opened wider as he listened. Tibor sat, staring at this man, shocked by the things coming out of his mouth.

Kaposi took a breath, folded his hands together, and as if what he was about to say would be even more painful, he bowed his head and continued.

"One month after the Russians arrived, they announced that all Hungarian men between the ages of eighteen and fifty were to report to County Administration Hall for *malenkij robot* — three days work. The men reported and were marched off to a town called Solyva where they were put into barracks. One man escaped and came home to his family in January. He told tales of deprivation — horrible conditions. Word got out that half of the men never made it to Solyva — they died or were killed along the way. Since that time, the ones who survived have been sent off to Siberia to work camps. No one, with the exception of this one man, has been seen or heard from since. You understand — thousands were taken from the entire region of Karpatalja."

Kaposi looked up at Tibor and Bela, noted the shocked look on their faces, and continued. "I would suggest saving yourselves a lot of suffering and pain. If you are determined to go back, simply buy yourselves a bit of rope and hang yourselves here at the closest tree. It will be a lot less painful than going back there."

Tibor realized the deadly truth in the man's black humour. Still, he had to ask, "But what about Hedy Weisz? Have any Jewish families returned?"

Kaposi looked at Tibor with a pained look on his face. "Some of those Jews who returned, who survived the war and the camps, even they have since been deported for *malenkij robot*. There are no exceptions to the cruelty of this regime."

At that moment the train right next to them started moving, very slowly, in the opposite direction. The compartment doors were open on both trains.

Tibor was still talking to Kaposi when Bela became quite agitated and announced to Tibor, "I've heard enough. I'm not going back there."

With that, he deftly stepped over from one train to the other slowly moving train — the one heading in the opposite direction, southwest toward Hungary. Tibor thanked the stranger, said goodbye, and with a heavy heart, stepped across onto the other train after his brother.

THE NEXT MORNING SUTI headed out to see his family home. He was positively obsessed with the idea of stepping into the house where he and his siblings were born. It became the central focus of this trip. It was as if this past year had all been some dreadful surreal nightmare.

Tentatively, he knocked on the door. After a few more attempts an elderly woman opened it. His hopes evaporated. Suti explained that he and his family once lived here, and asked if he could come in and take a look around. The old woman, dressed in black except for a colourful shawl, became nervous and defensive. As if to explain herself, she blurted out, "This is our house. We were given it legally. We didn't steal it."

"I didn't come here to get the house back," Suti explained calmly. "I just want to take a look around. I was born in this house and my mother passed away here."

Reluctantly, the elderly woman let him in, and watched suspiciously and followed him as he moved from room to room. The furniture was different, but the rooms were arranged in the same way as when the Weisz family lived there.

All through this, the elderly woman seemed nervous and made it clear she wanted him to finish whatever he was looking for and leave as soon as possible.

As Suti came out of the house, his dog Buksi, who had been Suti's constant playmate and companion, started to bark at him angrily. Suti just stared at his former friend. He realized maybe the dog didn't recognize him, or maybe he did and was angry with him. After all, Suti thought, I was the one who abandoned him.

While he was still in the yard of his former home, looking at the apiary, a neighbour who had trimmed and pruned the fruit trees on the estate came by. He was incredibly tall and thin and, due to his appearance, was nicknamed Tall Steve. Tall Steve looked nervous when he saw Suti, and started to proclaim in a loud voice, "Don't believe those who will tell you that I took your family's things from the house. I know they will say that, but don't believe it. I only took a few things and am willing to bring them back. Your cousin Sanyi took most of the contents."

Suti stood silently while the disclaimer went on. He thought the behaviour of Steve was very strange indeed. What would I do with my father's clothes and household items?

Suti stared at Tall Steve and as he turned to walk away said, "Don't worry, I don't want anything back."

Within a short time, a former assistant to his father in the operation of the estate, Heder bacsi, also appeared. Suti couldn't believe how quickly the news had spread that he was back. Heder bacsi seemed especially anxious. Out of breath upon his arrival, he wiped the sweat from his forehead with a coloured handkerchief.

"Are you back, Sanyi?"

Suti looked around and didn't quite know how to respond. It was self-evident.

"Yes, I'm back."

Without asking how he was or what had happened to them, Heder bacsi went right to the point.

"Is your father coming back as well?"

Suti looked away for a moment before replying, trying to control his rising anger. He looked toward the flower garden and noticed how overgrown and neglected it had become. He heard a pair of mourning doves cooing in a nearby tree.

Finally, Suti said, "No, my father is not coming back. My father is dead."

Hearing this, Heder could not hide his visible relief. Suti saw in Heder's eyes what was running through his mind: if Vilmos Weisz was not coming back, then undoubtedly he would become the new estate manager.

Realizing he had to get as far away from these people as possible, Suti walked briskly toward the centre of town. He inquired from a stranger if there was a place where he could get a meal and take a shower. They pointed him in the direction of Vasut utca (train street), where the Jewish Relief Committee had set up an office for returning Jews to register for meals and accommodation.

Suti was registered as the 145th Jew to return to Nagyszollos. His name and number were registered into his ration card on July 2, 1945. The ration cards were modified little booklets formerly used by public nurses to register the weight of newborns. Now they were used by returning concentration camp survivors to register the meals they consumed. Suti was overcome with a feeling of satisfaction when he received it — the booklet was one of the first pieces of documentation, stating who he was, and what town he lived in. It was the first piece of official identification he received since his identity had been abrogated over one year ago. He inquired everywhere about his sisters, Hedy and Aliz, but no one knew anything about them.

The Jewish Relief Committee also gave him a house to compensate him for the home taken from his family. Suti's new house was centrally located and the communal kitchen was close by. The house was empty except for a straw-filled mattress on the floor and a small table. Suti settled in for the night.

Word spread to even the nearby villages: little Sanyi Weisz had come back to Nagyszollos. Uncle Moritz from the neighbouring village of Fancsika harnessed one horse to a cart and rode to Nagyszollos to embrace his nephew.

Uncle Moritz and Suti sat and talked for hours about their family, much diminished now. Through tears they tried to reconstruct all that had happened. Uncle Moritz lost his youngest son, Bumi, who was roughly the same age as Icuka. Suti told his uncle he had seen his other son, Lajcsi, as they were leaving the Gunskirchen when the concentration camp was liberated.

At one point, the pain of hearing all this simply overwhelmed Uncle Moritz. In a fit of crying, he went to the cart, pulled out a bottle of vodka, and with a few gulps downed half the bottle. In the next twenty minutes of wordlessness between them, he continued to down the entire bottle of the fiery liquid.

Becoming quite inebriated, Uncle Moritz then turned to Suti and said emphatically, "From now on, you are my son. You will come to live with us! Etu, my daughter and your cousin, returned as well. She will cook and run the household. We will be one family."

Suti listened to his uncle and realized that what he was proposing was the last thing he wanted for his future. Although the details were still taking shape in his own mind, he had been thinking about going to the Jewish homeland for some time. His mother's stories about making *aliyah* so many years ago stayed with him and inspired him.

"I can't come with you. I'm going to Palestine."

"I won't hear of it," bellowed Uncle Moritz. "You are underage — you can't live on your own."

Uncle Moritz was deaf to Suti's pleas for understanding, and grabbed his nephew by the shoulders and plunked him on the cart. Without letting him say another word, Uncle Moritz pulled himself up to his place on the cart next to Suti.

As the horse began to trot steadily, Uncle Moritz's head slumped forward, and within seconds he was asleep. When his uncle began to snore, Suti jumped off the slowly moving cart and watched it as the horse, carriage, and his Uncle Moritz headed out of Nagyszollos toward Fancsika. The horse kept going, Uncle Moritz kept snoring.

INTERESTINGLY, THE TRAIN GOING southwest in the direction of Hungary was packed with passengers. Bela and Tibor found two seats close to the door where they entered in the third-class cabin. They noticed there was an ominous sense of quiet in the compartment. Then they saw why.

Militias in khaki drab uniforms — not military but paramilitary guards — were walking down the aisle asking questions of the passengers. Tibor noticed they had pistols and nightsticks and were wearing black ribbons tied to their right arms. No insignias or identification were evident to indicate what country they belonged to. They spoke in a mixture of languages as they went up and down the aisle interrogating people. There were dozens of them, studying the faces of passengers. Tibor realized they were looking to see if they could find anyone who was involved with the previous regime. The militias were intense and seemed to be very young, some of them even teenagers.

Bela looked at Tibor nervously and whispered, "Now we're in trouble. The only ID I have is my military-school ID, and if I show that they will kill us both for sure. And if I get rid of it now, that will be sure to raise suspicion."

"Look," Tibor whispered back, trying to look nonchalant, "we've done nothing wrong, there is no reason to fear. Just look out the window and ignore them."

A few rows before the militias would have reached them, a man got up and rushed to the door. Seeing this, one of the men pulled out his nightstick and started beating the fleeing passenger. Everyone watched, frozen with fear. Then more militiamen came and dragged the unfortunate man away. By this time he was bleeding profusely from his mouth and ear.

The train seemed to be moving even slower now. Somewhere in the cabin, a child was crying, and the more his mother hushed him, the more adamant he became in his cries. It was hot and stuffy inside the train cabin. A general feeling of unease could be felt — no one knew who was going to be next.

Around twenty minutes later, several militias entered their compartment again. Among them, Bela saw an old schoolmate, and whispered to Tibor, "Look, there's Marta Grosz. Do you remember the family? We were in the same class — she's younger than me."

Marta was dressed like the others in the severe paramilitary uniform. From the end of the cabin, she pointed directly at them as she kept speaking to the others. There was no sign of friendly recognition on her face. Her hair was cropped short. She looked so different than when they went to school. An ominous feeling descended on Bela as he looked at the emotionless, icy expression on her face.

Tibor sat stone-faced. He thought he recognized one of the militias as well — a young man from their hometown who was jealous of Tibor because of Hedy. Tibor wasn't even sure of his name anymore.

As the train reached the railway station at Satoraljaujhely, inside Hungary, they noticed the train was surrounded by dozens of paramilitary guards. Four members of the paramilitary, who had travelled with them over the Soviet border into Hungary, walked up to Tibor and Bela, arrested them, and escorted them to the Russian police and military headquarters. They didn't give any reason for the arrest.

The Russian command station was several blocks away from the train station. As they walked behind Tibor and Bela one of the militias stepped on the back of Bela's bare feet with his boots, ripping his tire sandals and scraping away the skin on his heel with each painful step. After a few hundred metres of walking like that, Bela's bare heels were bleeding, the skin completely scraped away from the action of the militia's boot.

As they were being escorted, Bela noticed a family friend and distant relative, Imre Rez, walking toward them on the same side of the street. Bela didn't want to give a sign of recognition for fear that Imre would be taken into custody as well for knowing them, but crossed his hands at the wrist, as if they were tied together, and showed this gesture to Imre bacsi, hoping he would realize what was happening to them and know the best way to help.

They arrived at the Russian command headquarters and were shoved toward benches in a waiting area. Tibor avoided looking at Bela. What could he say to his younger brother now? They were exhausted, starving, and in Russian custody. And it was because of his own stubbornness that they had ended up in this godforsaken place.

The Russian guard was a husky man with an enormous round head, framed by tufts of dark brown hair. His eyes were like chestnuts sunken into a mass of skin, puffed up from the copious amounts of lard that he obviously consumed on a regular basis. With his olive skin and slightly Asiatic appearance, he looked like a Kyrgiz tribesman. The Russian military uniform was stretched at the buttons and, as he sat looking at his Soviet army-issue rifle, he held his fat finger on the trigger.

Bela, who couldn't get his eyes off the guard since they sat down, turned to Tibor and whispered, "This is what we're going to do: I will jump on him and then he will shoot us and we'll be done with this whole thing."

Tibor started to tell his brother what a bad idea that was, when the Russian bellowed at them.

"*Zatknis! Eb tvow mat!*" ("Shut up, motherfucker!")

Flies buzzed around the room. After what seemed like an interminable wait, the guard signalled it was time for their hearing. It was around noon.

They went into a hearing room, with a portrait of Stalin hanging a bit crookedly on the wall. A longish, hastily made table stood at one side of the room, where three persons could sit and face the accused. Two chairs were occupied, one on the right by a civilian translator, and one on the left by a uniformed soldier. The guard motioned the accused to face the table and remain standing. This was their courthouse.

As a Russian major came in, both occupants of the chairs stood up and waited for the major to take the chair in the centre, then they all sat down. He was a muscular man, slightly above average height, with a meticulous appearance. The seams of his pant legs were perfectly ironed.

The major's first order was to have the prisoners searched again, and the contents of their pockets emptied onto the table.

As Bela surrendered his military-school identification card, the little ray of hope he still had about getting out of there alive evaporated.

The hearing began with the major asking what the charges were against the two accused. It became obvious when the civilian started to speak and translate the words of the major that he was the translator sent by their family friend and relative, Imre Rez.

The two militias who brought in the accused began the accusations. The one who had been responsible for grinding Bela's heel into a bloody mess spoke first. Not more than twenty years old, he seemed confident and arrogant for his age.

"Will it please this hearing, we have found two war criminals. The one on the right," he pointed to Bela, "was influential in the deportation of the Jews from Karpatalja."

The other militia, anxious to begin speaking as well, interrupted him. "And taunted them and beat them while they were in the ghetto."

The two were eager to expand on the details of the charges, interrupting each other frequently.

"The one on the left is a rich businessman and landowner in Nagyszollos. They live in the biggest and most modern house in the middle of vineyards. Hundreds of people who worked for them were abused and kept in line by their estate foreman."

"They are the sons of a famous general who was the military commander of Karpatalja. Through them, we can find out where he is."

During this time, the major, with the identification card in hand, had a private conversation with the translator — they were examining the card in great detail. During this conversation, the major's relaxed and controlled facial expression slowly changed, becoming more and more agitated and finally turning beet-red from anger.

Without warning, his body language changed. Throwing the ID down on the table, he stood up he began yelling in a harsh, uncontrolled voice. Tibor and Bela couldn't make out much of what he was yelling except for the fact that his diatribe was dangerously angry, and obviously directed at them. The seemingly interminable outburst continued for a number of minutes.

At the end, the major shouted orders at the guards and left the room. As they were being led away by the guards, Tibor and Bela were convinced he had ordered the guards to take them out to be shot. Instead, the guards led them out of the room, down the stairs, and pushed them out onto the street.

Tibor and Bela stood stunned, looking at each other. They couldn't believe what had just taken place. In a daze, they picked up their papers and identification from the ground and stood in the shade across from the building from where they had just been ejected, not quite knowing where to go or what to do.

The translator came out of the building and motioned for them to follow him.

"My name is Peter. I was sent by your relative, Imre Rez, to translate at this hearing. I knew your father well." He kept his voice low so that only they could hear what he was about to say.

"What happened in there?" Tibor asked.

"You are two very lucky young men. The major comes from an educated background. His father was an officer in the Russian army during the First World War. When he saw your military-school identification, he quickly realized you couldn't have possibly been involved with the deportation of the Jews — you were fifteen years old. He became furious with your accusers because, as it turned out, his father was shoved under the frozen Volga alive, murdered on the basis of false testimony. The major ordered your accusers to be locked up. Let's keep moving, your relative has asked to me to take you to his house and I think it would be wise to get you off the streets as soon as possible. Who knows what kind of repercussions could come out of this hearing."

Bela simply couldn't cope with the incredible twists and turns of the events swirling around them. The heat, thirst, hunger, and exhaustion finally took their toll; there was a buzzing sound in his head.

He woke up the next morning between clean sheets, after sleeping some sixteen hours at the home of their relative. They were offered eggs, bread, sliced meats, and tea for breakfast — a seemingly sumptuous meal after living on scraps for days. Never had a meal tasted so wonderful. Imre bacsi hired a detective to escort them to Budapest. On the train, the detective behaved as if they were his prisoners. The detective explained he had to do this so that another group of militias wouldn't arrest them.

"It is a very dangerous time we are living in," he told them.

chapter 25 | summer 1945

WHEN TIBOR AND BELA arrived in Budapest in summer of 1945, after the harrowing experience in Satoraljaujhely, they went to their father's apartment, but it was crammed full of the in-laws of their older brother. Istvan and his wife occupied the study, his mother and father-in-law occupied the master bedroom, his brother-in-law and wife slept in the dining room on a chaise lounge, his sister-in-law and her husband were in the main parlour. Another brother-in-law slept on the floor of the kitchen. The entire family fled from Nagyszollos and had nowhere else to go. "What was I supposed to do?" queried Istvan. "Tell my wife's family to go somewhere else?"

The only spot remaining for Tibor and Bela was just inside the front entranceway — in the hallway on the floor. They slept there on a few coats — there was no more bedding left.

The Budapest they remembered had been completely devastated since the last time they were there. The siege of the city went on for three months, with advancing Russian forces pounding from the east, while the retreating German and Hungarian forces were inflicting terrible damage from the west. All the bridges connecting Buda to Pest were blown to bits by the retreating armies in the spring of 1945 in order to slow down, if just for a little while, the relentless push by the Russians westward. The once-proud Chain Bridge looked pitiable, its massive chain links, like broken arms, plunging vertically into the river.

Hardly a street survived without bombed-out buildings and piles of rubble. Homeless families created makeshift shelters out of tin sheets, loose stones, and bricks — whatever they could find. Fresh fruits, vegetables, and meats were a rarity. Water and electricity were only available during certain hours of the week, if at all.

Hungarians had always been wary of greeting the Russians as "liberators" — there was a widespread feeling among the population that one oppressor was being replaced by another. In a short while, their worst fears were confirmed. The residents of the capital were subjected to a brutal campaign of rape and looting by the army of liberation. Anyone stopped on the streets without proper papers could be incarcerated without reason, or worse, put on a train and sent to work camps in the gulags of Siberia.

After a few days, Bela decided he had enough of the crowded living conditions. Everyone was starting to get on his nerves, including Tibor. Bela was determined to make a go of it alone.

Bela remembered the address of Imre Laszlo, his friend from military school. He found Laszlo and together they decided to look for ways of eking out an existence. There was a tremendous need for movers in the city — tens of thousands of people had to get their possessions out of bombed-out buildings and move them to some other location. No horses or carts were left in the city. Everything with wheels seemed to have vanished with the military or fleeing population. Bela and Laszlo were lucky — somehow they found a cart, hitched themselves to it, and started an impromptu moving business. The idea went well for a few weeks until an elderly woman asked them to transport her furniture to the other side of the city. The apartment she was moving into was on the sixth floor of a building that had no elevator. When Bela and Laszlo finished transporting the piano up six floors, they looked at each other and realized they were both thinking the same thing: enough of this!

A distant relative, Sara neni, offered Bela a place to live. She didn't have any children herself and always considered Bela the son she never had. Through a contact, she secured a job for Bela spray-painting timepieces at a clock factory.

Bela loathed this job as well, but he didn't want to quit right away because he felt he might hurt Sara neni, who was constantly helping him. Inflation in postwar Hungary was out of control. He realized that this job was a complete waste of time. By the time Bela got his pay at the end of the week, he had enough money to purchase his weekly transit pass, and nothing more. And he had to run to the train station for fear that the cost of the pass would go even higher in the twenty minutes it took him to dash there. He didn't know how he was going to pay Sara neni for room and board while making nothing wages.

On a brilliant August Saturday morning, Bela dropped by his father's apartment. Istvan and his wife's family were all seated around the dining room table having lunch. They invited Bela to join them. Bela's eyes grew wider as he saw the cornucopia of delicacies on the table: smoked ham, cheese, real butter, plump fresh tomatoes, and pickled beets. Bela tried not to let his eyes give away how amazed he was, but he hadn't seen ham in a half year, let alone seen such a sumptuous feast in the ruins of Budapest. After eating a delicious meal, he pulled his brother aside and asked him how he was providing like this for his family.

Istvan was working at a shipping company, along with his friend and former business partner, Bela Friedmann — they were loading and unloading cargo containers. Lately they were packing containers of salt. Istvan explained they had obtained a few cartons of salt that "fell by the wayside."

"We made sure we took the packages in such a way that no one would ever miss them," Istvan explained. "The only way to make real money in postwar Hungary is on the black market. The small towns and villages in the countryside have meat, vegetables, milk, cheese, and butter. It's a simple barter system, really. The newspapers are full of condemnations of the black market — but what is the present regime thinking? Until they get inflation under control, and people can earn a decent wage and support their families, the black market will flourish. Go try your luck — but be careful." With that, Istvan gave Bela several packets of salt, wrapped tightly in wax paper.

Bela had heard about the black marketeering that went on between the city and the countryside, but he never imagined there would be so many people on the train heading west toward Gyor. The train was packed on Saturday morning, with hundreds of men and women even climbing to the top of the train and hanging on. This is where Bela finally found a spot. Carrying knapsacks and suitcases held close to their bodies, they were mainly dressed in grey, brown, and black work clothes. Could all these people be heading to sell things in the countryside? Bela tucked the precious cargo into the safari pants he still wore — it had many closable pockets.

As the train pulled out of the Nyugati train station, another slow-moving train was just pulling in. It was also packed to the rafters with people coming back from the countryside. The two trains passed each other and a great cry went up: "Death to the black marketers!"

I guess this is what will greet us on the way back, he thought.

TIBOR'S DAY USUALLY BEGAN before dawn. He awoke, dressed, and drank a cupful of something that distantly resembled the taste of coffee. It was instant coffee laced with chicory, and no matter how much of it one drank, there was never the feeling that one had consumed enough caffeine. What I wouldn't give for a good cup of espresso, he thought.

By five in the morning he was out of the apartment, looking for places where Jews from Karpatalja might gather — looking for anyone who might have any bit of information about Hedy. He would search the streets until 8:00 a.m. when he went to his uncle's restaurant to work. After working all day, he would go back to walking and searching. He usually got back to the apartment late at night after darkness fell on the city.

Over the past few weeks, he had felt that he had walked down every street, side street, and alleyway of the city. His feet ached by the end of the day — he barely felt the pain anymore. The soles of his shoes were nearly worn through. He remembered with regret the many pairs of shoes he had left back home. He wished he had taken just a few more pairs. Yet he kept walking, relentlessly, knocking on doors, making enquiries.

Sometimes he was met with a smile of a neighbour — a Jew from Nagyszollos who remembered his family. Sometimes he was greeted with disdain and suspicion. Often he was asked to explain himself: "What do

Karola Aykler and Domokos Aykler as refugees in Austria.

you want with the Weisz family?" But most of the time people just stared back at him when he asked about Hedy Weisz, the daughter of Vilmos Weisz and Terez Leizerovich from Nagyszollos.

One day in early August, fortune smiled upon him. He encountered a young woman named Sara who remembered that the Aykler-Schroeder family had sent yeast into the ghetto — with it, she had been able to bake bread for her family. This young woman had seen Hedy's younger brother, Suti, in an apartment block around Nagymezo utca. Tibor was elated.

The next morning at five he walked to the building on Nagymezo ut. It wasn't even dawn, yet Tibor felt it would be another hot summer day. There was a bit of a hot breeze, reflected off the concrete buildings and streets. He waited until seven, when people started entering and leaving the building. Tibor didn't recognize Suti at first — when he saw the skinny kid walking toward him, he looked twice, then three times. Suti slowed down as well — the young man standing at the entranceway to the building had a familiar stance about him.

"Sutikam," Tibor said.

Suti smiled — a big warm smile. They hugged each other.

"I'm just going to work," Tibor began. "I'm working at my uncle's restaurant cleaning up rubble. Will you come with me and talk to me while I work? I'm desperate to find out about what happened to you and your family."

Suti agreed to come along so they could talk. He saw anxiousness in Tibor's eyes.

As they walked along, the questions started pouring out of Tibor: How long had he been in Budapest? When had he returned? What had happened to them since he had last seen them at the train station in Nagyszollos?

Finally, he blurted out, "Did you know I am in love with Hedy?"

Suti stopped, turned to Tibor, and replied, "Yes, Hedy told me you were in love with each other and that you were engaged to be married. She told me on the train, once we left Nagyszollos. She was holding the prayer book you gave her on the platform."

One tear slipped inadvertently out of Tibor's right eye, and he wiped it away quickly.

"Is she all right?" Tibor asked quietly, tentatively, almost as if he feared hearing the answer.

Suti started telling, slowly at first, then sentence by sentence, what had happened to them since he last saw Tibor on that fateful day more than one year ago.

Suti explained the last time he saw Hedy was in January, when they emptied the concentration camp Auschwitz-Birkenau. "It was a horrible place in Poland. Icuka was taken away on the first day when they arrived. She got into the wrong lineup — the one for small children and elderly women. They went into a building that was a human crematorium. That was the last time anyone saw her alive." Suti could see the colour drain from Tibor's face as he spoke.

"Hedy and Aliz were together," Suti continued. "They shaved their heads. I don't know where they are today. I hope they are all right. But I know I wouldn't be alive were it not for Hedy encouraging me to fight to survive. Father died a few days after we were liberated — he was very sick with typhus." Suti's voice cracked with emotion.

They were still walking side by side, Tibor's face ashen, his whole being visibly shaken by all he had heard. After minutes of silence, as if he needed the time to absorb all of this, he reached over, gently putting his arm around Suti's shoulders. "I feel like a boxer whose head has been pummelled by too many blows. There are no words to express how sorry I am for the suffering endured by your family. If only I could have done more ...." His voice broke, and no more words came out. There was nothing more to say.

They walked the rest of the way in silence until they arrived at the restaurant where Tibor worked. His job was to salvage what was salvageable — mainly glass from the rubble. Window glass was of great value in the city, so much of it had been smashed during the bombardments. Suti offered to help. Tibor demonstrated how to gingerly place the glass in rows. They worked silently side by side, both immersed in their own thoughts, in all that had been said.

The sun crept higher and higher in the sky. It wasn't even 10:00 a.m., yet the day was already turning into a scorcher. Both worked without gloves — gingerly lifting and carrying the useable pieces of glass. But Suti's hands were sweating from the heat and one of the large pieces of glass slipped out of his hands and came crashing down onto the concrete sidewalk, breaking into what seemed like a hundred pieces. Tibor was aghast and although he didn't say anything, he realized within a few seconds that the look on his face was one of "how will I explain this to my employer?" Tibor could see that Suti felt terrible about the accident and despite Tibor's assurances that it wouldn't be a problem for him, Suti quickly said goodbye to Tibor and left. Tibor continued working in the scorching sun, hoping no one would notice the tears streaming down his face as sweat poured off his brow.

THE CLANDESTINE GROUP WORKED in a dimly lit office in an old apartment block on Nagymezo ut in the heart of Budapest. Ten people sat around a massive table, all of them focussed on some aspect of creating official-looking false documents. The windows were covered with thick, dark paper to block prying eyes from seeing what was going on inside. Between the slats of the hastily pasted black paper, streams of hot August sunlight fell on the working group. Everyone had their specific role in the operation. Two young men concentrated on folding the document, making sure that the paper was the right weight and size. They worked with a Gestetner stencil machine. Each copy was made slowly, carefully, with the turn of a crank. Each name was written in by hand. Others were typing the created identities: place and date of birth, false addresses, made-up occupations. New identities for individuals who had lost or destroyed their identity papers during the war. These Jews had made it through the war. Some, through luck or chance, survived the concentration camps, others stayed alive by hiding in the basements and attics of Budapest, or in rural areas. The forged papers re-established their identities, allowing them to ultimately leave Hungary and travel to Palestine.

In the centre of this working group sat a thin, almost emaciated young teenager, looking much older than his fifteen years. Suti felt he had regained a semblance of his identity within this group of left-wing Zionists. The people he worked with never saw him smile. He deadened himself to the pain of the past year.

He believed in nothing. His religion, his home, his childhood memories were all extinguished within him. He considered himself no longer Hungarian. After all, the Hungarians had betrayed his community and family in the cruelest way: by loading them all onto cattle cars and sending them and hundreds of thousands of others from Karpatalja to Nazi concentration camps. It didn't matter that they were brutalized by the Nazis in those camps; Suti held the Hungarians responsible for the act of being evicted from their homes, loaded onto cattle cars and transported to Auschwitz-Birkenau.

The past year had awakened the Jew in him. While being persecuted as a Jew, he ultimately found his Jewishness. For the first time in his life, he wore a Star of David on a simple chain around his neck. And he started calling himself "Itzik," a derogatory name used by some Hungarians for Jews. It was comparable to calling a black person "nigger."

Suti had a very important role in the group. He knew the Cyrillic alphabet — the seemingly incomprehensible language of the Russians, who presently occupied Budapest. The creation of identity documents was one of the most critical and most lucrative services one could provide in 1945.

Suti created the Russian signatures and the stamps, which were so crucial for the veracity of the documents. Without the prominent red stamps, nothing was official as far as the Russians were concerned. Some of the Russian soldiers who were stopping citizens were illiterate, but when they saw a large red stamp with Cyrillic lettering, they felt reassured that everything was in order.

Zsigmond Perenyi, the son of the baron, discovered through Tibor that Suti was living in Budapest and sent a message that he should come for a visit. Suti had always admired the baron's son. He was a curiosity: Oxford educated with a skinny American wife. Eleanor Perenyi didn't speak a word of Hungarian — nor did she try to learn. She kept herself aloof from most of the residents. She became pregnant during the war and went back to the United States to give birth to their child.

Zsiga wasn't alone in the apartment when Suti arrived. Terez Alexander was there as well. Terez came to Nagyszollos during the war and lived with the Ilkovics family — she was one of the refugees from Slovakia fleeing persecution. Terez sat silently as they spoke, occasionally wiping her eyes with a handkerchief. At one point, she stood up and said she was going to the kitchen to make a pot of tea. It was then that Zsiga quietly confided to Suti that they had fallen in love with each other. He was determined to marry Terez once his divorce from Eleanor came through. Nothing else mattered, he said.

Young Zsiga looked contented as he spoke of their love. Suti was moved that Zsiga would confide in him about their love affair. They sat quietly. By this time Terez had returned with a pot of tea. Terez was so thin she looked breakable. Suti suspected she had lived through the camps as well.

Suti told them about his intention to go to Palestine. When he stood up to leave Zsiga guided Suti down a long hallway to the door, stopped, and quietly slipped him some money. "You will need it for your trip," he said in a half-whisper. Zsiga apologized that he couldn't give him more. Suti was surprised, stunned, and moved by his gesture. Suti reflected on their humble circumstances — it looked as if the two of them had just enough to eat, but nothing more.

SUTI WAS WORKING AMONG the forgers when a stranger came to see him. The man introduced himself as Gyula Berger, and claimed he was a cousin from his mother's side of the family. Gyula had a strange-looking round hat on his head — part of a military uniform Suti had never seen before. Suti had never met this relative and was skeptical about whether he was indeed a cousin. At this point in his life, contacts and family members were critical for Suti. Gyula explained he had already made *aliyah* to Palestine in the 1930s. Suti queried him about dozens of family members — they went through the entire family tree before Suti's skepticism became allayed. He found out his cousin was an officer in the British army contingent in Palestine.

Gyula informed Suti that his brother, Bandi, was alive and already living in Palestine. Gyula claimed to have his brother's address — not with him, but in Milano where he was stationed. After a long night of talking, Gyula convinced Suti that he should go to Milano in Italy, where his unit would take him to a place where he would be well-looked-after. Suti was still a bit wary of this man in the strange uniform when they parted, but realized, during their conversation about Bandi, that his desire to go to Palestine and find his family was overwhelming. Ostracized by his homeland, he needed a place in this world where he felt at home. He believed in Zionism and wanted to build the new Jewish homeland. He heard all about the kibbutz system and wanted to live in and help build such a place.

Suti realized his cousin's offer would take him closer to his dream of making *aliyah* to Palestine, the place his mother often talked about. He needed to get to the sea, where ships could be boarded that would transport him to the land of his dreams. The Zionist organization Bricha established a network to help Holocaust survivors flee from Europe and arrive in Palestine, which was at the time under British mandate.

In the fall of 1945 Suti and a group of seventy young people were sent off on their journey by foot toward Szentgotthard in western Hungary. Their first obstacle was to get from the Russian zone to the British zone. With the assistance of a guide, they made it to Graz, where they were caught and taken to a camp for displaced persons in a small town named Judenberg near Stiermark. They spent two months in this place, receiving medical help and three meals a day. A doctor determined that Sandor Weisz was to receive double portions because he was so thin. Suti enjoyed this, and spent the time slowly gaining weight, but by November, he and twelve others decided it was time to move on.

Again with the help of the Zionist network, they hired a truck to take them to the Austrian-Italian border, over the Alps. The truck broke down and the driver, who had already taken their money, disappeared, leaving them stranded. Austrian border guards caught the group and took them to a small local prison. It was November 6 and very cold. They were hungry and ill-prepared for the plunging temperatures. Without blankets or mattresses, they slept fitfully on the stone prison floor.

Before dawn, Suti awoke to the most incredible sound of high-pitched yelling. Never in his life had he heard anything like this sound. It sounded like human barking. The Austrians unlocked the cell and abruptly ordered them out. When they were led outside, they saw that a British officer was yelling his head off. The officer looked and sounded very intimidating: he pointed to a truck and ordered them to climb into the back, all the while yelling at the Austrians. Suti and his friends didn't know where they were going or why the Austrians were handing them over to this British officer as they didn't understand a single word of English, but they had little choice — they had to go. When the truck drove away from the police station there were two officers in the front seat: the driver at the wheel, and the sergeant major who had until then been barking. Just two kilometres down the road the sergeant major pulled back the curtain separating the front cabin from the back, smiled, and quietly said: "Shalom." The until-then fear-inspiring officer introduced himself as Sergeant Major Leon Ostreicher, head of the transportation unit of the Palestinian contingent of the British army. Ostreicher took the twelve youngsters to his company near Klagenfurt. When they arrived, he ushered the group to the front of the line of soldiers waiting for breakfast, cut into the line, and told the youngsters to eat as much as they wanted. In the next few days, Ostreicher arranged papers for the twelve — papers that would grant them safe passage into Italy. The British army unit transported them with trucks as far as Mestre (near Venice) where they boarded the train to Milano.

As the train rambled through the mountainous region of northern Italy — the Dolomites — Suti felt as if all the cruelty and hatred he had experienced in the past year was melting away, drifting further and further from his mind as the distance increased and kilometres clicked past. For the first time in his short life he sat and marvelled at the breathtaking scenery unfolding around him.

The train stopped frequently between Mestre and Milan. There was nothing to eat along the way and Suti was starting to feel quite famished. At one station, the train stopped for a longer layover. Suti heard one of the food vendors yelling: "olivero, olivero!" A vendor was selling what looked like black, bite-sized round objects soaking in an oily tub. It must have been the curious look on Suti's face as he stared at the giant containers of produce that compelled the vendor to ask him if he would like a taste.

Suti didn't know what to say, as he didn't understand Italian. Where-upon the vendor took a bit of newspaper, wrapped it into a cone shape, and plopped about a half kilo of black oily beads into the cone. While handing it to Suti, he announced his produce with pride: "olivero!" Suti pulled out his pants pockets to show the vendor he had no money to give him, but the vendor insisted he take the olives gratis.

Suti never tasted anything so wonderful.

In Milan the group went to the headquarters of the Zionists at Via Unione 5. Here Suti was separated from the rest and sent to Selvino, where an organization had established a boarding school for orphans of the Holocaust. The rest of his group were determined to be too old and were sent on to Rome.

The military truck made its way slowly up the winding, snake-like narrow road, through the dense forest, to an altitude of more than nine hundred metres above sea level. There the road let to a small village of Selvino, north of the Milan-Venice highway. A few hundred metres beyond the village, on the mountain's slope, stood an elegant, four-storey villa.

The truck stopped in front of the villa and Suti stared at the magnificent garden extending down the slope with pine, cedar, and cypress trees and showy pink and yellow flowering shrubs. The Italian Alps peaked out from behind the trees.

As they started to disembark from the truck, someone started yelling from one of the upstairs windows: "Suti, Suti!" Suti turned and saw his old friend Vili Teszler came bounding out of the house toward him. Suti couldn't believe it — the last time they saw each other was in Mauthausen. Suti was elated: here he was alone again in a strange place, a bit lost in this world. Meeting Vili was like being reunited with a family member.

Selvino was created to prepare orphaned children of the Holocaust for the transition to life in Palestine. The school was established by Raffaele Cantoni, an Italian Jew and ardent Zionist, Mathilde Cassin, his partner who travelled from convent to convent looking for Jewish children, and Moshe Ze'iri, a member of an agricultural collective in Palestine. There was an incredible mix of children: those who had been with the partisans during the war, children who had been hidden in convents and forests, and children who had survived the concentration camps. All were orphans. Most had not attended school during the war, so there was a tremendous gap in their education.

The students slept thirty to a room — dormitory style. After lights-out, Suti occasionally saw a girl crawling out of her bed, kneeling down, making the sign of the cross to pray. It was obvious she had spent the war hiding with a Christian family or in a convent. Suti was shocked to find some boys and girls who weren't able to read or write — it turned out they had been hiding in the forests in Ukraine for four or five years.

Other children had nightmares and cried out in terror night after night while dreaming.

Food was scarce. Everything was rationed out in small portions. No support was being sent from Palestine. The food came from UN rations for refugees and from the Jewish Brigades, who sent flour, sugar, rice, and dried beans.

The children had one roll at each meal. There was little variety: jam, margarine, soup, gruel, small portions of army bully beef, and small amounts of fresh fruits and vegetables from the nearby villages.

It was cold in the house. By the time Suti arrived in late November, heavy rains were falling and winds were raging through the mountains. There weren't enough warm clothes or adequate blankets for every child.

Moshe Ze'iri, who was in charge of the home, directed it according to his own principles as a kibbutz member who had been educated in a movement based on "self-fulfillment through co-operation." The school was run on the principles of self-sufficiency, shared responsibility, and shared property. Every activity around the school, whether scholarly or leisurely, was infused with the principles of life of the kibbutz system. The daily chores were divided between the children themselves: cleaning, kitchen duty, serving food, keeping the house heated, doing the laundry, sewing, caring for the garden and plants, and guard duty at night. The older children were entrusted with the care of the younger ones.

All classes were taught in Hebrew and even when they were not in class, the children were expected to speak among themselves only in Hebrew. The day began with morning roll call and raising the blue and white flag of the Jewish people, while everyone sang "Hatikvah."

After a full day of classes and chores around the house, the late afternoon was left free for games in the courtyard, in the garden, on the football field, at the ping-pong table, at the chess board. After supper, everyone would gather for singing, dancing, storytelling, and parties. The chorus, conducted by Moshe Ze'iri, became the focal point of the cultural activities of the house. The motto of the choir became "We sing not of blood and battles; we sing of life and creation." Other teenagers started their own school newspaper, called *Nivenu*.

There was no talking about the past, about the concentration camps, about the horrible things so many of them had experienced. The future was what counted, and preparing for the future in Palestine was the focus of all their work in Selvino. The personalities, character, and entire being of these children had been permanently affected by the traumatic events of the past five years, yet they couldn't talk about this trauma. Occasionally, a few children went crazy. One boy tried to hang himself in a nearby forest. Another couldn't sleep and convinced himself he was going insane. He was sent off to a sanatorium in Milan. When he came back with his head shaved, he never spoke again of his past.

Suti spent his days learning Hebrew and learning as much as he could about his new homeland, Palestine. At night, he also had nightmares, but mainly, he dreamt of life back in their home with his mother and father and sisters and brother. He missed them all tremendously — there was an ache in his heart that he could never quell. In Jewish tradition, the one-year anniversary of the death of a parent was marked in a special way. It was called *Jahrzeit* in Yiddish. Suti couldn't mark the one year anniversary — he was in Auschwitz on his way to Mauthausen in January 1945. But the second anniversary of the death of Terez Weisz was fast approaching. Suti quietly, clandestinely wrote a poem to commemorate the anniversary of her death.

chapter 26 | fall 1945

HEDY LAY ON A straw-filled mattress — awake, but keeping her eyes shut tight. She pulled the blanket closer, trying to remain in her semi-conscious dream state, immersed in memories of Tibor. Images of sitting behind him on his motorcycle — her arms wrapped around his waist, her face buried in his back to shield it from the wind. As he was driving, Tibor grabbed one of her hands every once in a while and kissed it. At least in her daydream, she was going somewhere ... anywhere.

Her sister, Aliz, kept intruding on this most pleasant daydream, sitting on the side of her bed, talking to her gently, trying to rouse her. Hedy knew if she opened her eyes the wonderful images would vanish.

She resisted opening her eyes.

Back in Nagyszollos again, with Tibor — walking along the pebbled shore of the river Tisza hand in hand. A small groundhog lay on the pebbles in front of them. They almost missed it as the rodent blended in among the brown and grey stones. It remained motionless, but opened its eyes and raised its head a bit when the two of them approached. It didn't flee. Hedy had a few scraps of bread in her knapsack; she tossed them gently near the groundhog's mouth. The animal didn't react to the bits of bread. There weren't any visible wounds on the fur. After watching it for a little while, the two of them surmised the creature had simply lost its will to live.

Hedy finally acknowledged her sister's attempts to wake her. She pushed the covers back and slowly crawled out of bed. A little hand mirror was hanging on the wall and, unintentionally, she caught a glimpse of herself in it.

What would Tibor say if he saw her now? Her hair had grown back somewhat —not blond anymore, but a dull brown. It was still barely long enough to comb out. She ran her fingers through it and decided it didn't matter how she combed it, it always looked unkempt. Possibly it was the water they used to bathe or that awful-smelling soap in the showers, but she felt her hair would never be soft and shiny again.

She had lost so much weight she felt like a skeleton of her former self. The only clothes they were provided were drab, over-washed army issue coats and pants — all uniform, all ugly. No matter how many times she looked in that tiny mirror, she couldn't believe the face reflecting back at her was her own. In her reflection, she saw a much aged, tired-looking woman staring back at her. She honestly felt that no man could ever be attracted to her again.

In her pants pocket was a small, folded-up postcard, still with her after almost a year. The postcard had arrived at Auschwitz, addressed to her at a fictitious place called Ebensee. She only received it because her friend had worked in the sorting area of the camp. Hedy had no idea how the note from Tibor had arrived at Auschwitz. On the postcard he had written, "I am waiting for news from my wife, I hope she is well." Nothing else. A message from him had filtered through — a message that he still loved her.

If Tibor still loved her, Hedy thought, he was in love with a woman who no longer existed. She realized he could never understand all that she had been through. Hedy could never, no matter how well he listened, explain to him the unbelievably dreadful events that had taken place since they had last seen each other. The environment they had to endure. The human deprivation and cruelty. There were no words to describe it. She had been irrevocably changed.

Hedy and Aliz last saw their brother, Suti, on January 18, 1945, when they were separated while being ordered out of Auschwitz. They didn't know his fate, or the fate of their father or Bandi.

After three days of marching in freezing cold and snowy conditions, they were put onto open cattle cars and ended up at another concentration camp called Neustadt Glewe near Mecklenburg in northern Germany. They continued to work there under dreadful conditions until the Americans liberated them in early May 1945. Within a few days the Russians took over the administration of the camp and transferred them all to another camp called Prenzlau, near Stettin. Following liberation, an overwhelming exhaustion enveloped Hedy, followed by the unspeakable hollow feeling of depression. All the rules of survival changed; she simply couldn't garner the strength to go on.

While they were in captivity, Hedy looked after Aliz and protected her, provided for her, coaxed her out of her negative thoughts. Now everything had reversed: Aliz had become the caregiver, the one who brought her sister tea and soup and coaxed her to get out of bed.

The weeks stretched into months. The Russians made long and ex-haustive lists and allowed the citizens of Yugoslavia, Romania, Hungary, Poland, and Czechoslovakia to return home. Hedy and Aliz and the 120 or so who declared that they were from Karpatalja were not allowed to leave. They were unaware that Karpatalja had been ceded to the Soviet Union at the end of the war. According to the records of the Russian camp authorities, those from Karpatalja were considered "stateless." The Russians were unwilling to send ethnic Hungarians back to a region that was now part of the Soviet Union.

By mid-October 1945, Hedy realized that she had to flee this desolate camp in order to regain her will to live. Aliz was elated by the decision. Finally, her sister wanted to do something other than lie in bed, curled in a fetal position.

"Where shall we go, my dear sister?" Aliz asked.

"I don't know where we'll go and I don't know how we'll get there," Hedy replied, looking around to make sure no one could overhear them. "All I know is that we have to leave this soul-destroying place as soon as possible."

September 1945
Budapest

My Dearest Hedy,

There is so much in my heart that I've been aching to tell you. The distance of one year of not knowing how you are and where you are is unbearable and weighs heavily on me. I have sent many messages to the refugee centres at the International Red Cross and IRO (International Refugee Organization), but all my searches have turned up nothing.

I am writing these words from Budapest, where I'm living in our father's apartment along with my older brother, Istvan, his wife, Eva, and practically every one of Eva's relatives. It is very cramped. Each day I would leave the house at 5:00 a.m. and go to places where I might possibly find out about you. I did this until I found out from a Jewish woman from Nagyszollos that Suti is living here as well.

Suti and I met. Oh, what a heartfelt and joyous occasion it was for me to finally hug your little brother! I felt that finding you had to be a breath away. You can't imagine the sadness in my heart on hearing of what happened to all of you. In my mind I've gone over and over the events of the days before you were taken away, and although I know that this type of thinking of how things might have been different is all useless, I can't help but think I might have been able to do something else, something more to save you and your family.

Since you were taken away, I've felt like a blind man in a dark room. I've decided to write you. Although I don't know where you are and don't have a place to mail these letters to, I will continue to write them, as I am afraid I will lose my mind if I don't get these thoughts down on paper. You are not only the love of my life, but my very dearest friend, with whom I could share my most intimate, private feelings. I miss you and our long talks terribly.

I haven't stopped thinking about you and loving you since the moment at the train station when we were pulled away from each other. Nothing matters, except seeing you again, being with you again.

Your loving fiancé,
Tibor

ALONG WITH TWELVE OTHER women from Karpatalja, Hedy and Aliz found a broken slat in the fence surrounding the perimeter of the camp, squeezed through it, and walked away. The escape wasn't difficult, but deciding how they would fend for themselves once they were out was more challenging. Without money or any identification, the group walked all that day until darkness fell and they stumbled into an empty barn to sleep on top of a pile of hay. Again, the next day they continued walking until they became quite famished. They entered what looked like a deserted farmhouse to look for food. They found a few remnants of flour, and some carrots and turnips, but also came across a room full of bales and bales of clothing. The five women gleefully tore through the bales, helping themselves to real clothes.

At one point, as they were pulling apart one of the stacks, Hedy noticed a child's sweater — knitted light blue with flowers and butterflies on it. Her heart stopped a beat as she stared at the size and style. There was only one such sweater she had ever seen in her entire life. It was identical to her little sister Icuka's — the one their mother had knitted for her. The coincidence was more than she could cope with. With a lump in her throat, she commanded herself not to cry. Hedy bundled the sweater in among others then loudly called out that they had better leave before someone came home.

They travelled by train to Berlin. There they made their way to a refugee centre where the food was much more varied and nutritious and they were given more civilian clothing. There was even a resident hairdresser who finally evened out the zigzag lines of their regrowing hair. Hedy began to be transformed into a young woman again.

The authorities provided official papers based on their declaration of where they were born. Hedy and Aliz spent untold hours combing through reams of lists of missing and located individuals, but couldn't find Suti, their father, or Bandi. Hedy's eyes occasionally wandered to the *S* part of the lists, looking for *Schroeder*, but she didn't know what she would do if she actually found his name and his location. Could she face him?

Hedy felt that Tibor had always placed her on a pedestal. The experience of the past year made her realize she could no longer live up to his inflated image of her. The romance, the engagement with Tibor, felt like a very pleasant but distant dream. She didn't know what she would say if she saw him, how they would even begin to pick up the pieces of where they had left off.

Nussbach, Austria
March 1946

My Dearest Hedy,

Since I wrote to you last, I left Hungary and am now living with my mother, father, sister, and her husband, Erno, in a little town called Nussbach in Austria. Things in Hungary have gone from bad to worse as the communists are tightening their political power. I'm sure you must have heard the economy is in tatters. We have heard that our home is no more, ransacked and plundered by Russian soldiers.

My parents still actually have it in their minds to return. We argue with them all the time about it. They bring it into the conversation quite often. My mother naively thinks we will all go back and carry on as before.

When I first saw my father, I realized that, physically and spiritually, he has become a broken man. His hair and his beard have turned completely white. He worked for the American army, creating lists of ex-enlisted men and organizing the repatriation of these men and their families. Once that work was finished, my parents no longer received ration coupons. Since then, all three of us — Picke, Erno, and I — have been supporting them by working for the farmers in the neighbouring villages, doing whatever work is available in return for some flour, milk, lard, eggs, or even chicken or rabbit meat, when available. The neighbouring community treats my parents with respect; they refer to my father as "Herr Oberst von Aykler."

My father feels he is a burden to the family, and that, because of his ailing health and heart condition, none of us will be accepted as immigrants to a third country.

My younger brother, Bela, has been drafted into the new Red Army of Hungary. He was given the rank of sergeant, works for the border patrol, and seems to be doing well.

Inflation is out of control everywhere in Europe and the black market is the only thing that flourishes. Still I felt it urgent to help my parents in their desperate time of need.

I don't mind not having anything — I feel I am young enough to rebuild my life — but my parents feel they've lost everything and that their lives are too advanced to start over. It's very difficult to deal with their depression and overwhelming feelings of sadness.

I have asked Suti to stay in touch with me, and if by some chance he finds out about you, to send me your address right away. The searing pain in my heart will never be healed until I know you are safe.

Your loving fiancé,
Tibor

STILL SEARCHING FOR MEMBERS of their family, Hedy and Aliz heard of an even larger refugee centre near Hannover and hitched a ride with a driver who was transporting a group of refugees there.

As Hedy and Aliz were helping each other climb into the back of the truck, someone nearby yelled, "Hey — you there — Hedy — it's me!"

Hedy couldn't believe what she was seeing or hearing. It was Fabri Berliner, one of the Berliner brothers from home.

"This isn't a chance encounter, you know. We were meant to meet. I'm going to marry you!" Fabri quipped.

Even in Nagyszollos, Fabri was known as a bit strange, but to start a conversation this way led Hedy to believe he was more than a bit abnormal. She pretended she didn't hear his statement and began questioning him about friends and family.

"Fabri, were you home? Who has come back?"

"Don't ask me that," Fabri replied with a hurt look on his face.

"Did anyone come back?" Hedy persisted.

"Your father didn't come back. They say he passed away after liberation."

Hedy turned white when she heard the news, she stopped for a beat, but the next question came straight from her heart.

"And what about Suti?" she asked, holding her breath.

"Suti came back but only for a little while, then left again. No one knows where he went."

"For God's sake, Fabri, why didn't you tell me first that Suti is alive?" she said as tears welled up in her eyes. "The sadness knowing my father has passed away is not as great as the joy I am feeling right now just knowing that Suti is alive!"

The good news injected strength into Hedy's tired bones. The two sisters said goodbye to Fabri and decided to go to Prague. They no longer had a reason to go to Hannover — they had found out that Suti was alive and well!

Life was simple in Prague. Hedy and Aliz were provided three meals a day and a warm bed at the Red Cross centre. They met and conversed cautiously with a few other residents they knew from home, but otherwise kept to themselves. They didn't want to get engaged in any kind of special activity. One young Czech soldier, who lived in an army barracks nearby, brought a message from an officer by the name of Emil Hosek. The soldier inquired if Emil, who knew the Weisz family from Nagyszollos, could come for a visit. Neither Hedy nor Aliz remembered the name, but replied that of course he could come to see them.

As Emil walked into the main meeting room, Hedy didn't immediately recognize him, but there was something about his presence that comforted her. As soon as she laid eyes on him, Hedy instantly remembered that this was the suave man she always noticed driving a Czech-made Jana motorcycle in a long leather jacket.

Before the war, Emil was an insurance agent who worked in Vasut utca in Nagyszollos. Emil's last name had been Klein. He had indeed known Hedy's father well and came to the family home often.

An officer in the Czech army, Emil was a soft-spoken man who exuded strength and determination. He had a thick head of curly, dark-brown hair and widely set brown eyes. When he smiled, two deep dimples made his smile more engaging.

During their first visit he introduced himself and said reassuring things about Nagyszollos, their community, and their family. He bought a single rose for each of them.

After his first visit, Emil asked Hedy if he could come again. She nodded, not believing he would return. It was so unusual to encounter someone who was considerate of her as an individual again. For the past year, all she had experienced was people barking orders at her, telling her what to do and how to do it. All of a sudden, here was Emil asking her permission if he could come for another visit. It was so unexpectedly refreshing.

The second time Emil came to visit, he asked Hedy if she would come for a walk with him. While they walked in the historic castle district, Emil told Hedy that his wife, who was also from Nagyszollos, had died during the war. He spoke softly, but Hedy could sense that he was deeply affected by the loss. His grief was present in his tone.

Emil quietly told Hedy, in a matter-of-fact tone, that he had rented an apartment for her and her sister. "You can't possibly stay here in the Red Cross centre forever," he explained. Emil informed Hedy that he had inherited a house with a metal-working shop on the main floor and a walk-up spacious apartment on the second floor. The place had lots of room for both of them. With the business, he could easily support all of them.

Hedy was moved by the generosity of Emil. He seemed to quietly accept all that she had been through, making no demands of her. It was comforting to know that Emil knew her family and was from the same background — there was an unspoken understanding about their past.

Most importantly, Emil was willing to take care of both Aliz and herself in offering them a home. Without being intrusive, Emil took the lead in organizing their lives at a time when Hedy was incapable of doing so.

Within a few months, Emil asked Hedy if she would be his wife. She agreed. They were married according to Jewish laws and traditions.

Hedy with her husband, Emil Hosek, and their daughter, Chaviva.

chapter 27 | 1947—1954

IN SELVINO, SUTI AND the other young residents were taught that this era would be remembered by history as a period of struggle and rebellion against the British Mandate and about the work of thousands who were working clandestinely for the future of their homeland within such Jewish organizations as Haganah, the Palmach, the Irgun and the Lechi. Boatloads of illegal immigrants set out from Italy and France for the shores of Palestine, but most were stopped by the British patrols. The passengers were taken to detention camps in Atlit and Cyprus. The British government's White Paper decrees were imposed, setting limited quotas of fifteen hundred per month for Jewish immigration, but the struggle for unlimited immigration and the right to settle in all areas of the new Jewish homeland continued.

Secret arrangements for illegal immigration (*aliyah bet*) became better organized, manned by soldiers of the Jewish units and emissaries of the Haganah. A network of wireless communications stations sprang up in villas and hidden in the mountains, from Bari and Metaponto in the south to Milan and Como in the north. Operations for forging passports and other documents were established. Ships were purchased or acquired, along with fuel, foodstuffs, and arms, and secret agreements were reached with the Italian police and bureaucracy to undermine the work of the British intelligence forces to prevent Jewish immigration to Palestine.

Suti and a group of ten others slipped out of the school at Selvino one evening in the early spring, determined to finally make their way to the land of their dreams. They were convinced that they had heard enough about the details of the journey to be able to make their way. They heard about the places where boats secretly embarked. They hitched rides toward the seaside of Italy, through Genoa, Bolgliasco, La Specian, finding themselves south of Aral, near a little seaside hamlet called Metaponto. It was the place of an old Greek ruin. Here, Haganah was hiring local fisherman to take groups across the Mediterranean. The Haganah organizers recruited Suti and his friends to assist in ferrying the pontoon boats full of people to fishing vessels anchored four hundred metres offshore. When these ships left for Palestine without them, Suti and his group complained to the organizers, saying they wouldn't help anymore if they would be left behind.

The authorities of the Haganah complied, and sent an old fisherman's vessel, the *Shoshanna*, to take Suti and his friends, along with 150 others, across the Mediterranean. It was a harrowing journey — they encountered a vicious storm while they were passing through the Greek Islands. The tremendous gale-force winds forced the ship off course to take shelter in the shadow of one of the islands.

The overcrowded ship carrying Suti finally landed on a sandbank just a few hundred metres offshore from Palestine. Suti, determined as ever, jumped into the ocean and swam ashore. It was his birthday — March 12, 1947 — and he wanted to be in Palestine by the time he turned seventeen. It was an emotional moment in Suti's life, but he didn't have a second to savour it. Zionist groups, waiting for the passengers onshore, pulled them out of the sea and hurried them onto a bus — a regularly scheduled bus route operated by South Yehuda. Jews and Palestinian residents alike used the bus service. The Zionists ushered the new arrivals onto this bus in the hope that they would enter the country unnoticed. The bus route ran directly through two English military camps, and to the great chagrin of Suti, the busses were halted and everyone on the ship was eventually rounded up and taken into British captivity in Cyprus.

Suti spent one week in Cyprus. He was questioned at length about the customs, movies, geography, and general life in Palestine. He responded to every trivia question correctly. The British officer interrogating Suti finally took out a coin, flipped it through the air, caught it, and asked, "What was that?" The official answer was "fifty mil," but they were trying to see if Suti knew the slang for the coin. He did, answering "a shilling." The officer told him to go home to Palestine.

The Zionists spirited Suti away to a kibbutz. He was a young man with no identification whatsoever, and it was explained that until a new ID was created for him, he was not allowed to walk the streets or go anywhere in Palestine. Even inside the kibbutz, called Givat Brenner, he was told not to talk to anyone about how he got there. He was allowed to go to the mess hall and eat three meals a day and instructed to do nothing else. It was here that Suti saw for the first time what a glorious, abundant paradise this place called Palestine was. The sun was always shining. Date and avocado groves thrived inside the kibbutz, and he marvelled at the wonderful scent of the fruit trees. Everything was in bloom.

A man was leading a donkey pulling a little cart of ripe oranges. When the man noticed Suti staring at the oranges, he asked if he would like one. Suti nodded eagerly and took one. The man kept watching the young refugee and asked, "would you like some more?" Suti nodded again. "Then take as many as you would like." Suti grabbed about a half dozen oranges and hightailed it back to his room.

Within two days, Sandor Weisz officially became Yitzhak Weisz and a resident of Palestine. He knew which kibbutz he wanted to go to, but first he wanted to find his brother, Bandi, who lived in Natanya. Yitzhak disembarked from the bus in the centre of Natanya and didn't quite know how to find his brother. He looked around and, amazingly, recognized someone from home — Karoly Aushpitz from Kaszony, a neighbouring community in Karpatalja. Yitzhak went up to him and asked in Hebrew, "Do you speak Hungarian?"

Karoly turned, stared at Yitzhak and replied, "Why do you ask?" Yitzhak explained he was looking for his brother.

He thought the reaction of the man was very strange indeed — Karoly knew his entire family back home. Yitzhak realized there were grave security issues to worry about in this country and attributed these security concerns to Karoly's strange behaviour. Karoly took Yitzhak to his own home and locked him in a room until Bandi came back to the city. Bandi was the chauffeur of the Mayor of Netanya.

Karoly went to tell Bandi the news, and Bandi hurried over to see his younger brother.

The brothers were elated to be together again. They spoke for two days — every waking hour. Yitzhak again related everything that had happened to him. Every once in a while a tear flowed down Bandi's cheek as Yitzhak related what happened to Icuka, Hedy, Aliz, himself, and their father. Then Bandi spoke about his service in the Hungarian work brigades and his escape through Romania where he got caught and came within a hair's breath of being executed.

At one point in their discussion, Bandi asked his brother: "Why couldn't you save Father?" It was a turning point. The question made Yitzhak realize that Bandi really couldn't comprehend what they had gone through. He had no answer, but the question hurt him to the core.

Gradually, bit by bit, Bandi told Yitzhak he was a member of the Irgun, the top secret information-gathering agency. Headed by Menachem Begin, this underground organization was responsible for blowing up trains, robbing banks, and kidnapping British officers. One of the main goals of Irgun was to destabilize British rule in Palestine. Once Yitzhak learned all this, he understood a bit better the mindset of his brother. He also realized that Bandi was conservative in his political beliefs, whereas Yitzhak had been inculcated with leftist beliefs. They agreed to disagree on many subjects.

Within two days, Yitzhak once again said farewell to his brother and departed for his ultimate destination: the kibbutz in Merhavija. There, Yitzhak immersed himself in the life of a kibbutz. Hard work was emphasized, and he and the other young people switched jobs every day. They cleared vast fields of stone, transforming the land into tillable soil. Once crops were planted, they harvested cucumbers, tomatoes, and peppers. Large herds of dairy cows had to be fed and tended to. The daily assignments included work in the blacksmith shop where all the agricultural equipment was maintained, repaired, and replaced.

Leftist ideology seeped into every aspect of life at Merhavija, however, and family life was secondary to the building of the kibbutz. It was emphasized on a daily basis that every member of this kibbutz was equally important, but they should forget about their own biological families. Everyone was encouraged to work for the homeland, to die for the homeland. Nothing else mattered. The organizers of the kibbutz knew Bandi well and were aware of his conservative mindset. Yitzhak was told outright to cut all his ties to his brother.

The leaders of the kibbutz simply didn't know how to handle survivors of the Holocaust — they were an enigma. Of the three hundred or so young people at the kibbutz, twenty were survivors and special efforts were made to keep them separated from the rest — and in particular, from the youngsters born on the kibbutz. With time, the survivors were made to feel like they had some incurable infectious disease. The organizers held separate ideological sessions with the survivors, and inculcated them with the belief that the past had no effect on their lives anymore — it was only the future one should focus on.

In September 1946, after six months at Merhavija, Yitzhak quit the kibbutz. He was fed up with being told over and over again that Bandi is "not one of us." They forced him to make a choice between Bandi and the kibbutz, and Yitzhak chose his brother. He was sick of waking up and going to bed to revolutionary music and of the communist ideology seeping into every aspect of his life. He desperately wanted to help build this new Jewish homeland, but realized that he had to find some other way.

Yitzhak went to live with Bandi and his cousin Gyula Berger — they sublet a single room with three cots. He briefly worked as an apprentice in a diamond-cutting factory, but realized this, again, was not something he wanted to do for the rest of his life.

Yitzhak was haunted by a song that was popular in Hungary during the war: "A Cowardly Nation Does Not Have a Country." The words of this song rang in his ears and made him realize that he wanted to become a soldier in service of the Jewish people. He enlisted with the Haganah, which was at the time a "sports organization" working clandestinely on organizing the Jewish armed forces. When he volunteered to join, one of the first questions they asked him was his age.

"I'm seventeen and a half," Yitzhak replied.

Major Yitzhak Livnat with his wife, Ilana, circa 1955.

"Oh no, that won't do. Our minimum age for recruits is eighteen."

Suti gave the recruiters a stern look.

"Okay, if you don't take me, someone else will."

They enlisted him on the spot.

Yitzhak Weisz decided to join the signal corps — the unit that trained in basic signal communications, like Morse code, wireless, and field telephone units. He was chosen for signal-school training because he could read and write Hebrew highly proficiently. A large percentage of the new army recruits were European-born or newcomers who hadn't yet mastered the Hebrew language. In February 1948, Yitzhak was enrolled in a one-month signal course. By the time he finished in March of 1948, the state of Israel was declared and the armed forces were made official. By 1954, Yitzhak Weisz was a major and second in command of the main school for signals.

The signal school organized a Hanukkah party late in November 1953. Yitzhak was one of the hosts. At the party he met a stunning, self-confident young woman named Ilana. Yitzhak's commander introduced her as his younger brother's fiancée and asked Yitzhak to look after her. Yitzhak was happy to comply.

Before Ilana met Yitzak, her parents had warned her about "the walking skeletons" who were arriving from Europe. They were damaged individuals, her parents said. No matter how promising a young man may be, if he was a survivor from Europe, it was best not to get involved with him.

But something about Yitzhak touched Ilana to her very core. There was something different about this man. He was also an officer in the Israeli army — an intriguing man who exuded an inner strength, as if there was nothing in the world that could intimidate him. The more time Ilana spent with Yitzhak, the more she wanted to be with him. When they were apart, Ilana thought of the captivating young officer constantly and began to have grave doubts about her engagement.

Within a few weeks, she broke off her engagement and Ilana and Yitzhak became inseparable. They married a short time later, much to the chagrin of her parents.

With time Ilana found out he was Hungarian and had changed his name to Yitzhak Weisz from Sandor Weisz. Other than that, there was little Yitzhak would share with her about his past. One day she noticed the number tattoo on his upper left arm. When she pleaded with him to tell her more about what he went through during the war, he put his arms around her, hugged her tight, and said very firmly, "At this point I want to forget about everything that happened. I left the damn bloody continent of Europe behind and really never want to see it again. I have buried my past. I love you and want to build a future with you here. That is my story."

chapter 28 | 1946

ON ONE OR TWO evenings during the week, Bela and his friend Laszlo Imre went to a social club where dances were held for young singles. Organized by the Catholic church, it was an ideal place for the two handsome young men to meet eligible young women. The church-sponsored socials were intended to give hope to young people to rebuild their lives, marry, and start families. But most of these young people had seen too much and they were fed up with the deprivation and suffering of the many years of war. The prevalent feeling was still "let's live for the moment because who knows what tomorrow will bring."

Bela and Imre were naturally attracted to the women who wanted to party. When things developed to the point where the female partner indicated her willingness to meet one of them privately, the two young men even had a furnished apartment to take them to. The "love nest" was in an abandoned building with a distinct feeling of openness: the walls had bombed out holes and one wall was completely missing. The entire apartment was like an open, covered veranda. But it had been a relatively warm summer and they could continue to use it for several months into the fall. It was just one of many such buildings, abandoned since being bombed, declared unsafe — but it made a quiet, secure love nest.

With the exception of his exhilarating social life, Bela's life in Budapest became quite routine. He had a steady job at the clock factory — a loathsome, tedious job, but one he hoped would eventually lead to a trade. On Saturdays he continued to travel to the countryside to trade blocks of salt for bacon, butter, ham, and eggs on the black market.

But his sense of security melted away on the day Bela received a letter ordering him to report to the nearby Hungarian army barracks on Ulloi ut. Since the devastating experience in the American-run prisoner-of-war camp, he had sought to divest himself of his military past — to irrevocably cut those ties. Now, it seemed, his years at military school kept a grip on him that he couldn't seem to eradicate.

Bela had little choice. As ordered, he reported to the army barracks. He was directed to the inner office, where he noticed a first lieutenant overseeing the operations.

The first lieutenant looked familiar. Then, slowly it dawned on Bela: the man, named Ferenc Rokus, had dated his sister, Picke, back home. For a while, the two were very much in love.

Bela realized he couldn't greet Rokus or make any sign of recognition. This was simply the reality of their time. If Rokus had become an ardent communist, he couldn't admit to knowing the Aykler's without denouncing them as being part of the old world order. Once the denunciations happened, it would be a matter of hours or days before Bela would be shipped off to labour camps in Siberia. Not a day passed that Bela and Imre didn't learn about someone being taken away, with no hearing and no possibility to defend themselves. He felt faint.

Bela handed over his papers and looked away nonchalantly. Feri looked at him and smiled.

"Don't you recognize me, Berci? How is Picke?"

Bela smiled back, feeling a genuine warmth emanating from Ferenc.

"It's good to see you," he replied. "I believe my parents and Picke are either in Austria or Germany somewhere because they left before me — I've lost touch with them."

After reminiscing a while about the past in Nagyszollos, Bela asked quietly, "Could you tell me what is going to happen? Have I been called in to be sent to Siberia or what?"

"No way," Rokus replied. "There is a shortage of non-commissioned officers and we are reorganizing the army right now and recruiting any-one we think can contribute to that."

Bela was grateful for the reassurance, although still a bit distraught

Bela as a refugee in Austria.

about being forced back into military life. He would desperately miss his lovers in Budapest. Still, it was far better than his job of spray-painting clocks. After registering he received his orders, was given the rank of sergeant, and was told where to pick up his new uniform.

Three days later, Bela reported to a commanding officer at the Nyugati train station at 5:00 a.m. There, on the platform, were hundreds of newly arrived former prisoners of war. Bela first noticed the acrid, choking smell emanating from the group, who had evidently not washed in a long time. Bela learned that most had been in prisoner-of-war camps for at least six months, some as long as one year.

Some wore army issue shirts and pants — their clothes were thread-bare and dirty. They had nothing with them other than the clothes on their backs. The one thing they all had in common was a tin can hang-ing from a button or button hole, attached by a single string or a wire. Bela recognized from his own experience that this tin can was the most prized possession that any prisoner of war could have: a tin can in which they got whatever was being passed out, be it water, a bit of soup, or gruel.

A container to sustain their strength, their life. He saw in them a reflection of his own past life.

Everyone was ordered to board the train. Bela and other non-commissioned officers sat separately in a regular passenger compartment. Bela didn't know the other men — his future colleagues — but was grateful that they were separated from the others and didn't have to endure that unbearable smell.

The former prisoners of war were ordered to board cattle cars, where benches had been loaded. All the passengers on that early morning train, whether in the passenger cars or cattle cars, seemed to be relieved when they realized the train was heading west instead of east. Bela and other non-commissioned officers sat separately in a regular passenger compartment.

Many hours later, the train pulled into Szombathely, where more officers were waiting for them. Sergeant Aykler was assigned a platoon of thirty men. They were given two wagons with four horses to take the platoon to their final destination. The platoon was provided with one machine gun with a short row of twenty-five to thirty bullets and thirty single-bolt action guns (First World War era) to be handed out later to each soldier. Each gun was supplied with only five shots of ammunition. Bela reflected on the symbolic meaning of this: the lack of trust demonstrated by the Russian occupying forces toward the new Hungarian army. In contrast, the Russians had tanks and trucks, and each soldier carried a submachine gun that disgorged seventy-two bullets within seconds.

The final destination of the platoon was a village called Henye. The men were all quartered at homes in the village.

The villagers of Henye reluctantly took the soldiers in — not less than two to a home. Most of the homes did not have furniture or heat in this room. All the soldiers were given iron bed frames and a sack to be filled with straw as a mattress. Bela, their commanding officer, had to make sure everyone was provided with a metal bed. He gave his men a little speech about how they were here to win the villagers over with their correct behaviour, not to cause any problems for the locals.

Bela was assigned the best spare room in the village — a front room in a spacious house owned by a family called Nemeth.

All the men in the platoon were older than their commanding officer by at least three to four years. The army supply depot provided them with rations: two sacks of beans, a sack of flour, and some lard. It wasn't much to feed the men, especially since there was at least a kilogram of small stones in the sacks of beans. Bela thought whoever had sold the army the beans had cheated the supply depot.

Bela learned that the village was constantly being raided — livestock was stolen on a regular basis. It was time for this to stop or they would have nothing to rebuild their farms with.

Bela set up a security zone in the three surrounding villages: Henye, Pac, and Alsohid. The men of his platoon worked in teams, and each team was assigned to the houses at each end of the villages they were determined to defend. There was still a curfew in existence in the region — nothing moved after eleven at night until five in the morning.

Within one week, the platoon captured two Russian deserters who had murdered a peasant in the nearby village. When the prisoners were taken into the nearby Russian command post, the commanding officer took out a pistol and shot one of the men in the head at point-blank range. The other was sent to prison. While the body was being dragged out of his office and the blood washed up, he ordered two glasses and a bottle of vodka to toast the platoon's good work in capturing the renegade soldiers.

Through a translator, Bela was told that these two had been on a rampage, robbing and raping for two weeks. The murder had outraged the Russian commander. Yet, despite sending scouts out to find the deserters, his men were unable to apprehend them.

"Good work," the commander kept repeating. Each time they toasted, he slapped Bela's back in a bold expression of praise and admiration.

The capture of the Russian deserters was a tremendous coup for the platoon.

Instead of being looked upon with suspicion and resentment, they were perceived as the defenders of the local populace. Bela made arrangements to have the men fed at least once a day by the locals.

It was a time of tremendous political turmoil and battles. The Communist Party, backed by the occupying Russian troops, was attempting to consolidate power by first allying themselves with popular parties and then amalgamating these popular parties into the Communist Party.

Each time in his relatively short life that dramatic changes had occurred, Bela had been somehow able to find a way to mould the situation, to transform the disastrous events to his advantage. But this changed when he was named commander of a border guard unit near Szent Gotthard. He realized that he would not be able mould situations any longer — the nature of the work was so black and white, while Bela was beginning to think in greys. The main function of the border guard was to make sure only those citizens with proper identification papers were able to leave the country. The guard duties included sifting through the personal data of each returning refugee, especially anyone with a military past.

The command of the unit was shared with a sergeant named Patak — the two men took turns commanding the border patrols for one week at a time. A small guard house was their command headquarters.

Every ten days, the border guard commanders received updated "watch lists" of those formerly enlisted Hungarian men — officers as well as non-commissioned officers — who were to be taken off the train and interrogated upon their return. The problem was that no one instructed the border guards as to what kind of information they were looking for while interrogating them. While Bela was in command, he identified a few of the men on the watch list, but if they were with their wives and small children, didn't pull them off the train as instructed. In two instances, he found his father's signature on one of the repatriation orders. Bela instantly memorized the place — underneath his father's signature was an Austrian town called Nussbach. Both men in question were low-ranking corporals. That week Bela realized that his days at the border patrol were numbered — surely someone else would soon recognize his father's signature as well.

Each time Bela returned as commander to the inconsequential little border-crossing station, he started to suspect that something was amiss with his co-commander Patak. The men assigned to Patak would complain bitterly to anyone who would listen about his brutality. They said Patak would order men and women off the train on a whim, hardly looking at

Susan M. Papp

Hedy in Canada, circa 1960.

the list. After finding blood spattered in several areas, Bela suspected that there was truth in what he had heard about the brutal rapes and beatings that took place. But Bela wasn't supposed to listen to rumours, so he snuck back to the guard house one evening to surreptitiously find out if he could verify what the men were saying. A woman's heartbreaking cries could be heard from a distance. Bela didn't go to look through the window — he couldn't bear to listen. The screams haunted him all night, long after he was kilometres away.

The next day, Bela confronted Patak. He couldn't report what he had heard — he wasn't supposed to be near there — but he could make a formal complaint about the blood inside the guard house. Possibly it would end there.

"According to article 5.1 of the guard rulebook," he began, maintaining an air of professionalism, "we are commanded to hand back the station house in clean and good order."

Patak looked up at Aykler.

"What the fuck are you talking about?" he replied briskly.

Bela realized Patak was in a fowl mood, but persisted.

"For the past couple of times you have handed the command of the border post over to me, this guard house has been filthy, sprayed with —"

Before he ended his sentence, Patak clenched his teeth and yelled, "Why you little spoiled shit! You were barely out of diapers when I was already in the army." Then, without a moment's hesitation, he slapped Bela across the face with a force that made him briefly lose his balance, but didn't knock him down.

Bela had had it with the cruelty of sadists like Patak. The screams of the defenceless woman as she was being assaulted were still ringing in his ears, and the knowledge of Patak's brutality with other victims fuelled his rage. He jumped on top of Patak, grabbed his head with both hands, and smashed it against the cold concrete floor. Over and over and over again, Bela smashed Patak's head on the floor until three of the men from his platoon came in and physically pulled him off.

An ambulance was called, and Patak was taken to the nearby hospital. Within a few hours, after changing his bloodied clothes, Bela went to one of his superior officers and told him what had happened. The officer advised Bela to leave the country immediately, but did give him written permission for a leave for the purpose of "work study."

Bela told his platoon guarding the border that night that he was leaving the country permanently. The moon was just bright enough as he walked west toward Austria. It was a relatively mild November evening. With each step he hoped one of his men would shoot him in the back — after all, they would have been justified, since he was escaping across the border. For the second or third or fourth time in his life — he had lost count — Bela just wanted it all to end. He wanted to die. But the shot never came.

Bela Aykler, dressed as a member of the Canadian Scottish reserve in Cornwall, Ontario.

chapter 29 | 1947—1948

Nussbach, Austria
November 1947

Dearest Hedy,

    Father passed away at the end of November. He was sixty-one. Another shock to the family, especially my younger brother, Bela. I have to tell you honestly, the combined forty-two years of military service broke our father. He was a ghost of his former self here in Austria.

    The day he passed away, he went to see his doctor, a military surgeon, a Dr. Szollosi. They say he requested a shot of some kind — his heart had been ailing. By the time he returned home, he collapsed on the cot, said goodbye, closed his eyes, and died.

    My mother and my sister prepared him for the burial, and washed and dressed him in his finest dress uniform. All his medals were gleaming on his chest for the few local farmers who came to see him and pay their respects. I hammered together a simple wooden coffin, and a nearby family donated a single plot in the local cemetery. We had no money to pay the priest who said the burial mass, but we promised we would pay him as soon as we could. From the surrounding farms, people came to the house, graciously offering milk, sugar, and flour so that Picke and my mother could make a few pastries. After the funeral, we were able to invite some of these kind people over for tea.

I will stay and help my mother for a few more months, but in February I am determined to leave for Paris, where friends of ours have already secured a visa and passage to Argentina. I am told they are looking for qualified, European-trained engineers in Argentina. I am willing to go anywhere where hard work is rewarded and a man is able to make something of himself.

I am still desperately awaiting news from you. I need you more than ever.

Your loving fiancé,
Tibor

Paris, 1948
Spring

Dearest Hedy,

One of the most difficult things about living in Paris is that I am reminded each minute, hour, and day that I am alone here. It is a city full of lovers and it is difficult to be reminded of the state of my sorrowful heart each time I take a walk or look out the window.

I have applied for a visa to go to Argentina, and while I am waiting for the bureaucrats to do their job, I wander the streets by day and night. I have been told that I am scheduled to leave aboard the ship Partizanka *in two weeks, on May 9. While I wait, unfortunately, I am unable to get any kind of work visa. There are literally hundreds of thousands of refugees seeking jobs while their cases are being heard and processed by third countries. It's very hard to be poor in Paris, especially when one is alone.*

My brother, Bela, is now working for the United States Army. He hopes to gain entry to either the United States or Canada through his connections. Think of it: the great northern country of Canada.

275

I've always thought of it as the land of ice and snow, but I hear it is an enormous country with a small population. They are looking for farm labourers and domestics. I am neither. We've decided that when I land in Argentina, or Bela in Canada, whoever gets settled sooner will eventually sponsor the rest of the family.

I have received a letter from Bandi. He mentions you only in passing, that you are healthy and living in Czechoslovakia. That's all. It seemed to me that there must have been further news that he simply doesn't want to divulge. I don't understand why I haven't heard from you, but I don't blame you for that. Possibly you have simply fallen out of love with me. Until I hear officially from you that it is over, I will continue to dream and hope.

With much love,
Tibor

chapter 30 | 1948

THE *MARINE PERCH* ARRIVED in Halifax early in the morning on July 25, 1948 and docked at a place called Pier 21. The pier was shrouded in mist, and it was still dark. Bela couldn't believe they had actually arrived at a city — it looked like a deserted rocky outpost. He could barely make out a few surrounding warehouses. Many of the sea-weary passengers skipped the breakfast being served on board, their stomachs churning with excitement and apprehension.

The ship was eerily quiet. Most people had slept little, knowing their arrival to their new homeland was just a few hours away. They were elated that the frequently rough seagoing journey was coming to an end. That expectation soon turned to disappointment and depression, however, on seeing the port of Halifax.

A small group of stern-looking immigration officers stood waiting for them as they disembarked. The officers got to work, checking lists, making sure everyone's papers were in order, handing out tags. The tags were affixed to the jacket or blouse of each newly arrived passenger, like luggage identification labels — everyone was "labelled" according to destination.

Bela's tag read "Cornwall Employment Office."

The immigration officers seemed anxious to process the group quickly — they barely looked up at them as they checked for their names on the lists. No one said any welcoming words, no one smiled.

Where had they come to? After leaving the beautiful port of Genoa, Bela thought they had arrived at the ends of the earth.

There was little processing to be done — they had passed their medical exams in Europe. After they received their tags they walked through the warehouse and were directed to board trains standing behind Pier 21. The individual train cars were elegantly emblazoned with "Canadian National Railway."

Bela grabbed a window seat in a compartment with his fellow Hungarians. The inside of the train was sweltering. Bela had put on his dress pants, black shoes, and a white shirt in preparation of meeting his new employer. The sweat was already gathering in the small of his back.

Officially, Canada took in 10,151 Hungarian displaced persons between 1948 and 1952. Displaced persons could enter Canada under two schemes: the Close Relative Scheme, whereby an individual could be nominated by relatives living in Canada, and the Specialized Workers Scheme, whereby immigrants were contracted to work in a specific industry for one year. Canada required men for employment in heavy industry, farm labour, rural construction work, building construction, lumber camps, and mines.

At mid-morning the train pulled out of the station and headed west, they passed through what must have been the outer edge of Halifax. Houses made of wood, here and there painted light blue and green, occasionally yellow. Hardly a building of note to be seen. An ad for Black Cat cigarettes painted on the side of a garage. In a short time, there were fewer and fewer houses. The train ploughed through seemingly endless low-growing brush, trees, and bushes, rushing past glimmering lakes and over rivers.

The locomotive slowed each time they passed through a smaller community. Bela was surprised to see black people in front of tiny houses that looked more like sheds. Little children were playing in front. The adults stared silently and sadly at the train as it passed, as if they wanted to get on board themselves.

They travelled all that day, and through the night, making a number of stops along the way, arriving in Montreal some twenty-four hours later.

When they finally arrived in Montreal, Bela felt relieved that there was life in this country: they rode past roads with row upon row of big automobiles, the kind military officers rode around in in Europe, and saw multi-storey buildings. As the train slowed, they saw the sidewalks were crowded with elegantly dressed people.

Bela's friend, Janos, the mechanic, who had been dozing through most of the journey, suddenly became animated.

"See that?" He was pointing to a large black sedan. "That's the newest Ford. I read about that one in Europe. It has a lounge car interior, and hydra coil for a smoother ride in front."

Bela didn't know what any of that meant, but nodded anyway.

As they pulled into Montreal's massive train station, they saw there were dozens of lines and thousands of people milling about, conductors blowing whistles, couples hugging and saying goodbye, children crying.

Another passenger, Dora, had been translating French billboards along the way. As the train came to a full stop in the station, she suddenly became gravely quiet. Then she started to quietly translate a billboard at the station, and something in the timbre of her voice forced everyone to become silent.

"The Liberals will allow into our country 180,000 immigrants who will grab your homes, your businesses, your work, your capital, your farms, your future, your positions. Duplessis won't bring or allow —" Dora stopped and questioned her translation, then continued after taking a breath. "Any more immigrants."

"Who is Duplessis?" someone asked.

But no one in the compartment knew the answer. They sat quietly and pondered the message — the excitement of arriving in Montreal vanished.

The trip to Cornwall from Montreal was forty minutes, just on the Quebec-Ontario border, but in Ontario. Bela and his travel companions were pleased to get off the train. It was hot, they had slept little, and they were hungry.

Cornwall must have been even smaller than Halifax. Two men in uniform were there to greet the seven Hungarian men who got off the train. They all had contracts to work as farm labourers for one year.

One of the uniformed men asked, "Do any of you speak English?"

Bela raised his hand a bit and the official said, "Okay, you'll be our translator. Will you tell everyone to follow me?"

Bela translated.

The seven men were led to a truck, benches on two sides on the inside, light coming from one window in the back. They sat quietly, tired from their long journey. The short ride led to the employment office. The first person Bela noticed was a bald short man with wire-rimmed glasses pacing up and down impatiently outside the office. When he saw the group coming toward him, he stopped and grimaced, looking at his watch.

"You told me they would arrive by nine this morning," the bald, short man barked at the official. He spoke about them as if they weren't yet there.

"I told you, Mr. McGee. These things cannot be predicted precisely. The train was late."

The new arrivals were lined up. Other local men started to arrive.

"Does anyone speak English?" the bald man McGee asked.

"I do," Bela said tentatively.

McGee looked at Bela's form and asked, "What's your name?"

"Albert."

"So, you're Bert," he replied.

Bela nodded.

McGee went over to one of the officials, signed some papers, then told "Bert" to come with him.

Bela was led to a blue Ford Fairlane covered in dust. He recognized the car from the many American magazines he had seen in Europe.

McGee started the engine and drove. The engine sputtered a bit, then ran smoothly.

"What nationality are you?" McGee asked, giving Bela a sidelong glance.

"Hungarian."

"So, you are the enemy."

"No," Bela tried to explain. "Ex-enemy."

McGee's lip hardened.

"No," McGee remained adamant. "Enemy."

Bela again tried to argue the point and clarify his official status.

"The war is over, and my official status is 'ex-enemy.'"

"No, no, you're wrong," McGee stated in deliberate manner, without taking his attention from the road. "The war is just starting between you and me."

Bela glanced at this bald man and thought he undoubtedly had a small brain to match his small body.

He realized there was nothing further to say.

What was there to argue with someone who was well-sheltered from it all here in Canada?

Why should I bother, Bela thought, explaining to him what it feels like to lose your home, your country, to have your family ripped up and scattered about in all directions?

They sat in silence. The car passed a sign that read, "BAINSVILLE," then shortly afterward McGee turned down a short driveway and stopped before a small, ordinary farmhouse. It was midday.

McGee showed Bela to his room and said, "Get changed. We're going to bring in some hay."

Bela's little room was tacked on to the house like an afterthought. It was built above the mudroom, and the stairs leading up to it opened from the kitchen. It had a tin roof. It contained a bed, a chair, and nothing else. The room was sweltering.

He changed and found a washroom where he threw some cold water on his face and took a drink with cupped hands directly from the faucet, giving some relief to the parched feeling in his mouth and throat.

Suppressing his hunger, Bela gritted his teeth. "If it's war the old man wants," he decided, "then it's war he shall have."

chapter 31 | 1950

Resistencia, Argentina
July 29, 1950

Dearest Hedy,

I am writing this letter to you on my thirty-first birthday, my heart and mind still immersed in thoughts of you.

I feel I have some good news to tell you: I finally have a well-paying job in my field, as an engineer working for the company hired to prepare the work for building a hydroelectric dam at Iguazu. I am told by my colleagues that Iguazu is an amazing, powerful, thundering waterfall and that the work to harness its powerful force for electricity will be a marvel of mankind.

We are en route to the majestic falls in the jungle more than two thousand kilometres away, and I honestly can say that this has already turned out to be an amazing adventure. There are ten of us — all engineers — travelling in five black sedans, similar to the large Tatra sedans we knew at home. The district around Resistencia, where I am writing this letter, is very flat. The road runs directly parallel with the railway lines. There are hardly any residents in this region — we pass a few houses here and there every forty or fifty kilometres or so. The colour of the earth has been variable as we go further and further north from Buenos Aires. First it was red, then black, now it is the grey colour of clay earth.

Occasionally we will see a gaucho riding past us, always in a hurry, rushing to wherever gauchos rush to in great urgency — probably to some emergency with his grazing cattle.

The wildlife is unusual as well: enormous birds with long legs making the most horrible screeching noises. Others sit, roosting on top of telephone poles, just watching us, waiting for us to pass. I've lost count of all the snakes we've seen, and when it rains, as it often does, you really have to hurry to higher ground, as they will float by, pushed and pulled by the rushing water. It is an amazing world, and I am quite enjoying its raw beauty.

At present it is thirty-three degrees Celsius with a bit of a breeze, which makes the temperature quite comfortable. The dust is overwhelming at times and the road can be quite rough, as it is not really a man-made road, just a path beaten down by cars and trucks. We pass many overturned vehicles, which always serves as a warning for our drivers to slow down and take it easy. Our cars are so packed with gear and supplies that they really can't speed anyway. Special soldiers from the Argentine army are escorting us, guarding us along the way. It is reassuring to have them along, as bandits are quite common along this route.

When the rain comes, we have to wait for hours, sometimes days, as the "road" becomes quite impassable. Yesterday, in a place called San Nicolau, I got out of the car for just two minutes to check out a road sign, and got completely soaked when the water flooded into my boots from the downpour. As soon as I was able, I changed my wet clothes, and my colleagues passed over a shot of brandy.

The consumption of alcohol is otherwise forbidden for the crew and closely monitored, but they knew it was my birthday and shared one drink with me — to congratulate me on getting this far in life, I guess. If only they knew how my heart aches still because of the most poignant loss in my life. I feel the heartache every day and realize, with the greatest sadness, that you will probably get on with your life — possibly you have already forgotten me.

When we left Resistencia, we took a ferry to Corrientes, crossing the Parana River. What a breathtakingly beautiful sight to behold:

perfectly calm water, lush vegetation on each side of the river, with the occasional cawing of a bird. This is paradise! I feel you with me each time I see such stunning sights. Probably just wishful thinking. I wish I could empty you from my mind, my heart, but I can't. I can't imagine loving another human being was meant to end with such a feeling of desolation and pain.

I'm still sorting through all these feelings. When darkness descends on the region, it is pitch black, so much so that I cannot see my fingers in front of my face. Once the electricity gets turned on, the crew makes dinner and usually retires to bed directly after eating. I find that I am completely exhausted by nightfall.

With much love
Tibor

chapter 32 | 1956

ALTHOUGH ILANA REALIZED THAT what her husband had been through during the war was a taboo subject between them, Yitzhak was otherwise a loving husband and father to their ever-expanding family. Their first son was born in 1955, followed by two more sons and a daughter.

Hedy, her husband, Emil, and little daughter, Chaviva, came to Israel in the early 1950s. They intended to stay and make a new life for themselves in the new Jewish homeland. Hedy hardly recognized the skinny little brother she had last seen in January of 1945. He was now a self-confident, rugged-looking soldier. It was a joyous reunion. Emil wanted to join the army while retaining his rank of major from years of service in the Czech army and was very disappointed when the Israeli military system refused this request. Emil found the transition to living in Israel to be too difficult, and they moved on to Canada after a few years.

Major Yitzhak Weisz had already been named to the rank of lieutenant colonel — the rank was to become official in 1957. But in 1956, after serving ten years in the army, Yitzhak applied for a low-interest loan from the army in order to buy a home. Despite promises that he would be eligible for such a loan, the application was turned down.

When Yitzhak left the army, determined to find some means of supporting his family, Bandi invited him to join him in building a transportation business. Yitzhak started driving a truck to study the business from the bottom up. In the late 1960s, Yitzhak and Bandi changed their family name from Weisz to Livnat.

The business thrived, and began specializing in trucks, cranes, and the logistics of moving shipments from one place to another.

Yitzhak Livnat began to travel regularly to Europe on business. Within a few years, he and Ilana enjoyed several short holidays in Europe. One of their first trips together took them to Zurich, Switzerland.

Ilana knew instinctively that her husband was hiding some horrific scars from the war. Being a perceptive wife, she also knew that by entombing those scars they would only fester and grow, like a boil or infection left untreated. She realized the boil that represented his scars had to be lanced, but still didn't know how to quite go about it.

In Zurich, an opportunity presented itself. Ilana noticed that a nearby restaurant was promoting Hungarian cuisine and folklore for one week. The brochure was brightly coloured — red, white, and green — with pictures of buxom young women with long braids, in national dress, holding platefuls of enticing delicacies: cabbage rolls, stews rich with red paprika, mouth-watering sausages. Across the top of the brochure was written, "Come and spend an evening in Hungary without ever leaving Switzerland."

That afternoon, when Yitzhak came back from his business meetings, Ilana was waiting with a proposal.

"I want to invite you out for dinner tonight, darling," she said warmly.

"Fine," Yitzhak replied. "Is it a special occasion?"

"No, nothing special," she replied. "But if you accept my invitation, then it has to be my choice of restaurant."

As they walked into the restaurant later that evening, Yitzhak stopped when he read the sign promoting the Hungarian event. He turned to his wife with a stern look in his deep brown eyes. Ilana touched her husband's arm and whispered, "Remember, you promised: the place would be my choice." He reflected a moment, then nodded for her to proceed through the doors.

Comely young women with braided hair, dressed in a stylized Hungarian folk costume, were offering free samples of Vilmos pear liqueur as an aperitif to everyone who walked in the door. Ilana glanced at her husband inquiringly. Yitzhak wasn't interested — he walked right by them. In a distant corner of the restaurant, a gypsy ensemble played, moving from one table to the next.

Yitzhak sat stone-faced as Ilana ordered one delicacy after another. For starters, she requested an appetizer portion of goose-liver pate with sweet green peppers and rye toast. Next, cabbage rolls with sausage and sour cream. Then, for the main course, veal paprikash with delicate egg dumplings. Initially Yitzhak had an air about him as if he was determined to get through this, but certainly wasn't going to enjoy it. By the time they'd had their third glass of wine, he was noticeably more relaxed, though still reserved.

The gypsy ensemble worked their way through the spacious restaurant, playing songs requested by the patrons. The gypsies noticed Yitzhak sitting with his wife at one of the tables. Normally the lead violinist, or *primas,* had an amazing ability to sense people who didn't want the musicians around them and would steer clear of such tables. But there was something so Hungarian looking about Yitzhak. Instinctively, the *primas* began to play Hungarian folk songs.

Yitzhak tried to look elsewhere, avoiding the eyes of the violinist, but he couldn't cover his ears and block out the song that went directly to the core of his heart. The third song the violinist began to play so masterfully was the song his mother had sung practically every day. The song, entitled "The Old Gypsy," was her song; he had learned the melody and lyrics from her as a child. Memories of his happy childhood flooded back. He was Suti back in Nagyszollos, and his mother was pinning wash to the clothesline. He was playing with Icuka among the wet and drying sheets, both of them squealing with laughter. The images of his mother and little sister — brought back by the music — were too vivid to block out.

Tears started trickling down his face, unleashing a veritable flood. His shoulders were shaking. With his eyes closed, more images flooded forward: visuals of the entire family sitting in the kitchen, of his father playing the violin, mother's rich melodious voice singing along. The gypsies kept playing, and Yitzhak continued crying, quite loudly now. Ilana sat calmly, remaining apparently unperturbed by her husband's uncontrolled sobbing. She knew it was therapeutic. The fortress her husband had built around his own childhood memories had finally been shattered. The healing of his long-suffering heart could finally begin.

Tibor Schroeder and his wife, Eva, circa 1960.

chapter 33 | june 1967

THE TRAIN TO MONTREAL left Union Station in Toronto at 8:00 a.m. Tibor glanced at his watch, and although he had calculated the travel time many times already, he reassured himself that the journey to Montreal would take six hours. He would arrive by 2:00 p.m., if all went well.

After more than twenty years, he was finally going to see Hedy again.

Tibor settled into a seat facing east. He always liked facing the direction he was travelling.

The song he heard late last night, "King of the Road," was still ringing in his ears. He had continued his lifelong hobby of listening to the newest songs. He had a new record player and was building a new collection of the latest recordings. Written and recorded by Roger Miller, Tibor felt the lyrics summarized his life — the life of a nomad, a wanderer.

Tibor glanced out the window and noticed an entire high school band on the platform. They were probably travelling to Expo 67, the international world's fair in Montreal, he thought. Clad in burgundy school uniforms, they carried their band dresses on hangars protected with plastic wrap. Some of the students transported small cases for violins, clarinets, and horn instruments; others lugged enormous cases for tubas, drum sets, and bass violas. They must have occupied several other cars, thought Tibor, as only a few students occupied some of the seats in the same compartment.

Tibor enjoyed the fact that he was a citizen of such a young country. Other than native Indian tribes, it was a country full of citizens making a new beginning. Expo 67 was created to celebrate Canada's centenary. The world's fair was an engineering marvel — built in record time, an unbelievable three years. The world seemed to be enamoured with Canada's newness. The country's bold new enterprise, Expo 67, attracted millions from around the globe.

Tibor had brought along a few letters in his satchel — letters he had written to Hedy while in Argentina, but had never sent. The letter eased the pain of his then-suffering heart. Tibor wasn't sure why he brought them along — surely he would never show them to Hedy.

Tibor had eventually found out from Bandi, living in Tel Aviv, that Hedy had married a man called Emil Hosek. He was devastated when he found out about the marriage and it took many years to get over the pain. He rehearsed in his own mind what he would not say to Hedy when they met. There would be no recriminations. He would not ask why she didn't attempt to contact him after the war ended or why she married Emil so hastily.

Bandi wrote Tibor a letter in which he told of Hedy's life in Canada, her daughter, and the death of her husband from cancer. Tibor wrote to Bandi, asking if it would be possible for him to contact Hedy. Bandi suggested he write to her directly, and gave him Hedy's address. He debated with himself for days before taking pen to paper and writing a few lines. To his great astonishment, she replied, and sounded interested in seeing him as well. Tibor was overjoyed when she invited him to Montreal for a visit.

How differently their lives would have turned out if ...

He blocked out the thoughts almost as quickly as they came to him. No recriminations, no speculating about the past, no could-haves, would-haves, should-haves.

Tibor was forty-seven years old and still in good physical condition. The years immediately following the end of the war had been the most difficult. He had lived in Hungary, Austria, and Paris, France. He had felt in his heart that Hedy was alive and also living somewhere in Europe, yet he had no means of contacting her. Then it dawned on him that she didn't want to contact him and that realization was more hurtful than anything. Then Tibor also learned the depth of the tragedy of what had happened to her, and to her entire family. With that knowledge came a deep understanding and acceptance of whatever she decided. He respected and loved her too much not to abide by her wishes.

The love became muted and was pushed to the back of his mind, into the distant corners of his heart. He wanted to emigrate to one of the furthest corners of the globe, hoping that the thousands of kilometres would eventually fade the memories and dull the pain. To further distract himself, he even had brief affairs with several stunning Argentinian women. But all his efforts to obliterate the memory of the one great love of his life seemed to only succeed in numbing the pain, and he was never able to forget about it completely.

Tibor began munching on a chocolate bar and thought about those difficult years in Argentina, where he experienced the most brutal working conditions of his life. They worked in the jungle building a hydro-electric dam near Iguazu. No shoes, boots, or materials existed that could keep their feet dry. The athlete's foot fungus, or "jungle rot," as they called it, seemed to eat through each layer of skin. The heat of summer was consistently oppressive: forty degrees Celsius in the shade. The workers couldn't eat or drink water fast enough — the environment sucked the energy and liquid out of them as quickly as they ingested it. Tibor lost many of his teeth.

If one could tolerate the endless days of living in the jungle heat and bone-numbing isolation, the pay in the end was well worth it. After Tibor settled, he sponsored his mother, sister, Picke, and brother-in-law, Erno, to join him in Argentina. Picke and Erno were expecting their first-born. They all lived in Buenos Aires and when Tibor could get out of the rainforest to the city on leave, they were together as a family. These occasions helped alleviate the never-ending feeling of loneliness that gnawed away at his soul.

Bela had been granted immigrant status in Canada, on the opposite end of the hemisphere.

After several years of back-breaking work as a farm labourer, Bela established himself as a tobacco farmer near a place called Delhi in Ontario. After he bought his first house, he sponsored the family and they all came to Canada. Tibor was fortunate to find work in Toronto and met his wife, Eva, a divorcee with a young son. Eva was a vivacious woman with a voluptuous figure and legs that were seemingly endless.

Tibor and Eva were married in 1954. What a day full of promise and expectations! Their daughter, Judy, was born two years later.

On the train, Tibor thought about what a tremendous amount of joy Judy had brought into his life. An inquisitive and sensitive child, Judy had lovely brown eyes and a heartwarming smile. Tibor and Eva learned early in their marriage that if there was a misunderstanding between them, they could never argue in front of Judy. The dear, sweet child would burst into tears at the slightest argument. Tibor thought of his daughter as a gentle soul who needed tender nurturing.

When they were first married, Eva woke night after night to his nightmares. He was yelling at ghosts, screaming, waking up drenched in sweat. Once he was awake, he refused to talk about the images haunting him. Tibor knew he had lingering nightmares from the war, but didn't realize until he was married how frequently they still dominated his dreams. After Judy was born, they agreed to sleep in separate bedrooms. Eventually, they drifted apart. Tibor became completely absorbed with his work as an engineer. Even after he came home from his day job, he retired to the basement after dinner, where he set up a workshop for carpentry projects. Lately, he had begun to work in creating decorative lamps and plant holders out of wrought iron. It calmed him to create objects with his hands. He concentrated on staying busy and focused.

The couple lived disparate lives under one roof, and maintained the guise of marriage for the sake of their much-loved daughter.

The trip passed relatively quickly, thanks to the constant activity of the high-school band. It was entertaining to listen to them teasing each other, telling jokes, and sharing lunches. Tibor concentrated on not closing his eyes; that's when all the loving images of Hedy came drifting back to his mind. How things could have been, should have been ... indeed.

When the train arrived in Montreal, he managed to find rue Wilderton, number 6280, easily enough. It was strange to observe the different building styles in this city — the stairways to the upstairs apartments were outside the two-storey structures. Tibor had never seen anything like that anywhere else in the world.

He stood outside the building where she lived for a while just watching, observing the sounds and sights of the street. It was summertime and the tree-lined thoroughfare was crowded with a group of children playing ball. One line of a poem by Petofi ran through his head — it was one that they had often recited to each other, especially the last line: "and I clung to her lips silently, like fruit on a tree."

The poem was about a young man on a train, pondering about what his first words would be to his mother, who he hadn't seen for years. At the end of the poem, all the rehearsed opening sentences went out the window as he flew to her arms.

Finally, Tibor gathered his courage, walked up to the front door, and knocked gently.

After a few seconds, Hedy opened the door.

They stood silently watching each other for a few seconds. Tibor looked into her eyes — they were as captivating as ever. Neither said a word. There in the doorway, he put out his arms and they melted into each other's embrace.

"Oh, Tibor," he heard her say over and over.

"My lovely Hedy," he whispered. They stood there, locked in each others arms for what must have seemed to the nosy neighbours a very long time.

Hedy was the first to pull back after the long embrace. She turned away to wipe the tears from her face.

"Let me make you some tea," she said. "You must be parched from the long train ride."

Tibor nodded, still choked up with emotion. With that she went into the kitchen.

Tibor collected himself, and wiped his tears with a handkerchief while she put the kettle on to boil. He looked around — the apartment was small and sparsely furnished, with lots of bookcases filled with books. One chaise-longue chair stood in the corner of the room, with a beige-coloured two-seater couch and Swedish style teak coffee table in the centre. He noticed a framed picture of Hedy and what must have been her little girl as a toddler.

Hedy came back with a pot of tea, two cups and saucers, and a plate of almond cookies. She began to set the dishes out on the coffee table in front of them. Noticing that Tibor had been looking at the picture she said, "Her name is Chaviva, now twenty years old. A real blessing in my life."

"I know how wonderful daughters are. I have one as well," Tibor replied. "Her name is Judy — she's ten."

Hedy began to pour the tea. They sat quietly and talked about the joys of children.

Tibor realized there was little they had to explain to each other despite the years of separation. They didn't owe each other explanations or apologies. Life simply happened. They were separated by disastrous historical events and had to continue on with their lives. Tibor would probably never find out what made her marry someone else following the end of the war, but what would it matter today if she did divulge what went through her head and heart in those days, months, and years following the war? How could he now even begin to comprehend what she had been through?

But there were some things Tibor wanted to tell her; things he had to say.

"Hedy, I wanted to tell you about ...," he began, then stopped. A key turned in the door, the door opened, and a confident young woman walked in.

"Hello, my darling," Hedy said.

The young woman smiled and gave her mother a kiss and a hug, then looked at Tibor.

"Do you know who this is, love?" Hedy asked.

The young girl looked at her mother's smile, then at the man sitting on their couch, and replied, "This must be Tibor!"

The two of them smiled at each other, then at Tibor. She leaned over, shook his hand, gave him a kiss on the cheek, and said, "Hello, my name is Chaviva."

He was amazed. Chaviva had her mother's big round eyes and thick hair.

"But how did she know? She's never seen me," he queried.

"You know, a mother and daughter share many wonderful secrets," Hedy said, smiling.

They exchanged stories about their new lives in Canada, how interesting it was that they had both ended up here. They reminisced about growing up in Nagyszollos and laughed about the stories of the humorous characters of the town. Tibor asked about Suti and Aliz, Hedy inquired about Bela and Picke. At suppertime, they walked down the street to an Italian pizzeria. The place had a homey, neighbourhood atmosphere to it with checkered tablecloths and candles on each table. Frank Sinatra's "September of My Years" was playing on the record player. Tibor, Hedy, and Chaviva ordered pasta. Tibor sat across from Hedy and kept glancing at her, amazed at how she hadn't changed a bit. They shared a half litre of wine.

Tibor and Hedy ordered espresso, all of them had Italian ice cream — spumoni for dessert. Chaviva regaled them with stories of her school friends. It was obvious that she had inherited her mother's intelligence and quick wit. When they returned, they sat on the wrought-iron steps watching the children play in the streets. The evening was still pleasant, and dusk was long in its shadows. Hedy's face had a special glow in this light. They sat, side by side, arms intertwined. Chaviva was chatting with two friends who had come by to visit.

"You know, Hedy," Tibor whispered, "there is the saying: 'all is not lost that is delayed.'"

Hedy looked at him with a dreamy smile.

"It's been such a wonderful day."

Tibor stared at her eyes and continued with a very steady voice. "It would just take one word from you my dearest Hedy ... I would be here in a second."

A single tear inadvertently rolled down her cheek.

Tibor grabbed his handkerchief and tenderly wiped the tear.

He took her hand, kissed it, and held it for a very long time.

She never answered.

epilogue

TIBOR SCHROEDER PASSED AWAY in January 1982 in Toronto at the age of sixty-three from cancer. He was married twice in Canada. His only daughter, Judy, converted and married a Jewish man, Martin Chasson, in 1997.

Hedy Weisz lives in New York City. After her husband, Emil Hosek, passed away in 1966, she decided that she didn't want to marry again. Friends persisted, trying to arrange dates for her. It was only after friends informed her that they had set up a special date with a man called Tibor that she agreed to meet the man. She married Tibor Pivko in 1977.

Hedy's daughter is Chaviva Hosek, who at the time of the publication of this book is the president of the Canadian Institute for Advanced Research. During the prime ministership of Jean Chretien, she headed the Office of Research for the Canadian government. Chaviva married a Christian man — Alan Pearson — in 1979.

Bela Aykler built a real estate firm in Toronto, specializing in residential development and property management. He still works with his two sons and grandsons in running the business. In 1988 he married his second wife, Susan. Together, in 1994, they initiated the Students Without Boundaries program, which brings together 135 students who live in minority status in east-central Europe with students from Canada. In 2008, the program celebrated its fifteenth year — over two thousand students from five different countries, including Canada, have taken part.

Yitzhak Livnat, together with his brother, Bandi, built a successful transportation, shipping, and logistics business. His sons have branched out to run their own enterprises. Today, he spends his time travelling the world with his wife, Ilana, scouring archives, gathering the pieces of his family's lost past.

Yitzhak Livnat first came to the closing ceremony of the Students Without Boundaries program in 1997 after hearing of the program from his sister, Hedy. Since that time he has become an ardent supporter of the program and sponsors many of the students from Karpatalja. Each year, all of the participants are told what he went through when he was fourteen. He is a member of the board of directors of the Rakoczi Foundation of Canada, which is the sponsoring organization of Students Without Boundaries.

Bela Aykler and Yitzhak Livnat have both been granted the Officer's Cross of Merit from the Republic of Hungary for their outstanding business accomplishments. Neither has been acknowledged for their support of the education of Hungarian youth worldwide.

In addition to the citizenship from their adopted countries, Aykler and Livnat have requested the return of their Hungarian citizenship. Both applications have been denied.

suggested further reading

Applebaum, Anne. *Gulag: A History*. New York: Anchor Books, 2004.

Bacque, James. *Crimes and Mercies*. Vancouver: Talonbooks, 2007.

____. *Other Losses*. Toronto: Fenn Publishing Company, 1999.

Bakó, Ágnes, and Éva Szabó and Verő Gábor, eds. *Emlékezések*. Budapest: Magyar Auschwitz Alapitvany–Holocaust Dokumentácios Központ, 1995.

Braham, Randolph L. *The Politics of Genocide*. Vols. 1 and 2. New York: Columbia University Press, 1981.

Carp, Matatias. *Holocaust in Rumania 1940–1944*. Budapest: Primor Publishing, 1994.

Csernicskó, István, and Ildikó Orosz. *The Hungarians in Transcarpathia*. Budapest: Tinta Publishers, 1999.

Dupka, György. *Kárpátaljai Magyar Gulag Lexikon*. Budapest: Intermix Kiadó Ungvar, 1999.

____. *Keressétek fel a sirom, Szolyvai Emlékkönyv 1944–1959*. Budapest: Intermix Kiado, 2004.

Fedinec, Csilla. *A kárpátaljai magyarság történeti kronologiája 1918–1944.* Budapest: Nemzeti Kulturális Örökség Minisztériuma, 2002.

____. *Iratok a kárpátaljai magyarság történetéhez 1918–1944.* Budapest: Fórum Kisebbségkutató Intézet, 2004.

Friedrich, Otto. *The Kingdom of Auschwitz.* New York: HarperCollins, 1982.

Gilbert, Martin. *The Jews in the Twentieth Century.* London: Endeavour Group, 2001.

Gutman, Israel, and Bella Gutterman, eds. *Az Auschwitz Album: Egy transzport története.* Tel Aviv, Israel: Yad Vashem and Auschwitz-Birkenau Állami Múzeum, n.d.

Hokky, Charles J. Senator. *Ruthenia: Spearhead Toward the West.* Gainesville, FL: Danubian Research and Information Center, 1966.

Jan Van Pelt, Robert, and Deborah Dwork. *Auschwitz.* London: W.W. Norton, 1996.

Jelinek, Yeshayahu A. *The Carpathian Diaspora.* New York: Columbia University Press, 2007.

Kertész, Imre. *Fateless.* Evanston, IL: Northwestern University Press, 1992.

Kontler, László. *A History of Hungary.* Budapest: Atlantisz Könyvkiadó, 2002.

Lendvai, Paul. *The Hungarians: A Thousand Years of Victory in Defeat.* Princeton, NJ: Princeton University Press, 1999.

Susan M. Papp

MacMillan, Margaret. *Paris 1919: Six Months That Changed the World*. New York: Random House, 2003.

Magocsi, Paul Robert. *Historical Atlas of Central Europe*. Toronto: University of Toronto Press, 1993.

_____. *The People from Nowhere*. V. Padiak Publishers, 2006.

Marrus, Michael R. *The Holocaust in History*. Toronto: Key Porter, 2000.

Megged, Aharon. *The Story of the Selvino Children: Journey to the Promised Land*. London: Vallentine Mitchell, 2002.

Muller, Filip. *Eyewitness Auschwitz: Three Years in the Gas Chambers*. Chicago: Ivan R Dee in association with the United States Holocaust Memorial Museum, 1979.

Nemeskürty, István. *Requiem egy hadseregert*. Budapest: Magvető Kiadó, 1972.

Perenyi, Eleanor. *More Was Lost*. Boston: Little, Brown, 1946.

Porter, Anna. *Kasztner's Train: The True Story of Rezso Kasztner, Unknown Hero of the Holocaust*. Vancouver: Douglas & McIntyre, 2007.

Szakály, Sándor. *Hadsereg, Politika, Társadalom*. Budapest: Lánchid Kiadó, 1991.

Ungváry, Krisztián. *Budapest Ostroma*. Budapest: Corvina Kiado Kft., 1998.

SUSAN M. PAPP IS a television producer, director, and writer, who, after working for the CBC for fifteen years, founded Postmodern Productions, her own television production company. While at the CBC, she was awarded the prestigious Michener Award for her outstanding investigative work. She has written and published widely on Hungarian immigration to and settlement in North America. She lives in Toronto.